Africa: The Challenge

Africa: The Challenge
of Transformation

STEPHEN McCARTHY

I.B.Tauris & Co Publishers

LONDON · NEW YORK

Published in 1994 by
I.B.Tauris & Co Ltd
45 Bloomsbury Square
London WC1A 2HY

In the United States of America and Canada distributed by
St Martin's Press
175 Fifth Avenue
New York NY 10010

A full CIP record for this book is available from the British Library

Library of Congress catalog card number 94–60179

A full CIP record for this book is available from the Library of Congress

ISBN 1–85043–821–8 (hardback)
ISBN 1–85043–820–x (paperback)

Maps drawn by Russell Townsend based on originals by Carol McCarthy

Set in Monotype Ehrhardt by Ewan Smith

Printed and bound in Great Britain by
WBC Ltd, Bridgend, Mid Glamorgan

Contents

Figures

Abbreviations and Acronyms

ACP	African, Caribbean and Pacific
ADB	African Development Bank
AIDS	Acquired Immune Deficiency Syndrome
ANC	African National Congress
BBC	British Broadcasting Corporation
BDP	Botswana Democratic Party
CDC	Commonwealth Development Corporation
CPP	Convention People's Party
DAC	Development Assistance Committee (OECD)
EC	European Community
FNLA	Frente Nacional de Libertação de Angola
Frelimo	Frente de Libertação de Moçambique
GDP	gross domestic product
GNP	gross national product
HDI	human development index
HIV	human immunodefficiency virus
HPER	human priority expenditure ratio
IBRD	International Bank for Reconstruction and Development (World Bank)
IDA	International Development Association
IMF	International Monetary Fund
MPLA	Movimento Popular de Libertação de Angola
NATO	North Atlantic Treaty Organization
NDF	net development finance
NGO	non-governmental organization
NP	National Party (South Africa)
OAU	Organization of African Unity
OECD	Organization for Economic Cooperation and Development

OPEC	Organization of Petroleum Exporting Countries
PAIGC	Partido Africano da Independénçia da Guiné a Cabo Verde
PPP	purchasing power parity
RDA	Ruvuma Development Association
Renamo	Mozambique National Resistance Movement
SACUA	Southern African Customs Union Agreement
SWAPO	South West African People's Organization
TANU	Tanganyika African National Union
TASO	The AIDS support organization (Uganda)
UN	United Nations
UNCTAD	United Nations Conference on Trade and Development
UNDP	United Nations Development Programme
VSO	Voluntary Service Overseas
UNITA	National Union for the Total Independence of Angola
ZANLA	Zimbabwe African National Liberation Army
ZANU	Zimbabwean African National Union
ZAPU	Zimbabwean African People's Union

Acknowledgements

The writing and publishing of this book would not have been possible without the support given to me in different ways by the European Investment Bank, St Antony's College, Oxford and the development group, Mokoro. Between them they provided me with the necessary opportunity, time, resources, facilities and finance. Needless to say they take no responsibility for its content.

A full list of source books and references is given in the Bibliography, but some deserve special mention. The chapter on African history draws extensively on Professor Oliver's wonderful book, *The African Experience*, which is full of measured perspectives and love of Africa. Another book full of optimism is Pierre Pradervand's *Listening to Africa*, which I have quoted in a number of places to illustrate the argument. I also wish to thank Fr. Julian Black for permission to quote from his private letter (Chapter 1). On the economic side most of the statistical data are taken from either the World Bank's 1992 *World Development Report* or the 1992 *Human Development Report* of the United Nations Development Programme, except for Figure 5.2, which is derived from the World Bank's *Trends in Developing Economies*. Yet much of the inspiration comes not from books but from the many African colleagues, friends and acquaintances whom I have had the pleasure to know and work with over the years. Although this book is written from an outsider's point of view, I hope that they recognize the Africa which it portrays.

Many people read the text at various stages and several commented in detail. I particularly wish to thank David Bevan of the Centre for the Study of African Economies at Oxford, and Chris Colclough of the Institute of Development Studies, Sussex, for their comments on early drafts. Dr Colclough's own work on primary schooling has been instructive, as were in different ways the lectures and seminars of Professor Terence Ranger, Tony Kirk Greene and Professor Paul Collier, all of St Antony's College. Pip Bevan was the first person who actually asked for a copy of the text, a psychological boost to any author working away on his own. Many friends and colleagues have also given me useful advice, comments or support, especially: Peter Carter, Peter Christiansen and Lucien Peters, together with Daniel Ottolenghi, Luigi Genazzini, Roger Lavelle, Mike Stevens, Clive Keith, Sandy Grant, Pierre Landell-Mills and Kevin Cleaver. I have also benefited from the comments of some anonymous publishers' readers. Irene Sneesby helped with the checking and preparation of the figures, and Mary Betley proofread the text.

My wife, Carol, prepared the maps. More importantly, she and the rest of my family had to put up with many hours of my spare time taken up with a project which eventually took much longer than initially expected. It is for the reader to judge whether the effort was worthwhile.

S.J. McCarthy
Luxembourg, March 1994

Preface

We shall not cease from exploration
And the end of all our exploring
Will be to arrive where we started
And know the place for the first time.
(T.S. Eliot, *Four Quartets*, 'The Dry Salvages')

An Exploration

Africa is a continent of paradoxes. Ravaged by hunger, war, illness
and poverty, it seems to be lurching towards a catastrophe. Yet underneath something stirs. Over the last decade the picture has been one
of almost unremitting gloom. Look back a hundred years and change
and progress have been quite remarkable. What do we see when we
look forward?

The question is unanswerable, but we can throw some light on it.
This book aims to do so. It is an account of a personal exploration
into the state of Africa today. I have spent most of my working life on
development in Africa, initially in Africa itself, more recently in an
external aid agency. In the 1960s Africa was viewed with great optimism; at that time it was the Asian sub-continent for which Malthusian
predictions were made. Africa seemed empty, fertile and virginal. In
the first flush of political independence, it had enormous potential.
Given time, goodwill and a certain amount of external aid, there
seemed to be nothing that could not be achieved. Its spokesmen, such
as Nkrumah, Senghor and Nyerere, wrote of their vision for the future
of their continent. It was a socialist vision – but that suited the times
and, so we were told, the African cultural tradition.

This vision of progress and development also complemented the
spirit of the age. It was not too difficult to believe in the evolution of
mankind towards some common purpose, an ultimately benign goal –
perhaps Teilhard de Chardin's *Omega Point* (De Chardin, 1959). This
evolution would no longer be a matter of physical biology. Indeed,
purely biological characteristics – race, sex, physical ability – would
become relatively less important as society advanced, with intellectual
and social organization becoming more important.

Such aspirations are no longer fashionable, given that we are now weighed down by concerns over the environmental fragility of our small earth. Yet the intellectual and social progress has continued. Human society is increasingly complex and interrelated across the whole world. The sum of mankind's knowledge is millions of times greater than the amount that any single individual can know in a lifetime, and much greater than it was even 30 years ago. The tools man has created for thinking and doing are thousands of times more powerful than his own intellectual and physical strength. Yet to put all this knowledge to effect – to build this small computer on which I am working, for example – requires complex social and economic organization, which is also part of this evolution.

It is unacceptable that any part of the human race should be left out of this process. Yet just that appears to be happening to Africa. Since those heady days of the 1960s and in spite of all the efforts of Africans and sympathetic outsiders alike, the scene has turned from one of hope to one of disillusion – even despair. Expectations have been dashed; hope deferred. Most of the human race seems to be moving ahead, leaving Africa further and further behind.

Have things really gone so badly wrong and, if so, why? Are there any glimmers on the horizon? What can or should non-Africans do? These are the questions I set out to try and answer in this book.

The Ruvuma Development Association

My own awareness that all was not well actually goes back to 1968, when I went to Tanzania as a volunteer teacher under the auspices of VSO (Voluntary Service Overseas). It was my first acquaintance with Africa, and, if not the very first time I began to think about development, it was nearly so. My year as a teacher passed uneventfully, or no more so than that of any other enthusiastic, but untrained and inexperienced, teacher working in a strange physical and cultural context.

During my school vacations I used to go to the Ruvuma Development Association (RDA) to help out with the teaching in the village school. The RDA was a cooperative village movement, an experiment in socialism if you like, deep in southern Tanzania. It had been founded by ten Tanzanians who had listened to and taken to heart President Nyerere's advocacy of *Ujamaa*, national development through socialism. They had established a village, Litowa, where none

existed before, in which much of the food and crop production was
carried out communally with all the farmers working on a common
farm. In the first year there was a complete crop failure but three of
the original ten pioneers carried on to eventual success.
The underlying theory was twofold. By working together people
could pool their resources and be more productive. They could address
their problems together. By living in a common village, rather than in
single dispersed homesteads, which was the prevailing settlement
pattern in Tanzania, it was possible to provide common services such
as a village school and a clean water supply. Kate Wenner's book
Shamba Letu gives a lively, sympathetic account of life in Litowa and
reflects the mood of the time (Wenner, 1970).
The founders of the RDA had requested Ralph Ibbott to join them
and provide technical help. Originally a quantity surveyor by profes-
sion, he had become what one would call a community development
worker – though he would have rejected such a title, which would
seem to patronize the community. He had been involved in a similar
venture in village-level development in Southern Rhodesia, as it then
was. His job was in fact to be available to the villagers as required. He
and his wife Noreen were my hosts in Litowa during my time there
in 1968 and 1969. By then the RDA had extended to more than a
dozen villages, all working on similar lines and following the same
ideals.
The RDA was in some ways the precursor of the Ujamaa villagization programme that swept through the country during the 1970s.
What I scarcely appreciated at the time was that a great political
debate was under way. President Nyerere's Arusha Declaration in
1967 had proclaimed Ujamaa as the development path for Tanzania.
The establishment of Ujamaa villages was accordingly one of the first
practical priorities, and the RDA was being held up as a model.
Nyerere himself was impatient for progress. However, in fact, the
RDA philosophy was to move slowly, no faster than village people
themselves would consent to and support. Notwithstanding the presence of outside advisers, it was essentially a grass-roots movement. I
well remember the day that the Oxfam man called by, eager to provide
some finance, only to be told that nothing was really needed at the
time.
In the meantime local and regional government officials also had
axes to grind. They were suspicious of the RDA, which seemed to be
undermining their authority. The people of Litowa were growing in

assertiveness and self-confidence and so threatening the power and authority of the local and regional officials. No doubt there were many other undercurrents that an outsider would never appreciate. The result was that at the end of 1969, a few months after the end of my stay, officialdom moved in on Litowa. The RDA was forcibly disbanded. The Ibbott family was obliged to leave the country. Tanzania soon thereafter embarked on its compulsory villagization programme, making people move into communal villages rather than being scattered in small settlements throughout the countryside. This was draconian forced migration, which affected several million people, and contributed to the subsequent ruin of the Tanzanian economy.

Whether the RDA model of voluntary cooperation was sustainable or replicable is doubtful. The history of other production cooperative movements in the world is not particularly encouraging – except perhaps where they are limited in their objectives and very precisely structured. But the forced movement of people and the authoritarian top-down imposition of a particular mode of production, which the government-sponsored Ujamaa villages came to be, was clearly a development disaster, the very antithesis of the people-centred development philosophy which Nyerere liked to proclaim.

Encounter with Botswana

Two years later I found myself in the Ministry of Finance and Development Planning in Botswana, now doing a very different job, as one of those very government officials. I eventually stayed in Botswana for six years. Now if Tanzania has been a development disaster, notwithstanding the enormous external goodwill and finance it has enjoyed, Botswana has been a development success. Judged purely in economic terms, it was the fastest-growing economy in the world between 1965 and 1990. Other indicators of human welfare show similar progress. Most remarkably, it is a country with a multi-party democratic constitution, under which regular elections are held, and with a low level of corruption. Botswana is sufficiently important as background to the rest of this book and as a model against which to compare and contrast the rest of the continent, that a few pages are taken at the end, in a separate appendix, to consider in greater detail why it has been so different.

Since the late 1970s, however, my work has been on the other side of the development fence, that of the aid agency, where my areas of

> *Kate Wenner describes one of Nyerere's visits to the RDA:*
>
> When they arrived at the tobacco fields, everyone was at work pruning the plants and weeding between the rows. Nyerere walked up to Kalikenye who was busy pruning one of the plants and asked how the work was going ... 'Mzee, tell me, how far apart do you plant the tobacco?' There had been a rumour around that the farmers at Litowa had ignored the instructions of the Ministry of Agriculture and planted the tobacco plants too close together. Nyerere had probably been told of this ... Relations had long been strained between the local ministry office and Litowa.
>
> 'We measured off a yard between plants', Kalikenye answered. This was just as the Ministry of Agriculture required.
>
> 'Are you sure?'
>
> 'Of course. We mark it off with yard measures before we plant.'
>
> Nyerere reached into his pocket and pulled out a tape measure. He must have planned to investigate the rumour. He stretched the measure across from one plant to the next. 'One yard exactly', he said loudly. He repeated the measurement at another row of plants. The same, one yard exactly.
>
> 'Well you certainly are right, mzee. It's exactly a yard to the inch.' Nyerere turned to the agricultural officer beside him who now looked a little red in the face. 'Seems as if the tobacco is just as it should be. I don't know what you were complaining about.' (Wenner, 1970: 13)

interest have ranged across all of the 40 or so countries which make up sub-Saharan Africa. As I travelled to and from most of these countries during the 1980s, it became increasingly clear that the process of development in which I had believed during the 1960s, and which I had witnessed in Botswana in the 1970s, was simply not happening in the rest of the continent; indeed, elsewhere in Africa the process seemed in many ways to be moving backwards. Nevertheless, the impressions were not all negative. Oddly, the further one moved from the capital cities and into the countryside the stronger was the sense, if not of prosperity, certainly of stability, resourcefulness, underlying strength, even of joy and exuberance. It was as if some kind of African drama was being played out, an almost visible struggle between good and evil. It became ever more important to understand. So, with the help of a sabbatical from my employer and a year in Oxford, this book came to be written. My aim was not to write another African catastrophe book, but rather to make sense of these conflicting impressions and experiences for myself and perhaps for others too. If, at the same time, some of this sense of drama could be conveyed, then so much the better.

The scope of the book is sub-Saharan Africa, or black Africa, and 'Africa' will be used as a shorthand term for sub-Saharan Africa, except where the context indicates otherwise. This focus might appear somewhat arbitrary except that, for about the last ten thousand years, the Sahara has been a natural dividing line. Societies and countries along the Mediterranean littoral north of the Sahara have always been part of Mediterranean culture and history. They have had continuous contact with Europe and have been at various times part of the Roman, Arab and Ottoman empires. At the other geographical extreme, South Africa's history, politics and economics have been quite different from those of the rest of sub-Saharan Africa. Towards the end of the book, we shall consider briefly whether, as South Africa moves towards majority rule, it is destined to suffer the same travails and experiences as the rest of the African continent to the north.

Themes of the Book

At the outset of writing this book, I had wanted to emphasize the complexity of Africa's chronic problem of underdevelopment. The simple explanations which are proffered – an unfair international economic climate, declining terms of trade, foreign debt, external aid agencies, corrupt politicians, tribalism, overpopulation, environmental degradation – are each too simplistic. Rather, all of these things, and others, are in some way to blame.

Even if, as many believe, the crux of the matter is bad government, to say so does not advance the argument a great deal. Poor government is both a cause of underdevelopment and a symptom of it. It is partly caused by a weak sense of nationhood, inappropriate political philosophies, lack of human capital, highly unstable, difficult-to-manage economies and so on. In reality, a whole web of interrelated factors combine and interlock into a series of vicious circles, from which it is difficult to break out.

As time went on, other related themes emerged. I had thought that economic policy for development was now reasonably well understood – certainly that had been my experience in Botswana. The puzzle was why these policies were not implemented in practice? The answer of course lies in politics, but that is simply to beg the question. What is it about African history and culture that throws up unsatisfactory political systems? To answer that, one has to look back to before the colonial period.

Pre-colonial society was small in scale, geographically dispersed but strong and resilient, surviving more or less unchanged for over a thousand years. The comparatively short colonial period, and the African revolution which led to independence, imposed a superficial modernity but left the underlying structure of society essentially unchanged. Development failure in independent Africa can be attributed to the inherent difficulties of such societies in adapting to the ethos of the modern world and to the scale and requirements of the nation state. As a result, the newly created countries fell prey to the unrestrained personal rule of grasping politicians and the interests of narrow elites. Western aid, with its encouragement of the state as the major actor in development, supported these tendencies.

Nevertheless, as the journey of exploration continued, it became increasingly clear that a great deal is going on in Africa which is not captured by any of the continent's notoriously unreliable economic and social statistics. Beneath the surface of economic stagnation and widespread political breakdown, the underlying strength of African society is intact. Moreover, these societies are themselves rapidly changing. Basic education, which however has not yet reached the mass of African people, is the key to this change. With education, in the broadest sense of the word, a bridge is thrown across the divide between the small, isolated, self-sufficient societies, which characterized much of pre-colonial Africa, and the shared knowledge and increasingly universal values of the modern world. Without mass education there can be no enduring social, political or economic advance.

This is not a new insight. More than a hundred years ago Lord Brougham, observing Britain's own move towards widespread education, commented: 'Education makes a people easy to lead, but difficult to drive; easy to govern but impossible to enslave.' Yet, as I argue towards the end of the book, it is an insight which the development experts and external aid-givers appear to have forgotten for much of the last 30 years, as they focused mechanistically on paternalistic formulas and policies for economic development and on written constitutions for political change.

So, under the influence of education, slowly permeating through the towns and villages, a major social revolution has been simmering. Since the end of the 1980s this brew has begun to boil over. People are clamouring for democracy and for accountable political systems. In short, a second African revolution is under way.

The coming few years will be marked by great changes as people struggle to take charge again of their own destiny. A few countries, such as Botswana, democratic and economically successful, offer a model for others. However, these changes will not come easily to the whole continent and there will be much instability and, in places, continued strife.

In the economic sphere, structural adjustment, which aims to give men and women control again over their work and production, is beginning to show results. However, the pendulum of economic policy, which has been swinging rather strongly in Africa, as in the rest of the world, towards the ideas of individual incentive and market forces, is now almost certainly overshooting its equilibrium position. Very little is yet really known of what actually drives development forward, but it is certainly not the simple workings of unfettered markets. The state still has an important role to play in Africa, both in protecting its citizens and in providing a stable framework under which economic development can take place.

The external aid agencies can contribute to these social and economic changes. But they can only facilitate change, not direct it, as they hoped to do in the past. They need to take a much longer time perspective and redirect their activities away from supporting governments towards African people themselves. They should make a sustained commitment to fund basic education and health for a whole generation. In this way they will give the people of the continent the essential tools and abilities to realize their own potential and in due time to work out for themselves their own destiny in the modern world.

Structure of the Book

The book, first examines the state of Africa today, both descriptively (Chapter 1) and statistically (Chapter 2), though great caution has to be used in interpreting African statistics, even those which are published, often with little comment, by reputable international agencies such as the United Nations and the World Bank. Then, since an historical perspective is essential for an understanding of the present, an excursion through history (Chapter 3) brings us from pre-colonial society through the colonial period to a review of the main political developments since independence (Chapter 4). The narrower topics of economics and the causes of recent development failure are then broached (Chapter 5). External aid has been left to near the end (Chapter 6), since, although substantial, it is too often thought to be a more important element than it really is. Finally, the book considers the outlook for Africa (Chapter 7). The future is in the hands of Africans themselves. The continent is pursuing its own agenda, which is not greatly affected by outsiders, be they colonizers or donors. Trying to understand that agenda is the main purpose of the book.

The precise order in which the various topics are taken may sometimes appear rather arbitrary. However, the threads of the argument are interwoven, so the reader can start where he or she will and, with luck, still find that the fabric of the whole supports him or her.

Map of Africa

1 African Society Today – a Snapshot

I speak of Africa and golden joys
(Shakespeare, *Henry IV, Part 2*, Act V, Scene iii)

> Famine, strife and warfare may be common in Africa, but by no means affect the whole continent or all its people. African society remains essentially rural, built around small communities, tolerant and welcoming, and still in close touch with nature and the environment. The people of this vast continent are deeply spiritual, and display a joyful exuberance even in the face of poverty, illness and natural disasters.

Images of Africa

Images are powerful. A picture is worth a thousand words. Those of us who are not African, or who have limited experience of that vast continent, hold images of Africa which probably derive from magazines, television and film. The images are compelling and reflect reality. However, if they are not set in context they may frustrate understanding. Providing some context in order to promote understanding is one of the aims of this book. Nonetheless, it is useful to start by examining the images.

Popular Images

The first to be confronted is the catastrophic image, which is brought to our television screens at periodic times of crisis, such as the 1984 Ethiopian famine, or the Somalian catastrophe in 1992. It is a picture of brown, barren land, where crops wither in the sun, of listless children emaciated or with the swollen stomach of kwashiorkor, and of mothers, their breasts dried up, holding their lifeless babies, or burying them. In the refugee camps people whose whole lives have been torn apart just line up listlessly for their daily rations, while aid workers speak to the camera of how little they can really do with the resources they have. Elsewhere, rivers of people are on the move, struggling on foot through a wasteland, a bundle of a few possessions on the heads of the women, going who knows where, fleeing hunger or, more likely, war.

War is a more proximate cause of hunger than is drought. Other countries have been worse hit by crop failure and food shortage during the 1980s than Ethiopia was in 1984, but Ethiopia was also waging a bitter civil war, as were Mozambique and the Sudan in 1990. Many African countries have experienced civil war over the last 30 years – Nigeria, Zaire, Liberia, Ethiopia, Sudan, Somalia, Chad, Mozambique, Angola, Zimbabwe, Burundi, Rwanda and Uganda – to name just the ones which reached the news desks of the Western press. Many of these were proxy wars between the West and the former Soviet Union, which by supporting and selling arms to each side inflated what would otherwise have been a more limited conflict.

War conjures up its own images – undisciplined soldiers, perhaps little more than bandits, emerging from the bush with their machine-guns and ragged uniforms; children toting Kalashnikovs through deserted shanty towns; and torture, rape and unspeakable atrocities carried out to ensure loyalty or to punish treachery, real or imagined, or perhaps for no reason at all. Such are the pictures that at various times have come out of the Congo (now Zaire), Biafra, Zimbabwe, Mozambique, Ethiopia, Somalia, Sudan and, most recently, Angola and would have emerged from a number of other countries, if we were not already satiated with such pointless, inexplicable evil.

Hollywood offers more stylized, celluloid portraits of war. The forces of the Mahdi overwhelm Gordon in his solitary, stupid stance at Khartoum in 1884. Fortunately, Kitchener arrives some years later to restore a proper British order to affairs. In the same year, the vast, disciplined Zulu armies come over the hill to surround and overwhelm a small British force at Isandhlwana, only to be properly smashed themselves six months later in a return match. However, most of the scramble for Africa was not like that; the armies were smaller and more ragged on both sides, and negotiation and duplicity were at least as important as warfare.

The negative images also include those of present-day conspicuous consumption. In Swahili the *wabenzi* are those who drive in Mercedes-Benz cars, who are resplendent in traditional dress or city suits, dangling gold ornaments and followed by a retinue of subordinates and bag-carriers. The most repulsive are the super kleptocrats, many of whom have stolen what little wealth exists in their countries and stashed it away in secret Swiss bank accounts. President Mobutu of Zaire personally owns a great deal of land and property in Brussels but has made his own country so inhospitable that he now lives on a luxury yacht moored on the Zaire river.

Nevertheless, we also retain more positive images, such as the halcyon picture of a colonial Africa inhabited by Robert Redford and Meryl Streep. Here, simple tribes live in comparative harmony under the benevolent dictatorships of their chiefs. There is stillness, order and tranquillity. The whites have taken the natives' land but the latter don't mind too much since there is plenty to go around. Poverty certainly exists, but not real hunger, and much entertainment is to be had at times of tribal ritual. Of course change and modernization affect even these societies. Children come to school under the shade of a spreading tree and scratch out their ABCs on small slates. Missionaries build churches and encourage people to turn away from their primitive ancestor-worship. Colonial administrators settle disputes which are too complex to decide by customary law, or build roads and dams.

Then comes the powerful image of a Nelson Mandela emerging from 27 years' imprisonment, where he has grown old and grey, but displaying no anger or bitterness, and, instead, all the courage and strength of personality which led to his imprisonment in the first place. Here we see that most remarkable of African characteristics – the capacity to forgive, forget and to be reconciled. Ali Mazrui, one of the most respected of African intellectuals, calls it the 'short memory of hate', and it contrasts strongly with the European capacity to nurture hate over successive generations, as recent events in the former Yugoslavia demonstrate. African wars may be brutal but there seem to be few reprisals afterwards – not after the Biafran war in Nigeria, nor more recently in Namibia or Ethiopia nor, apparently, in Mozambique.

Africa has also witnessed much personal heroism, as we have seen repeatedly – for example, in Kenya on the part of Oginga Odinga, or Robert Ouku, a popular former foreign minister who was murdered in 1990, and others who would not accept the steady subversion of the state by President Moi. More recently, in April 1992 the Malawian opposition leader, Chakufwa Chihana, calmly and courageously returned to his country to certain detention and probable torture. As he got off the plane he began to speak: 'There comes a time in the history of every nation when all must recognise that change is not only desirable, but inevitable. For Malawi the time is now ...', at which point he was arrested and bundled away (*Economist*, 11 April 1992).

Realities

Although all of these images of course reflect some facets of the truth, there is more to be said. There are about five hundred million people living in sub-Saharan Africa. Nobody knows precisely, since even population statistics in Africa are subject to huge uncertainties. There are about six million refugees on the continent, more than in the whole of the rest of the world. So about one person in a hundred is a refugee. The number of displaced persons, people who have had to move, perhaps because of war but also because of drought or other natural disasters, is about 35 million, or one in 15 of the population (UNDP, 1991: 36).

Yet migration is one of the most prominent features of African history. There have always been great movements of peoples; the land was relatively unpopulated, there were few insurmountable geographical barriers, people possessed little, and they could live off the land as they found it. So moving away has always been a traditional response to problems. Part of that tradition has been accepting and supporting new immigrants and absorbing them into one's own society – not always, of course, but sufficiently often to be remarkable. Africans have an ethnic tolerance which puts Europeans to shame. Thus, for example, the Zimbabweans took in hundreds of thousands of refugees from Mozambique into a land which is already rather densely populated. This was not without tension but it happened. Other refugees went to Malawi. Were it not for such traditions, the six million African refugees would have made much more of an international stir. In fact, they are being absorbed in a time-honoured way.

Much more could be said also about famine and hunger. Amartya Sen has studied famines in many parts of the world, including Ethiopia. He has shown, strikingly, that famines are caused not by shortages of food in the area concerned, but by poverty, by people being unable to acquire food, or by the normal workings of the economy and society breaking down. Without doubt warfare has been the main cause of famine in Africa. Famine affects perhaps ten to twenty million people in a bad year, or between one in 25 and one in

50 of the whole sub-Saharan population. These statistics are numbing, incomprehensible and quite unacceptable. They are a damning comment on development efforts by governments and external aid agencies alike, but they do not amount to the whole population, nor even to a significant part of it. Nevertheless, hunger and malnutrition are still widespread throughout the continent, a topic to which we shall return below. On the positive side, the halcyon Hollywood image is also grossly oversimplified. Africans, as we shall see, have never been particularly successful at building large states, yet the bedrock of society has great underlying stability. There is also much greater social diversity than is commonly supposed, with striking differences of history and culture between Islamic northern and western Africa and the more Christianized eastern and southern regions. Can we paint an accurate portrait of African society today which reflects what is common but encompasses the diversity? Some would conclude that no useful generalizations can be made. If so, we must fall back on our mental pictures, which are just as generalized and perhaps even less accurate. So, perhaps, by selecting a very broad brush, a useful portrait can be drawn so long as it is viewed from a distance rather than subject to minute examination. We would encounter the same problem if we attempted to depict European life today in equally few brushstrokes. Europe, too, has some common elements, while encompassing cultural extremes as great as those between, say, Sweden and Italy.

Country Life

Most Africans are country people, a description which is more apt than peasants, which denotes people who live in a particular type of rural economy (Hill, 1986: 8–15). People live in the rural areas in villages or even isolated settlements. Although the towns grew rapidly soon after independence, they still account for only about a third of the population, compared with 15 per cent in 1960 (UNDP, 1992). Even the most urbanized of African countries, such as Zambia, have only about half of their population living in towns, and in Zambia's case this proportion could even decline.

In fact many town-dwellers are also country people. The population of the towns is constantly shifting, as men and women come to try their fortunes, to sell their produce, or to be educated or hospitalized, before returning home again to their villages. Income flows between the towns and villages. Cash earned in town is brought home to pay for school fees, funerals or weddings. Food grown in the country is sent to maintain relatives temporarily urbanized.

Farming and Land

The majority of country people farm. In the past, the farming cycle would have been surrounded by ceremonies and traditions to encourage fertility and favours from the spirit world and ancestors. In this, the chiefs, who generally combined worldly authority with spiritual powers, played a crucial role. In some communities, these practices continue in forms which may be little changed from the past or which may carry a great deal of more modern adaption and invention.

Farming methods and crops vary and change over time. Root crops, such as cassava and yams, are particularly important in the more tropical parts of West Africa, while grains, including maize, millet and sorghum, are grown in the drier regions. Few of these crops are indigenous to Africa.

Many societies, especially in eastern and southern Africa and certainly outside the forest areas where the tsetse fly is to be found, keep a few livestock, cattle or goats, in addition to farming crops. The two activities complement each other. Livestock represent a reserve of food and a store of wealth. They can be reared on land unsuitable for crops and on crop residues. In some parts of southern Africa, oxen are used for ploughing. In other places, pastoralists and agriculturalists may coexist in the same area. For example, the Fulani people are to be found herding and rearing their own and others' cattle throughout West Africa. Pastoralism requires cyclical movement – following the grazing from one area to another at different times of year. So some pastoral societies, such as the Somali or the Masai, are semi-nomadic or transhumant. Others, such as the Tswana people and others in southern Africa, have solved the problem by establishing large central villages from which the men and boys can disperse with their cattle to more distant grazing lands for months at a time.

Land-tenure systems also show great diversity. Perhaps in the precolonial past, before there was pressure on land, the whole matter of land tenure may have been simply irrelevant – just as in industrial countries the right to have access to and breathe clean air only became a matter of debate and regulation as clean air became less and less available. Thus, even now, in those regions where population pressures are not so great, Zambia or Tanzania for example, or where the land is not so fertile, the matter of land tenure is probably still vague and insecure. People, or families, or clans would have rights to use land but would not own it in the Western sense. Under such rotating systems of land use, most land would be left fallow for several years, before being reclaimed again for a few years in a slow cycle of cultivation. Such cyclical land-use systems should not be confused with the opening up for cultivation of virgin land which might previously have been forested. This opening up of new land does still occur, for example in southern Nigeria or Côte d'Ivoire, but is not part of a regular cropping pattern since, even with the help of fire, it is extraordinarily physically demanding.

Pressure on, and competition for, land is certainly growing, more so in the more densely populated west of the continent than in the centre and the east. Different land tenure systems have emerged to take account of different economic and political circumstances. Matters are still evolving and land rights are by no means clear-cut or codified. At one extreme, in much of Kenya for example, land has been registered in the names of individuals and can be owned, bought and sold and inherited. In part this was a reaction to land disputes with white settlers. In other places, landlord and tenant patterns have emerged. This seems to be the case in parts of Uganda and in southern Ghana, where the introduction of cocoa, early this century, encouraged powerful or entrepreneurial Ghanaians to acquire tracts of forest land which were previously of little value. Such land was then let out to tenants. In Botswana extensive *de facto* land and grazing rights were acquired by those cattle owners who had the resources to sink a borehole for water in a previously unexploited area.

Transhumant pastoralists are probably losing out most as a result of these trends, since semi-nomadism finds little place in modern land tenure systems. The fringes of their communal grazing lands are being steadily encroached on by settled cultivators. One such group, the Tuareg, whose traditional grazing areas straddle parts of Mali and Niger, is increasingly disaffected and violent.

Occupations and Income

At one time, economists used to think that so-called subsistence farmers were idle for much of the time and had time on their hands which could be used in new productive, cash-earning activities. This was and still is a gross distortion of reality. These farmers are busy, and are especially so at times of peak agricultural activity. They have different tasks to do or occupations to follow at different times – of the day, of the year or of life. The distinction, such as we would make, between what is work, what is household activity and what is leisure, is not clearly defined. All is part of day-to-day life.

Not all country people are farmers, and many who are also pursue other activities at various times. There are traders and transporters, craftsmen, especially the ubiquitous blacksmiths, seamstresses, brewers of beer, policemen and petty officials. There are doctors and medicine men, priests, bishops of the new spiritual churches or imams. Importantly, there are also agricultural labourers working on others' land for wages or for other remuneration. In addition, there are migrant workers who are employed in the towns or plantations but return as often as possible to their natal village.

Yet there is little employment in the Western sense, with family income coming from just one job or activity. Rather, it is earned in various ways at different times or seasons. One of those generalizations which need modifying in particular circumstances is that women are responsible for growing food and men for farming crops which can be sold for cash. Even in small villages cash circulates through the local economy. Nor is everybody on the same footing by any means. There is much inequality, with great disparities of wealth and of income among country people, from the 'big men', the wealthy with their four-wheel-drive vehicles and solid modern houses – landowners or traders perhaps – to the destitute, struggling on the margins of society.

In some cases, it is useful to think of a husband on the one hand and his wife (or wives) together with her children as constituting separate households, perhaps living in different huts in the same compound. Their incomes, including incomes in kind, would be kept separate. The forest regions of West Africa have a particularly strong trading tradition among women, who operate on their own account – not for their husbands or for some family income.

The lot of women is hard. On their shoulders falls the responsibility for family food production and preparation, for the bearing and rearing of children and for much of the fetching and carrying, for example of food and water – the Kikuyu in Kenya have a particularly bad reputation in these matters. Moreover, women often suffer from having limited rights of their own, for example over access to land, or inheritance and ownership of cattle, which means wealth in a pastoral society. As a result, the numerous households effectively headed by women, for example those of widows, deserted wives or where the man is a migrant labourer, can be very severely disadvantaged.

Notwithstanding the variety of rural life as a whole, most individual lives are far from a rural idyll but consist essentially of hard, tedious work. Each day is a struggle for survival, having to grow and prepare sufficient food and seek out ways of earning a small income. Pierre Pradervand, in his optimistic book *Listening to Africa*, quotes one woman from Burkina Faso, describing her typical day:

> We get up at 4 to 5 a.m. to fetch water. Then we sweep the courtyard, pound the millet, and prepare breakfast. After that we go and work in our husbands' fields – we Dagara women have no fields of our own. We return home at 7 p.m., prepare dinner, and go to bed around 10 or 11 p.m. It's because we have such a workload that we Dagara women get old so quickly (Pradervand, 1989: 34).

Poverty

How much real poverty is there? Researchers sometimes set a particular country's poverty line at the level at which people can survive, clothe and feed themselves, but have no resources left over for luxuries or saving. On this basis, it is estimated that about a third of Africans fall below such a poverty line. This figure includes perhaps one in five of the population who at any one time are so poor as to be actually hungry, or to be undernourished in a way which affects their health and their children's development (Lipton, 1992: 22).

Such estimates are of course very uncertain. What can be said is that poverty and limited food production go hand in hand. So poverty and hunger are more common among larger families, since there are proportionately fewer adults to produce food for the family. As a result, children are particularly prone to poverty and hunger. For the same reason poverty tends to be greater in the arid and semi-arid areas of the continent, where food production is most difficult and unreliable. Improving agricultural productivity in these regions would go a long way towards reducing absolute poverty.

Poverty kills, not perhaps directly through hunger but because undernourished bodies, particularly those of growing children, are more prone to other infections and less able to combat disease. Equally, ill health, often the result of endemic and debilitating diseases – such as malaria, sleeping sickness, bilharzia, tuberculosis, river blindness or venereal disease including AIDS – causes poverty by reducing the capacity for productive work.

In Africa, poverty is much more severe in the rural areas than it is in the towns, contrasting with the situation in Latin America. This fact crucially affects the impact of present programmes of economic adjustment, which are discussed in Chapter 5. It also contradicts the impressions of many outsiders, transient journalists and others, who visit the large cities and their shanty towns but fail to penetrate the hidden rural remoteness. Visitors can be dismayed by the highly visible urban poverty and urban problems of overcrowding and so on, without being aware of the much more widespread poverty and much more limited availability of services in the rural areas. One reason why urban people are less prone to poverty is urban bias; government-provided services are more concentrated in the towns than in the rural areas. Thus, for example, the infant mortality rate in the country-side is much higher than in the towns, and schools are much scarcer.

The main defence against poverty must be the strong African tradition of sharing, particularly of food. *Karibu chakula*, literally meaning 'welcome to the food', is a Swahili greeting. Helping the poor, particularly those from one's own clan or family, is a major social obligation, though not necessarily an obligation always entered into graciously or without resentment. In his book *Africa, Dispatches from a Fragile Continent*, Harden graphically portrays the dilemma of a successful civil servant going to visit his family in his home village (Harden, 1990). He wants to go home and knows he should go home, but he also knows that as soon as he arrives burdens will be placed on him to help out with the financial difficulties of all the extended family.

So the particularly successful 'big man', who has perhaps acquired a city job or made some money in trading, commands a special loyalty and respect among his wide family. However, like any true patriarch, he is expected to reciprocate with special help or favours when necessary. Hence arises the importance of patrimonial politics in Africa (see Chapter 4). The image of the big man cruising in his Mercedes needs to be modified by the invisible caravan of dependants behind him.

Environmental Stress

African soils are generally not particularly fertile, except along river valleys or in the old volcanic regions, such as those of East Africa.

There is little humus and much of the fertility gets washed away in periodic downpours. Tree cover reduces erosion and encourages humidity. However, trees are threatened, not so much in order to turn land over to cultivation but to provide firewood, which is often sold in the cities and towns. Indeed, it is roughly estimated that, on a sustainable basis, a family needs as much land for production of firewood as it does for growing food (Grove, 1991). The present demand for firewood may not be sustainable. Small local trees may be being chopped down for wood fuel faster than they can regenerate, and ownership of such trees and rights over their use is varied and uncertain.

This diffuse problem is somewhat intractable. For a start, the evidence is uncertain and mostly anecdotal. There are very few historic species surveys of specific areas which could be compared with the present situation. Thus, it is very difficult to know exactly what tree cover there was 30 or 50 years ago, indicating a need for careful monitoring in the future. Some African societies have a strong tradition of caring for trees as a renewable resource, while others do not. In any event, solutions are more likely to be found at a local level, rather than through draconian actions by central governments, which all too often are simply ineffective. In the meantime, there is no obvious alternative energy source for most people, though there have been small successes in designing and selling wood-burning stoves which utilize the firewood more efficiently. •

Perhaps as a result of the reduced tree cover, or perhaps because of global warming, drought appears to be recurring with greater frequency across the continent. However, this again may just be an impression, the result of better dissemination of worldwide news. Certainly the evidence for *long-term* climatic change is highly uncertain. 'It gives no indication either of stability or of steady progressive change in the rainfall. Rather there are sudden random variations underlain by oscillations of a quasi-periodic nature and sudden shifts in mean conditions' (Grove, 1991: 40). To say this of course does not diminish the gravity of drought, or the urgency with which the international community may need to respond, when it occurs.

As far as tropical forests, specifically, are concerned, the threat is somewhat different and perhaps more manageable. It is estimated that Africa is losing its tropical forests at a rate of just less than one per cent a year (IBRD, 1992: 6). Much of the demand for tropical hardwoods is external, coming from the USA, Europe and Japan.

Zimbabwe's Campfire scheme is an attempt to give some rights in ownership of wildlife to small communities. The local people allow land, which might otherwise be used for livestock, to be reserved for wildlife. In exchange they receive part of the revenues which the wildlife can earn – mostly hunting fees in practice – and which can make a substantial difference to the incomes of people living in remote marginal areas. The scheme is still small, experimental and not without tensions. It is not necessarily a model that could be adopted everywhere. But it points in the right direction.

Paradoxically this export demand may be more readily constrained than that for local needs, through the pressure exerted by international environmental groups that forests should not be exploited beyond their sustainable yield. Without our being complacent, it seems at least possible that the remaining tropical forest in Africa, as in other parts of the world, could eventually be stabilized and brought under international surveillance – though the industrial countries may have to pay for the preservation of these lungs of the planet. The real danger is that instability or anarchy in countries such as Zaire will create a political vacuum that will then allow uncontrolled destruction of the forests in these areas. It is argued in a later chapter that the world cannot just allow political vacuums to occur in Africa, and conservation of tropical forests is one of the reasons for this.

Nevertheless, there is a risk of tunnel vision in the international environmental movement and, at the limit, of environmental preservation coming to be seen as more important than the eradication of human poverty. For many outsiders, Africa's major environmental problems concern the conservation of tropical forests and of a few species of big game – notably elephant, rhinoceros and gorilla – from the predations of armed poachers and from the erosion of their habitat by farmers and pastoralists. No doubt there are other species, even more under threat, about which less is heard but whose loss may be even more serious. The destruction of venomous snakes, for example, can lead to a rise in the rodent population and consequent greater loss of stored crops and food.

To make progress in environmental conservation, local people, not just governments and their exchequers, have to be fully involved and allowed to share in the benefits of conservation – whether these be in the form of ivory from culled elephants or the fees charged to tourists for viewing living ones. Again, as with land and trees there are uncertain questions of ownership of wildlife in which the politically weak are losing out to the more powerful or to the ambivalent interests of the nebulous state. Zimbabwe's Campfire scheme shows one way forward.

Relations with God and Man

Kith and Kin

The nuclear household, considered to be the norm in Europe, is a less important institution in Africa. Polygyny is still widely acceptable and perhaps aspired after by more men than can actually afford it, just as serial polygamy (divorce and remarriage) is common in most Western countries. Polygyny is more widespread in West Africa than in the more Christian south and east of the continent. Nonetheless, the idea of marriage as a close, social, convivial and loving relationship between a man and a woman is still relatively new and again probably strongest where Christianity has taken root or among the educated, where Western values have penetrated most. Otherwise, men and women live separate if related lives, socializing almost exclusively with those of their own sex. Gender roles are rather clearly defined, though they are not exactly the same throughout the continent. Within a wide family group, children belong to all; they are not exclusively brought up by their biological parents. Indeed, parents frequently give one of their children to another mother or couple, perhaps who have recently lost a child or who have no children of their own.

A man or woman's identity and sense of belonging is to be found in his or her clan or extended family. Clan membership may flow primarily through the male lines, in a patrilineal society, or the female line in a matrilineal society – not to be confused with a matriarchal society, which is one where women are in charge. Both patrilineal and matrilineal societies exist on the continent, together with a few, such as the Ibo, which are neither. Patrilineal societies are more common. Clans may be allied to each other, more or less closely, by means of inter-clan marriages. These alliances are measured and sealed through the practice of bride-price, whereby a certain amount of wealth – cattle, cash or both – is given by the groom's family to the bride's family. Bride-price reflects the value accorded to women, not so much for themselves but as producers of food and of the next generation. It is still common, though increasingly resented by more modern young people. It is a tradition which contrasts with the old European custom of a dowry, in which the payment goes from the bride's family to the groom, reflecting a society of more leisured females, more obviously consumers than producers.

This sense of family extends outwards to a great distance and backwards to several generations, and may even include unborn children. So, whereas Westerners generally have little family awareness beyond, say, first cousins, and to map out a family tree would be no more than an amusing diversion, to the African such a mental map of his family is the focus and centre of his identity. It is partly in this sense that the spirit of the ancestors is so important and present. Funerals, carried out furtively in our society, are events which bring whole communities and villages together.

One consequence is that a person's occupation, so important to a Western sense of identity and belonging, is relatively less so in Africa, where kith and kin are so much more determinant. This is a critical factor in the way that African economies and bureaucracies function. An effective bureaucracy depends on the notion of people being treated in a neutral way, according to predetermined rules, regardless of who they are. It requires a strong degree of professional independence, integrity and distance among those who administer the rules. All these are relatively new and unfamiliar concepts. The implication for economies and governments is a topic to which it will be necessary to return.

Another important cultural difference is the attitude to time. The Western mind lives in the fleeting present and in the future. We scheme and plan for the future incessantly. Perhaps it is part of the Protestant ethic, with its emphasis on reward in the hereafter in return for austerity now. For us, looking back is for the old, who no longer have a future, and consequently very little status. For the African it is quite the reverse. He lives in the present and savours the past; old age is accorded great respect. The distant future is remote and will look after itself. Many African languages 'have no verb tenses to cover that distant future' (Mbiti, 1990: 21). For Muslims, of course, it is even blasphemous to predict the future, which will only come about *inshallah* – if God be willing. The tendency to look back rather than forward is neither better nor worse than our obsession with the future, but it does cause society to function in a different way. This different attitude to time, and consequently to productivity and investment behaviour, is one of the greatest causes of confusion and misunderstanding whenever the two races come into contact.

Those in the towns bring all these cultural attitudes into a very different milieu. Here an active tension exists between the social, clan values of the country and the modern, Western values of the outside world, with its emphasis on individual achievement and on relating to others according to what they are, rather than who they are. Obviously when, as a young migrant, you first arrive in town to try your fortune, you stay with your 'brothers' – a much wider concept than our idea of a brother – and cousins who have made the journey before you. This is where you feel at home. However, if you are successful and find work then you begin to move into a world where what matters is what you are capable of rather than to whom you are related. Although there are now second- and third-generation townspeople, many are still country people at heart, with deep attachments to a particular village and society in the country.

Spirituality

African religion, like its culture and law, was never written down and codified. It was not so much intellectualized as lived. There was a holistic quality to life, combining social and religious order and authority, and physical health and spiritual well-being. Faith healed physical and psychological illness. The spirit mediums and healers are still consulted at times of crisis, and fulfil roles similar to those of family practitioner, counsellor and psychotherapist in Western society.

Thus, at the very centre of existence is a deep exuberant spirituality, which is a source of great good. It can also be the source of great fear and evil, as when the spirits seem to be angry, or magic is performed on enemies. In the past people had to pick a delicate course through life, surrounded on all sides by wilful and unpredictable spirits and by powerful sorcery summoned up by one's enemies. In 1897 Mary Kingsley, one of the first white women to travel in Africa, wrote:

> They regard their god as the creator of man, plants, animals, and the earth, and they hold that having made them, he takes no further interest in the affair. But not so the crowd of spirits with which the universe is peopled, they take only too much interest and the Bantu wishes they would not and is perpetually saying so in his prayers, a large percentage

whereof amounts to 'Go away we don't want you.' 'Come not into this house, this village, or its plantations.' He knows from experience that the spirits pay little heed to these objurgations, and as they are the people who must be attended to, he develops a cult whereby they may be managed, used and understood. This cult is what we call witchcraft (Kingsley, 1897).

These spiritual forces are still important today.

For many, especially those who were confounded on all sides by such forces, Christianity must have offered an escape from a very threatening spirit world. It also offered, through mission schools, a door into a different kind of society. Certainly over the last hundred years eastern and southern Africa have drunk deep from Christianity like a man with a great thirst. It is difficult to find words better than those of Bengt Sundkler:

> The theme in all these cases is the same: groups of young men looking for a job in order to buy the best that money could give, a musket of one's own or a new rifle, and in the process finding a new religion. And then the triumphant return home, the people of the village congregated to welcome their intrepid young men. They lift their guns to shoot, and thus to punctuate their travel story. But in the evening they will gather their contemporaries, and show them their greatest treasure: a book, a Gospel of S. Matthew, or perhaps even a New Testament, and they can read from it (Oliver, 1991: 205).

Perhaps a quarter to a third of Africans are now Christians, and the Church in Africa is no longer a mission church but rooted in the continent itself. Missionaries now play only a minor role. Africans have brought to Christianity their own strong spirituality, their sense of God's presence in the world and a respect and reverence for his goodness, even in times of great adversity. As might be expected, the Catholic Church is the largest Christian denomination, accounting for about half of the total. However, there has also been a great flowering of homegrown Apostolic or Zionist churches, particularly in southern Africa, in which the African exuberant spirituality, articulated through music and dance, has more easily found expression. Interestingly, these local churches, while Africanizing Christianity itself, have also been more condemnatory of, and less compromising with, traditional religion and witchcraft (Hastings, 1976: 53).

Apart from the Coptic Church in Ethiopia, Christianity is a relatively new influence in Africa. By contrast, the northern half of the

Father Julian writes from his Kalahari mission:

Last Tuesday evening, having spent three days with a poor family, I drove across the sand dunes to a place where there were some dead trees due to a seven year drought in the area. The young Zambian student, who has been travelling with me for the past month, and I cut one of the trees up, loaded it on the back of the truck and took the wood back to the family as a way of saying thank-you for their hospitality. They were delighted, as wood is very scarce in the area. However, next morning as we were about to leave I noticed that the pile of wood was gone, only a few twigs remained. When I asked what happened to it the woman of the house with a big smile told me that she had been able to share it with all the people who came to Mass at their house the previous night. That simple desert woman taught me something about the meaning of the Eucharist.

Her seventy three year old husband is the leader of the Church community. He prays aloud beautiful prayers straight from his heart for the people – I have never heard anyone pray like him – litanies of petition and praise – sheer Setswana poetry which flows effortlessly from a deep faith in God's goodness. When you listen to him it is difficult to keep back the tears.

continent has long practised Islam, which first came to Africa in the first millennium. It was a force for modernization. For the first time it opened the continent to a larger written culture of the outside world and a system of written laws. It promoted trade and, with that, prosperity.

Over time local culture absorbed Islam and vice versa. So, for example, imams in northern Nigeria sometimes engage in prophecy and foretelling of the future, a practice which can scarcely be orthodox. More recently, Islam, or at least its more fundamentalist manifestations, has adapted too little to the modern world, displaying, for example, an intolerance of other beliefs and encouraging a repressive attitude towards women. Perhaps the real difficulty is that fundamentalism, whether Islamic or Christian, does not accept a distinction, which in Western culture has long been taken for granted, between civil secular society and the religious sphere. In fundamentalist societies, civil law and behaviour are subordinated to religious law, with little liberal tolerance of those who happen to belong to that society but profess a different faith.

Of course, these are matters with which the world has to grapple, not just, or even especially, in Africa. By and large Africans are not dogmatic in their religions – they live them rather than theorize them. This applies to Islam as much as to Christianity. So the recent rise in Islamic fundamentalism in Sudan is something of an aberration in Africa south of the Sahara. In Senegal, Mali, Mauritania, Niger and northern Nigeria, Islam will always be an important force but will be unlikely to dominate events to the extent that it does in the Arab world. As a French scholar, Jean-Louis Triaud, has commented, Islam in Africa is 'more manipulated than manipulating' (Vidrovitch, 1988: 2).

The Wider World

How much has the outer world penetrated into the lives of these people? After the ending of the slave trade, the first major external influence was probably that of the missionaries. A mission education was a passport into a different world. The decision to educate one's children is still a decision to come to terms with the outside world. In fact, this opportunity is still not open to all. In sub-Saharan Africa as a whole, about a third to a half of children receive no primary education at all. Moreover, average figures conceal wide variations from one country to another, from, say, Zimbabwe or Kenya, where most children now go to school, to countries such as Ethiopia at the other extreme, where school enrolment even at the primary level is extremely low. Throughout the continent, quality of education leaves much to be desired. Even those who do receive a basic education may never become literate or may lose their literacy after a few years. Literacy is not like riding a bicycle; it can be forgotten if not reinforced. There are still few newspapers and books, other than the Bible and the Koran, outside the towns.

Yet the modern world does penetrate in one way or another. The ubiquitous transistor radio, or ghetto-blaster, is a powerful source of information, even if much of it is distorted into government propaganda. For those with some education, the BBC World Service is still immensely important, particularly in times of crisis, when impartial information is unavailable. Otherwise, government is remote and of little apparent importance, and government officials and law-enforcers may well appear more as exploitive agencies of an external power than as servants of the people.

Nonetheless, for the most part, the round of daily life in the country consists of: hard, monotonous work, especially for women; a boring and inadequate diet with the constant threat of hunger; and limited access to manufactured goods, such as soap and matches, which are often difficult to obtain in rural remoteness. Illness is to be endured, as it always has been, since medical care of anything but the most basic kind is largely inaccessible. Yet, there are reliefs and entertainment: in football, which must be second in importance only to Christianity as a cultural import; in music and song, where the rhythms of Africa have been, through the slaves taken to America, its greatest cultural export and which now enliven popular music throughout the world; and not least in those great events such as weddings and funerals which sometimes impoverish the party-givers yet which affirm the continuity of society and of social relationships.

Disease

Although there are more exotic diseases in Africa than in any other part of the world, the biggest killers are simple water-borne diseases which lead to dysentery and death by dehydration, particularly of children. In many cases, were it not for the dysentery, the body's own immune system would combat the infection. So, one of the most important medical milestones of modern times has been the perfection of oral rehydration therapy, which allows dysentery to be controlled even by unqualified medical attendants. Eventually, this type of illness will only be reduced by widespread access to safe water supplies, for which about 300 million people, or 60 per cent of the population, are still waiting (UNDP, 1991).

Many of the most debilitating diseases, which slowly sap health and strength, are parasitic in nature. Malaria is the most widespread and shows no signs of abating; indeed it is becoming increasingly resistant to the available prophylactic drugs. Fortunately, some West Africans are genetically immune to malaria but for many others it is an ever-present threat. Bilharzia, or schistosomiasis, a parasite carried by freshwater snails, is widespread and has also increased as a result of dam-building and irrigation schemes. It is believed to infect up to half the population of West Africa at some time in their lives (Grove,

1991). River blindness, onchocerciasis, affects a million or so people in West Africa and moreover makes large areas of cultivable riverine land uninhabitable.

AIDS

The newest health threat is AIDS. Unfortunately, statistics on the AIDS pandemic in Africa are still limited and unreliable. However, it is estimated that more than one per cent of the adult population of Africa is HIV positive, or in other words is likely to develop AIDS in due course, though some researchers believe that other diseases are being misdiagnosed as AIDS, so the real infection rate may be somewhat lower (Chirimuuta, 1989). Whatever the truth of the matter, it is certain that in some regions and social groups the rate of infection is much higher than in others. The problem is particularly concentrated in the towns and cities of eastern and central Africa and wherever there are transient populations, for example, along main roads and trade routes and around the shores of Lake Victoria, or where armies have been on the move. Already, whole villages in Uganda, having lost their able-bodied men and women, are disappearing as the old and the remaining children, some of whom may also be HIV positive, move away.

In these high-risk areas, HIV infection rates of 20 per cent or more among the adult population are typically reported (UNDP, 1991: 36). This includes both men and women; in Africa AIDS has never been confined to the homosexual group and is largely transmitted through heterosexual contact. Moreover, educated people, perhaps because they have a wider range of social contacts, are more widely affected than those with less education. Africa is in danger of losing much of its already very limited skilled population.

In assessing the future consequences of AIDS in Africa, two questions are important. To what extent will the disease spread through the population, and are there any limits or is a slowdown in evidence? How will societies and economies deal with the problem? As yet, we have limited research and few hard facts on which to base answers. The ultimate extent of the disease will largely depend on how much contact takes place between the groups most at risk – sexually active townspeople and migrant workers – and the rest of the population – country people and those in stable sexual relationships. One review of the available evidence suggests: 'that without major behavioural change

---

TASO, The AIDS Support Organization, is a self-help group for AIDS sufferers in Uganda. It helps those who are HIV positive to adjust to and to cope with their situation. One of their counsellors, a medical assistant, has this to say of the epidemic:

Since the early 1980s we have been seeing this disease, but at that time it had no name. We thought it was only smugglers from Tanzania who got it because they were bewitched. But since we medical people don't believe in witchcraft, we were puzzled. Then we saw people affected who were certainly not smugglers, and who did not move about anywhere. I tried using strong drugs, but it still reoccurred and people died. As time went on, there were so many. It was such a worry, how to cope with them all. You lose credit because your patients don't get better and die. Some doctors won't even treat patients they suspect have AIDS. I've also seen many cases wrongly diagnosed – sometimes it's just a curable disease, but they stop the treatment because they think it's AIDS (Hampton, 1990).

... HIV incidence among African adults is likely to rise to 8–15 per cent in the next 15–20 years and then level off' (Becker, 1990).

Such calculations may seem dry and insensitive. What they show is that AIDS in Africa is a far greater problem than it is in the West, but: 'while all the projections indicate that hundreds of thousands of deaths will occur from AIDS, even the highest mortality projections do not give rise to depopulation' (Becker, 1990). The same study suggests that the population growth rate might ultimately be reduced by about 0.5 per cent a year in those countries which are most severely affected, say, from just over 3 per cent a year to just under 3 per cent a year, though other research is more pessimistic. So although AIDS is becoming yet another major African killer disease, which will decimate some groups of people and parts of society, its demographic impact will be to reduce the growth of population rather than to cause widespread depopulation of the continent as a whole.

For the spread of the disease to slow down, the first requirement is popular understanding of how it is transmitted. While initially AIDS may have been considered to be a consequence of witchcraft, more scientific explanations are now gaining ground, accompanied by a greater knowledge of how to reduce the risk. There is some scattered evidence that younger people are beginning to change their behavioural patterns as a result of the AIDS threat – albeit more towards reducing the number of sexual partners than to a widespread use of condoms (Barnett and Blaikie, 1991). Nevertheless, people can live with the knowledge of a danger but at the same time psychologically refuse to accept it, particularly where, as with smoking and cancer, the gratification is immediate and the danger postponed. According to a recent study of AIDS in Uganda, men are more inclined than women to make this psychological refusal.

So, for the time being, the rate of infection will increase and, in view of the time-lag between becoming HIV positive and the onset of illness and death, the number of adults dying from AIDS in the prime of life will rise until well into the early years of the next century – even if there were to be a very rapid change in behavioural patterns among the young. As a result of both death and disease, the proportion of able-bodied people in affected communities will fall considerably, compared with the numbers of dependent children and old people. The resilience of African society, with its particularly strong ties of family, will help to cope with the consequent social problems – supporting the ill, adopting orphans and so on. Certainly, as with refugees, it will be Africans themselves who will do most of the effective coping rather than agencies from outside. However, since labour is required for food production there will be greater hunger and poverty. The need for external food aid may be greater than ever.

The purely medical costs of treating people with AIDS are far beyond the capacity of the health services in all the countries concerned. Already, there are reports of hospital beds in the major cities being largely taken up with AIDS patients or those who have contracted other illnesses as a result of AIDS. Most AIDS sufferers will simply not be treated. However, there will be knock-on effects on the treatment of other illnesses as resources get diverted to AIDS patients. With a reservoir among AIDS sufferers, the incidence of other diseases, such as tuberculosis, may also rise in the population as a whole.

In short, in the absence of any vaccination or cure for the HIV virus, the outlook is bleak indeed, but, sadly, so it is for malaria and for other tropical infections. AIDS, as a disease of the educated and of townspeople, will get the attention and publicity, but it may possibly not be the greatest health threat to Africa.

2 Measuring Africa's Development

Progress, man's distinctive mark alone,
Not God's, and not the beasts': God is, they are,
Man partly is and wholly hopes to be.
(Browning, 'A Death in the Desert')

Development entails cultural change, or the accommodation by traditional societies to the values and beliefs of the modern world. As such, it cannot readily be measured. However, the rather unreliable economic and social indicators which are available suggest that there has been very little development in Africa as a whole for the last 30 years. All the same, the variations in development performance between one country and another are striking, with the more politically stable countries tending to be the more successful.

A Philosophical Interlude

We now turn to the matter of development, a topic which has been at the forefront of discussions about Africa for at least the last 30 years, and certainly ever since the time of independence. What do we really mean by development, and how much development have the people of Africa experienced over this period?

Development is a term which is used so loosely and freely that it has little precise meaning. Other words are available. The Victorians referred to the 'civilization' of primitive peoples. Historians talk about the 'modernization' of societies, by which they mean the process of organizing society around rational and secular concepts rather than spiritual ideas and values. All of these words imply change. More importantly, they contain the idea of other people's changing in order to adopt the values and mores of our own modern, Western society.

One of the problems of the development process is that we all take

One clash between two systems of values led to a major public debate in Kenya. It concerned the marriage between two thoroughly modernized and prominent Kenyans, he being Luo and she being Kikuyu. On his death his widow, following his expressed wishes when he was alive, wanted him buried on their private farm. But the Luo elders insisted that he be buried in the Luo region and according to Luo custom, even though he had effectively been detribalized and had lived in Nairobi for a long time. The issue was between the modern rights of a wife and the traditional rights of the extended family or tribe. The case was fought through the Kenyan courts, the widow eventually losing. It is dramatically recounted by Harden in his book *Africa, Dispatches from a Fragile Continent* (Harden, 1990), in which he argues that the Appeal Court's verdict 'was almost certainly fixed by Kenya's president'.

our beliefs and values for granted; they are the hidden assumptions of our day-to-day lives and thoughts. In exchanges with people from other societies and cultural and historical backgrounds, their hidden assumptions clash with ours. So, having spent some pages previously trying to understand African culture and society, it is worth a short interlude to examine our own and bring them to the surface. These hidden assumptions provide the framework within which, rightly or wrongly, development is conceived. Many educated Africans have to live out these conflicts between different sets of values within their own lives and respond to the inevitable tension they create.

Core Beliefs of Western Modernity

What are the beliefs and values which modern, Western culture purveys to the rest of the world and particularly to the so-called undeveloped, less developed or developing countries? Five elements are important for the present discussion.

First, the world around us, even if created and sustained by a god, is driven by rational, impartial laws which can be measured and investigated scientifically. It is not governed by the arbitrary, apparently irrational, whims of a spirit world, which characterize traditional African and other pre-modern religions. Spiritual beliefs are not denied in Western modernity, but become part of a private sphere which does not directly affect ordinary life. Thus, it is possible to be a scientist while retaining private spiritual beliefs, and the touchstone for the authenticity of secular, scientific knowledge is that it should be free of cultural values and transferable to other cultures. This pursuit of secular, scientific understanding is manifestly one of the most powerful features of modern values and beliefs, since it has enabled the control and manipulation of the material world to a degree which no other belief system has ever remotely achieved.

Second, whereas some cultures, including those of pre-colonial Africa, would assert the primacy of the social group, *vis-à-vis* its individual members, Western modernity, particularly the Anglo-Saxon tradition of Locke, reverses this priority. The individual person is the most important element in society. Individual human rights and free-doms take precedence over those of the social group. This is not to say that there can never be any restraint on individual freedom, but, rather, such restraint has to be justified on the grounds that, without it, the rights of other individuals would be compromised. For example, over the matter of private ownership, which is close to the core of such values, the individual is restrained from stealing because this limits the rights of others to have private property. This assertion of the primacy of the individual is not always accepted by those from a different cultural tradition, as we shall see later over the issue of human rights.

A third principle of Western modernity, which largely proceeds from the first two, is that of popular sovereignty. The ultimate arbiters of the legitimacy and acceptability of any particular form of human government are the people who are governed, and not some higher spirit world or god-figure who has determined rules for society and government. There is no longer any divine right of kings, nor for that matter any historical destiny of either the ruling or the working classes. The priest-kings, who, as we shall see, ruled African societies for many hundreds of years, have no place in this value system. Popular sovereignty is the basic principle of democracy. It does not, of course, explain how democracy is to be articulated in particular circumstances, which enables many dictatorial regimes to claim a bogus legitimacy on the basis of some interpretation of popular sovereignty. It also leaves unresolved the determination of which groups are entitled to self-government and which are merely minorities in a larger society, an issue which is troubling many parts of the world in the 1990s.

Fourth, Westernism plays down the biological accidents of particular individuals – whether of race, sex, kin or birth. Instead, it asserts the intrinsic equality of all people. Distinguishing between individuals on the basis of who they are is less acceptable than judging them on what they do, or what they have achieved. Out of this grows, first, the distinction, vital to our society, between a person and the various roles she or he fills and, second, the struggle for equal treatment for women *vis-à-vis* men, for people of all races, for children and old people against those in the prime of life, and for the sick and disabled against the healthy. Discrimination on the basis of biological characteristics, although it frequently occurs, is deviant behaviour which contradicts the norms.

Finally, Western beliefs and values include the notion of change, of human progress towards some end. This may be as prosaic as the economist's search for unending economic growth or as mystical as Teilhard de Chardin's *Omega Point*, where humanity evolves in some way into a more complex social form much greater than the sum of the individuals concerned. Indeed, those of us who have grown up in the Western world since the end of the Second World War have our own personal experiences on which to base this belief in change and progress. In our time and place in human history, we have witnessed rising economic well-being, stable and settled societies, relative social order and, perhaps most dramatically, an enormous increase in human scientific knowledge and technical capacity. One comes to believe that such progress represents the normal state of affairs.

Modernity and Development

A characteristic of this set of Western beliefs and values is its claim to universality, which goes beyond the particular culture and society of the Western world. If all individuals are of equal value, then people everywhere are entitled to be treated in the same way, whether or not they come from cultures which endorse these particular beliefs. Hence, the United Nations, whose very existence is itself an outcome of Western values, asserts universal principles of human rights – in which the rights of individuals feature prominently. Or, to put it another way, Westernism may advocate tolerance of other private beliefs and values, but would oppose societies based on radically different social norms, for example, that all individuals were not equal and thus that slavery or racial discrimination were legitimate bases for social organization. Similarly, since the idea of human progress is also a characteristic of modernity, Westerners are inclined to think, somewhat arrogantly, that development should also be universally available and be offered to, even imposed on, those coming from different cultural backgrounds.

It is thus important to consider, first, whether this complex of beliefs and values which make up Western modernity, and which outsiders, wittingly or unwittingly, transmit to African and other premodern societies, is indeed an essential part of development, and, second, if it is, can and should this system of values actually be transmitted to peoples coming from different cultural and social backgrounds?

The origins of Western modernity appear to lie in the European, Judaeo-Christian cultural background, with its strong emphasis on salvation, on a human destiny, and with its belief in a God who has a purpose for his chosen people or, in the Christian tradition, ultimately for all peoples. The belief in salvation and the modern notion of human progress and hence of development are intimately linked. Weber, who addressed this question, attributes the remarkable success of Western capitalism to the particular characteristics of Protestant Christianity.

Yet the examples of Japan, a developed nation by any criteria, and of other rapidly changing east Asian nations such as Singapore and Korea, suggest that, indeed, development can occur against quite different cultural backgrounds. Japanese modernity shares some characteristics with that of the West and demonstrates some differences. The common element is the privatization of the purely religious, spiritual sphere of life and the adoption of secular, rational, scientific values to govern ordinary day-to-day life. The main difference is that Japanese, like African, society is far less individualistic than that of the West, placing more emphasis on group and community values. This means that the detailed functioning of Japanese social organizations, from governments to large corporations, may be quite dissimilar to those of the Western world, even if the outward forms are the same.

Thus, it might be said that human progress or development does seem to have to draw on modern values, but does not necessarily require the wholesale adoption of specifically Western values – in so far as such a distinction can be made. Indeed, wherever development occurs there is likely to be some adaptation to the particular historical circumstances and culture of the country concerned. Japan did this very consciously during its Meiji period in the nineteenth century.

No doubt as time goes on this process of adaptive adoption will also occur in Africa. The outcome is likely to be a set of social and political institutions which will in part reflect the continent's own social history and in part draw on modern systems of beliefs and values which have proved capable of delivering material prosperity elsewhere. Thus, popular sovereignty may be acknowledged, without necessarily leading to Western-style democracy. The centrality of the individual may be recognized, without denying his or her role in, and duties to, the community. Rationality may be the guiding principle of ordinary life, without pushing the spiritual world to the background to quite the degree that Western society has done. In some of these matters the West may still have much to learn from its contact with African societies.

Yet development should not be confused with wealth. While it is difficult to think of any developed society which has rejected modernity, it is possible to think of wealthy societies which have done so. Saudi Arabia, for example, or at least its rulers, does not recognize the equality of all individuals regardless of gender, nor the principle of popular sovereignty, nor a distinction between the secular and the private religious sphere.

It is important not to push this discussion of cultural differences too far. Much that is pre-modern remains in today's Western society. When relatives of the US soldiers who died in the Vietnam War place personal objects before the memorial in Washington where all of their names are inscribed, they are engaging in an act of piety not dissimilar to ancestor worship. Those who take astrology seriously, or even only half seriously, appear to believe that there are or may be various non-rational forces at work in the world. Similarly, the mood of Christian fundamentalism which affects the United States is increasingly unwilling to accept the distinction, characteristic of modernity, between God's law and secular law, for example over abortion.

Finally, a major part, perhaps the major part, of life in modern societies is still lived in a private sphere of family and personal relationships, where the modern notion of impartial, indifferent roles has no place at all. A mother is a mother to only certain specific children; no one else can step into those particular shoes. Indeed, if one were to imagine a whole spectrum of human behaviour with the most intensely personal, such as motherhood, at one extreme, and the

In his book *Social Limits to Growth*, Fred Hirsch is pessimistic as to whether the tension between the individualism of the market place and the broader social restraints, both of which are necessary to make a modern capitalist economy work, can be sustained in the long term. Thus: 'The pursuit of private and essentially individualistic goals by enterprises, consumers, and workers in their market choices – the distinctive capitalistic values that give the system its drive – must be girded at key points by a strict morality which the system erodes rather than sustains.' And again: 'If judges were regularly to sell their services and decisions to the highest bidder, not only the system of justice but also of property would be completely unstable' (Hirsch, 1977: 117 and 143). Carrying over the subtleties of such an economic system to a completely different cultural background is not straightforward.

most impartial role-filling, such as the dispensation of justice, at the other, then perhaps the essential difference between modern societies and those of traditional Africa is whether they tend to draw their roles more from one end of the spectrum than from the other.

The Tension in a Market Economy

Having made the claim that development requires the adoption, more or less, of modern values, we now have to recognize that a serious tension exists between these very values and the effective functioning of a modern market economy.

Someone participating in a market does so for personal gain, not for the benefit of society as a whole or for some larger collectivity. Of course, as Adam Smith pointed out, the overall effect of many actors in the market pursuing their own individual interests can lead to a gain for the whole community. However, this does not alter the fact that the market is essentially driven by greed.

Market transactions and trade, except of the most primitive barter kind, need another element as well as individual greed. A degree of mutual trust is required between the participants. This can only develop where there is some common set of beliefs and values. For example, West African societies flourished for centuries through trade, partly because the unifying force of Islam provided the necessary common cultural framework. The early merchant, setting out across the Sahara, trusted that, when he arrived at his destination, his property rights in his trade goods would be respected; that he would not simply be set upon and robbed. Of course, mutual acquaintance of individuals was also an important element, just as it has been in the City of London for a long time.

In a complex modern economy, mutual acquaintance and trust have to be supported by laws of contract enforceable in courts, by agreed weights and measures, by common understanding of property rights and so on. Modern states have legal systems, bureaucracies of impartial officials and judges in order to provide and administer this framework. It is important for the prosperity of society as a whole that these administrators, in filling their particular roles, cannot be bribed or bought and do not give preference to those of their own social or ethnic group – or indeed to any particular individual. Of course, these practices do occur, but they are held to be deviant behaviour and are labelled as corrupt.

Thus, the paradox of the modern economy is that, while its great energy and inventiveness are driven by selfishness and greed, it is overseen by officials, judges, and indeed politicians who are expected to operate according to very different standards, in which individual selfishness for personal gain has no place at all. The overseers of the market have to restrain their own greed. Clearly, such impartial arbiters have to be rewarded in different ways – including that of a special social status. The British custom of awarding judges and civil servants honours and titles is useful in this respect.

Corruption

This tension at the very centre of a modern market economy, between two sets of values which have to run in parallel and be maintained in equilibrium, is at the origin of corruption, which of course is not exclusive to the Third World. Corruption emerges as a distinct problem as and when societies modernize and begin to assign specific roles, with particular powers to certain people, such as politicians and judges. A conflict then emerges between what the modernizing society sanctions as acceptable behaviour for these roles if the system is to function well, and what may be in the private interests of the individual concerned and perhaps be sanctioned, or even required, by more traditional beliefs and values.

The resolution of the tension is by no means the same in all societies, not even among all modern or developed societies. Indeed, if one compares what is regarded as acceptable behaviour in various Western countries, quite different, even mutually exclusive, norms appear. For example a British member of parliament (MP) can take directorships of companies, be sponsored by trade unions and generally have more direct links with the world of business than can a US congressman. Yet the notion of active political lobbying is more dubious in the UK than it is in the USA. To take an example from the world of finance, insider dealing in stocks and shares is a criminal offence in the UK and the USA, but is widely accepted in other market economies, including Japan.

From this perspective, the prevalence of corruption in developing countries is just a visible manifestation of the consequences of traditional and modern value systems running side by side and causing tension within individuals. The bureaucrat will certainly be torn between applying the modern value system, which requires him to act impartially and fulfil a particular role, and using his position for personal gain or to provide favours and rewards to his family members or those of his ethnic group. His decision will certainly be influenced by whether his role – in other words, his job – pays him well enough to live. If it does not, he may feel obliged to be corrupt in order to survive. Thus, a civil service which considers itself to be underpaid or under-rewarded, such as many African countries now have, is particularly susceptible to corruption, and this directly undermines the instillation of modern values into the government system.

In the end, different societies cope with corruption in different ways. Indeed, some modernizing societies, Indonesia for example, seem to have institutionalized a very high level of corruption, without fundamental economic efficiency being overly impaired. Somehow, many of the correct, that is economically efficient, decisions get taken anyway. Unfortunately, this is not the case in Africa, where the prevalence of corruption has led to many poor, that is economically inefficient, decisions being taken – though from the point of view of the corrupt decision-maker with his long chain of dependants, they may indeed be eminently sensible. In these circumstances, the social costs of corruption go way beyond the mere financial cost of the transaction itself and extend to the whole economy. Ultimately, if every administrative or political decision is taken with an eye to the pay-off for the decision-maker or for his circle, then rationality, the underlying principle of the modern state, is completely undermined. Those who may be trying to work the system honestly, of whom there are many in Africa, will become frustrated and ineffective. That many educated Africans recognize corruption for what it is and do not deny its corrosive effects on development, even when they are sometimes caught up in it, is a sign for hope. Many, no doubt, would like to get out of its web if only they could and so long as others did also. To help break this vicious circle, the United Nations Development Programme (UNDP) has proposed the setting up of a small international monitoring organization which would publicize information about corruption, as Amnesty International does with human rights (UNDP, 1992). Indeed, in 1993 such a group, called Transparency International and based in Berlin, was established as a private initiative but its success remains to be seen (Transparency International, 1993).

Indicators of Africa's Development

To summarize, development involves the steady adoption by a society of modern, though not necessarily Western, values, or at least their absorption into its own culture. Among these values is the belief in human progress – that life will not necessarily be just the same next year as it was last, but rather that we are entitled to expect that it will get better. Of course, the very notion of actually measuring human progress or development is a characteristic of modernity. The people and societies being measured may actually be rather indifferent to the result.

Statistical Problems

Before going further, some comment is needed on the problems of any form of statistical measurement in Africa, where all economic and social statistics are of very poor quality. In order to arrive at estimates of, say, income or production, complicated, detailed and regular surveys are required. These then have to be carefully analysed and interpreted. Such work is beyond the capacity of many African statistical offices, which, like so much else on the continent, are desperately short of skilled and educated manpower. The truth is that we have very little idea of even the most basic statistics on Africa, such as: the population of different countries, the number of children going to

A striking example of the fallibility of published African statistics is provided by those for Nigeria's population. In the absence of a reliable census for two decades, the World Bank estimated Nigeria's 1990 population at 115.5 million (IBRD, 1992). Yet the 1991 census eventually counted only 88.5 million people, far fewer than expected. The estimate was thus 30 per cent greater than the census figure. Not all African population statistics and projections are quite so uncertain, but many economic statistics are.

school, the level of agricultural production, the level of a country's exports and imports when smuggling is taken into account, or even the size of the external debt. Yet governments and outside experts will formulate important policies and decisions on the basis of very weak information. Of course often they have to: not to have a policy is itself a policy. Nevertheless, the robustness of a policy in the face of possible inaccuracies in the numbers should be examined more often than it is.

The same dilemma occurs in this book. Not to use the available statistics on Africa is to throw some information, albeit of poor quality, away. Nonetheless, to draw too precise conclusions from the data would be to place a greater weight on the numbers than they can really support. So in this chapter and in the rest of the book, we shall present various African statistics and indeed draw broad and tentative conclusions from them. The health warning about the inherent unreliability of the data will not always be repeated. Nevertheless, the reader is urged to bear it in mind.

Moreover, it tends to be the least developed and least politically stable countries which do not produce the statistics. To be able to collect them is of itself a measure of development. Thus, the published data tend to come most reliably from those countries which are modernizing the fastest. Most of the graphs which follow in this chapter deliberately leave out the very small countries, with a population of less than one million people. The attentive reader will notice that in each of the graphs some of the larger countries are missing also, for lack of published data. He or she can reasonably surmise that the missing countries would in most cases lie to the lower end of the particular indicator being examined. Thus, the lack of published data for some countries may give an upward bias to the overall picture of development for the continent as a whole.

Income Levels

We return now to the question of how to measure development. At this point, there is usually a sleight of hand in the reasoning, and the notion of economic development is slipped into the argument as a proxy for human progress. No doubt this reflects the materialist spirit of the modern age. Unfortunately, this sleight of hand is all too convenient, since many economic parameters are measurable, whereas social and political conditions are less so, and spiritual values certainly are not. In the following discussion, we shall start by considering economic indicators before turning to a number of social indicators of development.

The most common way of estimating living conditions in a country is to determine the average income of its people. Even as a purely economic measurement this presents some difficulties. First, there are definitional problems. Some work produces things which are used directly by the household itself. This is called 'income in kind' and would include food grown for family consumption, for example, or a house built for oneself. Other household activities, broadly corresponding to what Westerners would regard as domestic activity – food preparation, for example, which can take several hours of hard labour a day, or the long walks to collect water – are not considered to be productive activity at all, according to the agreed statistical conventions, and therefore do not generate income in kind. Thus, a major part of normal female activity is simply excluded from consideration.

On the other side, there are certain economic activities which take place in industrial societies and which are incorporated into the production and income statistics but which really reflect the ancillary costs accompanying a higher standard of living rather than directly improving human welfare. Pollution abatement would be an example, or the disposal of packaging materials. Much military expenditure falls into the same category, which is not to deny the right and duty of the state to defend itself. When national income statistics are used to compare levels of development or human welfare between countries it might be better to take all these activities out of the accounts.

The second problem is that the average income level for a country

National income, the expression used here, is broadly the same as Gross National Product, or GNP – the difference merely concerns depreciation. However, since the discussion is about living standards the concept of income seems more appropriate than that of production.

GNP measures what is produced by nationals of a country. Gross Domestic Product, or GDP, measures what is produced within a country, not necessarily by its nationals. For most African countries GDP would be slightly larger than GNP. In the case of Lesotho, it is the other way around – GDP is only about half of GNP. This arises because many Basotho work in South Africa. Thus, the national product is higher than the domestic product.

frequently conceals the fact that a few people in a country may be very rich while the majority live in great poverty. So, if one is interested in the standard of living of the majority of people, average income levels can be dangerously misleading. If strict comparisons are to be made between one country and another, then the income distribution of each should be taken into account. Income is more unequally distributed in Latin American countries than in those of Asia. Income distribution in Africa probably falls somewhere in between – though very few hard data are available on which to base this assertion.

Finally, in order to make inter-country comparisons, the average income for each country has been shown in the same currency, usually the US dollar. However, the official exchange rates, used to convert from a domestic currency to the dollar, may not reflect the different costs of living in the countries being compared. Considerable research

The *Economist* magazine makes rough and ready estimates of purchasing power parity by looking at the price of a McDonald's Big Mac hamburger in different countries. The comparison is not as frivolous as it may seem, since the product is more or less the same in different countries, it contains a number of important foods – including bread and meat – and the price includes some labour and energy costs as well.

is now being undertaken and coordinated by the United Nations Statistical Office to make international comparisons of the cost of living in different countries. From these are derived purchasing power parity (PPP) rates of exchange between different currencies. Purchasing power parity is the rate of exchange at which the overall cost of a typical selection of goods is the same in the different countries being compared. One of the difficulties with this work is that a selection of goods which may seem reasonable for one country may not be appropriate in another because of differences in taste and in consumption patterns. In general, however, such studies show that real income levels between countries are not quite so dispersed as the raw unadjusted data would suggest.

Despite all of these reservations, income per capita figures do tell us something about the state of economic development in a particular country. Figure 2.1 shows income per capita, or, strictly, GDP per capita, using PPP rates of exchange for different groups of developing countries for the years 1960 and 1989. The data have been adjusted to take account of the effects of inflation. On this comparison, the development performance of Africa has been very similar to that of South Asia, a region which includes India, Pakistan and Bangladesh, and which is as poor as Africa. African income has increased by about 90 per cent over these 29 years, or about 2.2 per cent a year, as has

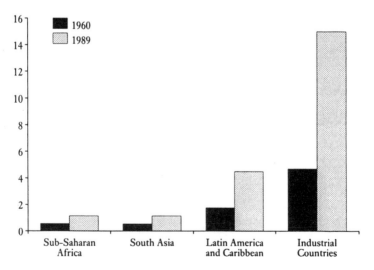

Figure 2.1 GDP per capita using PPP rates of exchange (US$ 1,000)

that of South Asia. The growth in other regions of the world has been far greater; the absolute income gap between Africa and the industrial countries or, indeed, Latin America has widened considerably.

If actual rather than PPP rates of exchange are used, Africa's performance looks even worse. The World Bank estimates income growth on this basis to have averaged only 0.2 per cent a year between 1965 and 1990, rather lower than for South Asia (IBRD, 1992). The gap between Africa and other parts of the world appears even greater too.

So, have incomes been stagnating as the latter comparison implies or actually growing at 2 per cent a year as Figure 2.1 suggested? It is a difficult question to answer. The slightly more hopeful PPP data are probably the more interesting, but the calculations behind them are subject to enormous uncertainties. The important point is that average income growth in Africa has been rather low compared with other regions of the world over the same period, though not, it should be said, low by historical standards, either for Africa or for the world as a whole.

One feature which is not apparent from these diagrams is that rates of economic growth have changed considerably over time. The first years of independence, up to the mid-1970s, saw significant progress in many parts of Africa. Since then, economic performance has deteriorated, particularly during the 1980s, when per capita incomes in most countries actually fell. Renewed growth may be occurring in the 1990s in some countries, as a consequence of what has come to be called economic adjustment. We shall discuss the meaning and importance of this in Chapter 5.

Social Indicators

Because of the problems of using average income as a measure of a country's level of development, various other indicators have been devised to attempt to capture some of the more social components of development. Unlike income measures, where the average can be dominated by the high incomes of a few people, social indicators are less prone to such distortions. There are natural upper limits for most social indicators, such as life expectancy or school enrolment, whereas there are no upper limits on personal wealth and income. Hence, social indicators offer a more reliable picture of the general social circumstances in which people live – their health, educational levels and so on.

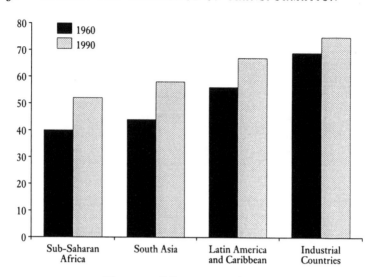

Figure 2.2 Life expectancy in years

Figure 2.2 shows life expectancy at birth for Africa and other regions in 1960 and 1990. Life expectancy in, say, 1990, is the average age to which a child born in 1990 can be expected to live on the basis of present circumstances. It is not the average age of a population, which is determined by other factors as well as life expectancy. It is generally considered to be the best single indicator of the level of health in a country, and perhaps of general welfare, since it encapsulates many social aspects. It is obviously highly influenced by the rate of infant mortality, which is high in Africa as a result of poor hygiene, polluted water supplies or unavailability of medical care to deal with normal childhood diseases. It is also influenced by adult experiences, such as nutritional deficiencies, endemic diseases, the welfare of mothers and so on.

Overall, the figure shows life expectancy in sub-Saharan Africa to be 52 years, compared with 40 years in 1960. Again, in historical terms this represents a major improvement. However, in comparison with other regions of the world, including South Asia, Africa still lags behind. The truth is that an African baby born today can expect to die more than two decades earlier than one born in the industrial West.

Figure 2.3 illustrates one of a number of possible educational indicators, the net primary school enrolment ratio as at the end of the

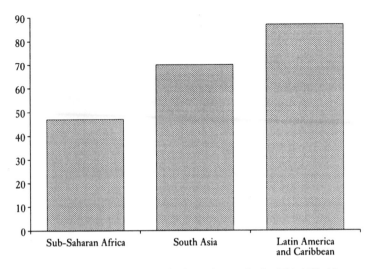

Figure 2.3 Net primary school enrolments in the Third World
(% of primary school age group enrolled, 1989)

1980s. This is the proportion of primary school age children who are actually enrolled in school. Other children may also be enrolled, but they fall outside the relevant age group. The net primary enrolment ratio in sub-Saharan Africa is estimated at 47 per cent, compared with 88 per cent in developing countries as a whole and even 70 per cent in South Asia, which in this respect has clearly pulled ahead of Africa (UNDP, 1992). Figure 6.4 in Chapter 6 shows the ratios for selected African countries individually. Chapter 6 returns to this indicator, arguing that its improvement ought to be the main target for aid agencies.

Availability of Food

Finally, Figure 2.4 attempts to compare hunger in Africa with that in other regions. It is estimated that, between 1965 and 1988, the average food supply in Africa fell from 92 per cent to 88 per cent of what is required, on the basis of theoretical nutritional calculations of what is needed to maintain health and growth. Hunger has thus been growing. The change may appear to be small but it is in the wrong direction. Other regions of the world, including South Asia, have seen an increase in the food supply over the same period, partly as a result of

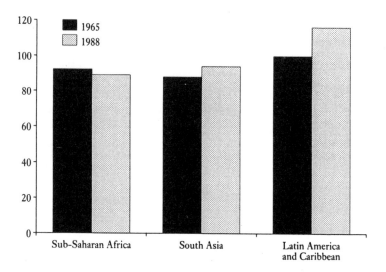

Figure 2.4 Mean daily food supply per head (% of daily requirements)

the Green Revolution. Moreover, since these are average figures, they conceal wide variations. Some people will be getting more than the minimum required, while others will be getting very much less. There are many things which hold back the food supply in Africa, though not generally a shortage of land: difficult climatic conditions, poor economic policy, the under-education of country people, and the absence of a technical breakthrough similar to the Green Revolution.

Overall, it may be concluded that, since the independence period, Africa has seen some increase in living standards and average income. How great that increase has been seems to depend on how the measurement is done. What can be said is that the development achieved in no way matches up to the enormous expectations of 30 years ago and seems a very poor reward for the efforts of Africans themselves and for the money of aid agencies and other outsiders. The gap between Africa and other parts of the world has not narrowed at all; indeed it has widened. Even South Asia, a comparable region, has pulled ahead in some respects, notably in feeding and educating its people and in improving their general health and life expectancy.

African Countries in Detail

Economic Indicators

However, African countries are not all the same and it is worth examining briefly the development performances for them individually. Let us start with the fallible but useful indicator of income. Figure 2.5 arranges countries by order of increasing per capita income using World Bank data, not corrected for PPP in this case. The most striking feature is that, even within a poor continent such as Africa, there are wide differences in average income levels between one country and another. However, the three countries at the top of the diagram – Botswana, Mauritius and Gabon – are all rather small and in different ways special cases.

Year-by-year economic growth rates, which are often given in great detail, are largely meaningless for African countries because of the unreliability of the underlying data. Nevertheless, something worthwhile can be discerned over a long period, say 25 years, as shown in Figure 2.6. The data are for the growth in income per capita, that is, after allowing for the increase in population, and after adjusting for inflation over the period. At one extreme, income levels in a few countries, such as Uganda, Niger and Zaire, have been falling by more than 2 per cent a year over the last generation. At the other extreme, the average per capita income in Botswana has been growing at 8 per cent a year. The difference between these extremes is enormous. African economic performance is not quite as uniform as it often seems, though once more it is smaller countries which, for one reason or another, have proved to be more successful.

Figure 2.6 also distinguishes between countries which have enjoyed political stability over the 25-year period and those which have not. Political stability, for this purpose, is taken to mean that there has been no military intervention in the process of government from independence until at least 1990 – see the discussion in Chapter 4 and particularly Figure 4.1. The politically stable countries cluster at the top of the diagram, demonstrating a clear association between political stability and economic growth.

The Human Development Index

Because average per capita income and economic growth are an unsatisfactory way to measure development, the United Nations

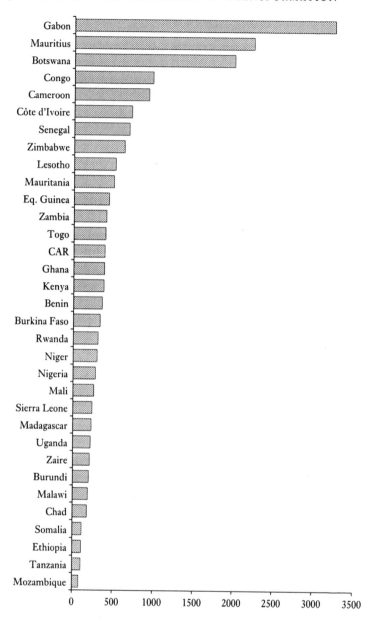

Figure 2.5 Per capita income levels, 1990 (US$)

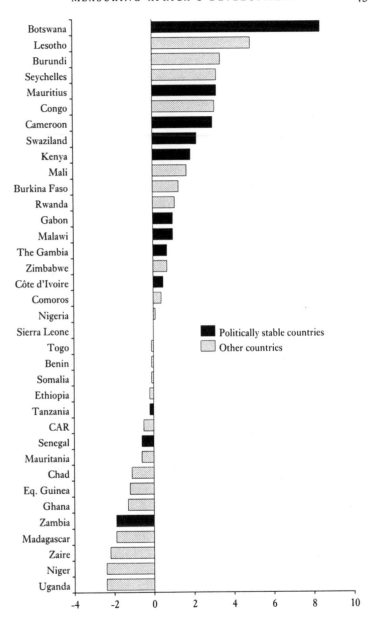

Figure 2.6 Average annual growth rate in per capita income, 1965–90 (%)

Development Programme (UNDP) has drawn up and published a composite social development indicator, which it calls the human development index (HDI). In its most recent form, it consists of four components for each country: average per capita income, life expectancy, adult literacy and mean years of schooling. Although the technical details of how the index is constructed need not concern us here, it is important to understand that it is just one possible measure of human welfare and inevitably includes a subjective element.

The HDI of a country can vary between 0 and 1. The higher the index number the greater the measured degree of social development – that is, the higher the average per capita income, life expectancy, adult literacy, etc. Worldwide, Canada and Japan head the list with indicators of 0.98. Guinea and Sierra Leone come at the bottom with 0.05 and 0.06 respectively. Almost all African countries are to be found in the lower third of the global list.

In Figure 2.7, individual African countries have been arranged in order of increasing per capita income, as in Figure 2.5 previously. The HDI for each has then been superimposed on the income data. As expected the HDI tends to rise along with income levels towards the top of the diagram. The relationship is by no mean uniform. Many countries, while remaining quite poor, have been able to achieve relatively high levels of human development. Tanzania, Madagascar, Kenya, Ghana, Zambia, Lesotho, and Zimbabwe stand out particularly in this respect. For others, such as Somalia, Chad, Sierra Leone, Mali, Burkina Faso, Guinea and Mauritania, the reverse is true: their HDI is relatively low for the income level attained. Clearly, the HDI is measuring something other than per capita income.

Finally, Figure 2.8 explores the relationship between human development and political stability. Countries are ranked in order of increasing HDI as estimated for 1990. Those which have been politically stable are shown in white; those which have been subject to military coups and instability are in black. The stable countries cluster strongly towards the top of the diagram. Human development, like economic growth, which was shown in Figure 2.6, certainly seems to go along with political stability.

Figure 2.8 also shows some tendency for the Islamic countries of West Africa to have lower levels of human development. The most likely explanation for this is the discrimination against women in Islamic societies and the consequently lower levels of educational attainment of women, tending to bring down the HDI for the country

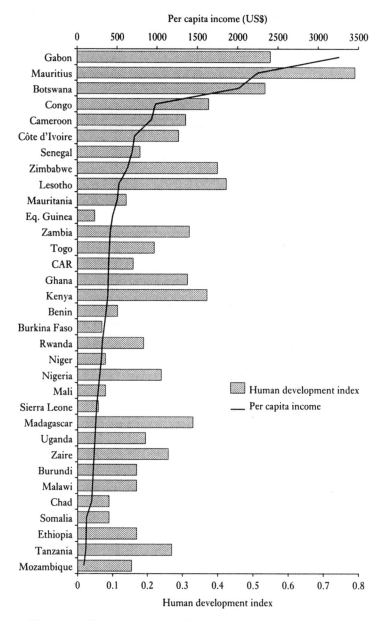

Figure 2.7 Human development index and per capita income, 1990

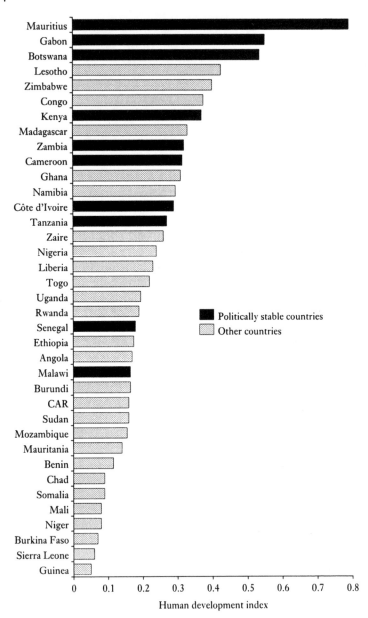

Figure 2.8 Human development index and political stability, 1990

concerned. We shall argue later that the education of girls is absolutely critical to Africa's future.

Sustainable Development

A fashionable topic in the present development debate is that of sustainable development, which means different things to different people. One strand of argument is that it is not possible for all of the poor nations to attain the material standards of the industrial countries without putting an unacceptable strain on the global environment. This view is perhaps best articulated in the book *Beyond the Limits* (Meadows et al., 1992), written by the same authors as *Limits to Growth* (Meadows et al., 1972) twenty years earlier.

Like the earlier study and unlike many other doomsday books, *Beyond the Limits* has the merit of attempting to model and quantify its case, not merely to state it. The authors' previous work had argued that, since the natural resources of the earth were finite, economic growth could not go on indefinitely. At some time, the earth would run out of resources. The sooner mankind anticipated this constraint, the easier would be the eventual adjustment. The more recent study used the same computer model with updated information. One thing which had changed in the intervening two decades was that, as a result of technical progress, natural resources, including energy, are being used more efficiently than they were in the earlier period, particularly in the richer countries. So, the constraint on resource availability has receded somewhat.

Nevertheless, according to the new study, there is still an ultimate limit, though this is now seen to be determined more by pollution and the problem of waste disposal than by the supply of resources in the first place. The global systems for absorbing pollution and dealing with waste products will, it is argued, soon be inadequate unless wasteful materialist habits and consumption patterns are severely modified or abandoned. Otherwise, there will be ever higher costs of pollution control and waste management, which may be necessary but, in themselves, add nothing to the quality of life.

The debate is clearly important, but it is a debate more appropriate for the rich world than it is for Africa. It would be quite wrong for the rich countries to deny the fruits of economic growth to those who still have so little material prosperity, simply because of a problem which they themselves have created. It is the rich countries who have to adapt first. If this ultimately leads to a different pattern of economic development, then the African nations and other poor countries, such as India and China, can follow.

A second sustainable development theme is rather more urgent for the poorer nations. The argument is that many such countries are achieving development through mining their resources, by which is meant not just physical mining but running down renewable resources, such as tropical forests, faster than they are renewed, with the accompanying risk of permanently damaging the environment. A good example, of which we have abundant evidence in much of Africa, is erosion of the fragile soils as a result of increasingly intensive cultivation without adequate soil protection – which the building of bunds along the contours would provide. Fortunately, there is also some anecdotal evidence in the other direction, of farmers beginning to see the merits in conserving the natural capital in their particular piece of land rather than simply, as in the past, expecting to move on elsewhere after a few years. We argue later, in Chapter 5, that basic education increases agricultural output. It is in small ways such as this that it does so.

A National Asset Register?

For sustainable development, there are no development indicators. Conventional economic analysis does not measure environmental degradation or the depletion of other natural assets. All of the economic income data which we have used and referred to is exactly that – a measure of a country's annual income. Data on GNP or GDP say nothing about national assets or capital stock. It is like examining the

---

The members of a women's group in Burkina Faso report:

We set up an anti-erosion committee because we saw that our fields were completely decimated. They really were finished. The wind carries everything away. When rain falls, an hour later it is as if no rain has fallen. We saw that to save our soil we had to undertake water and soil conservation. With small retaining walls and compost, we will succeed in regenerating our fields (quoted in Pradervand, 1989: 39).

finances of a company with a profit and loss statement but without a balance sheet.

Economists are increasingly turning their attention to this problem. For example, a recent study of Costa Rica modified the national income accounts in order to allow for the fact that the country's trees were being cut down faster than they were being replanted (Repetto et al., 1991). A similar study, on Papua New Guinea and published by the World Bank, estimated that national income is overstated by between 1 per cent and 10 per cent if the depletion of its natural assets is taken into consideration (Bartelmus et al., 1992). In other words, countries such as these, and there are many similar examples in Africa, are partly living off their wealth or their natural assets. This important new trend in economic analysis needs to be pursued in other countries.

Ideally, one would go further and derive a total national balance sheet, or, more correctly, a national asset register. If this were to be done each year, then the changes in a country's assets from one year to the next could be monitored. It is the annual changes in national assets which are interesting, rather than the absolute totals. Table 2.1 lists some of the elements which might be incorporated.

Table 2.1 A National Asset Register

National assets	Changes during a year
Natural resources:	
Renewable	Rate of reforestation or deforestation. Rate of soil reclamation or erosion, etc.
Non-renewable	New minerable deposits discovered. Less minerals extracted.
Physical assets:	Gross investment in roads, factories, housing, etc., as measured for GDP data. Less depreciation of existing capital.
Human capital:	Changes in literacy rate. Changes in school enrolment. Changes in morbidity and mortality.
Financial assets:	Changes in foreign exchange reserves.
Less:	
External debt:	Repayments less new borrowing.
TOTAL ASSETS	TOTAL ANNUAL CHANGE

Natural resources could be divided into renewable and non-renewable. The former, which we take to include environmental assets, have already been discussed. The latter refer to mineral and oil extraction, which obviously leads to a reduction in the stock of natural capital. A debatable point is whether the discovery of new mineral deposits should be considered to be an increase in non-renewable resources. It probably should, since prospecting is certainly a form of investment and since unknown mineral deposits can hardly be said to be part of a nation's capital wealth. As a matter of fact, it is probable that only a small fraction of Africa's surface has ever been prospected for minerals and certainly not using modern techniques. Most of present-day mining activity arose out of prospecting work done many decades ago.

From a strictly economic point of view, drawing upon natural mineral wealth is not necessarily undesirable. The critical question is whether it is being turned into other forms of capital – human capital or a manufacturing base, for example – which would eventually be more productive. The national asset register would enable one to assess this. The point is illustrated in the case study of Botswana in Appendix A. That country has reinvested a major part of its mineral wealth in education and health services, in other words into human capital formation. Other countries seem to have reinvested little of their natural resource capital in this way. Niger, Zaire, and Zambia, which have seen a decline in incomes over the last generation, as shown in Figure 2.6, have been drawing on a depleting mineral resource over this period without now having much to show for it. In short, Africa's natural capital stock, whether renewable or not, would almost certainly be shown to be being wasted away on present trends if this accounting exercise could be done.

A second form of assets include those which are man-made – roads, power supplies, dams, buildings and so on. Although there are no estimates of their total value or magnitude, GDP statistics do tell us how much new investment is being undertaken each year, both to increase the stock of capital and to replace worn-out and depreciated assets. What we do not know is how much of this new investment is necessary merely to replace old assets as these wear out or come to the end of their useful lives. Around 10 per cent of GDP may be a rough estimate of what is required for this purpose (IBRD, 1989: 26). Anybody who has travelled in Africa in recent years has witnessed a steady decline in infrastructure – roads not being maintained, power supplies collapsing, worn-out factories, abandoned irrigation schemes and so on. There is thus much circumstantial and anecdotal evidence that insufficient resources are being used for this purpose. Moreover, the gross rate of investment in Africa, both to replace old assets and to provide new ones, at 16 per cent of GDP, is lower than in any other region of the world, and, during the 1980s, investment levels actually fell. Therefore, the accounting exercise would most likely show that there was very little new accumulation of these man-made assets from one year to the next and in some cases there might even be a net loss as old assets were run down without being replaced.

Human capital cannot be left out of the exercise, and fortunately, as discussed previously, Africa's human capital, as measured through literacy rates, mean years of schooling and so on, is rising, if rather too slowly. The real challenge of the exercise would be to measure these increases in human potential in such a way that they could be usefully compared with the other forms of capital – natural resources and man-made assets.

Finally, a complete measure of a country's assets would have to incorporate financial assets – the holding of foreign exchange reserves on the positive side and the accumulation of external debt on the negative side. In most countries, foreign exchange holdings would be too small to be significant, while the external debt would be important. Since the independence era, external debt has increased from virtually nothing to about the equivalent of a whole year's income, proportionately far more than Latin America's external debt ever was (see Figure 5.3 in Chapter 5). As with the depletion of natural resources, if the accumulation of the external debt is used to build up other forms of productive national assets, then it can be beneficial. Sadly, in Africa this does not seem to have been the case.

This type of exercise, even if done only crudely, could well be revealing. However, for most African countries, the conclusions would be very disheartening, showing a steady drawing down of the continent's natural wealth.

An Overview

These first two chapters have presented a rather mixed picture of Africa today. On the one hand, African society, particularly rural society, appears remarkably robust, notwithstanding a natural environment which is sometimes extraordinarily hostile, with its catalogue of drought, erosion, famine, pestilence and disease. The catastrophes tend, quite rightly, to get reported through the world's newspapers and television; unfortunately, the underlying resilience of African society does not.

Similarly, the present chapter's attempt to measure change and human progress in Africa also gives mixed results. The purely economic indicators are not encouraging: there has been little economic growth in Africa over the last 30 years, notwithstanding the apparent priority which has been given to development; indeed the continent is to some extent living off its capital. The various social indicators do give some indication of progress, but, even here, Africa still lags behind every other region of the world.

Perhaps most interesting of all is the variation in performance between one country and another. Among all of the indicators of development presented earlier in this chapter, three countries consistently stand out as having been successful, finding themselves at the top of all the various charts. They are Mauritius, Botswana and, to some extent, Gabon. Mauritius, a small, densely populated island in the Indian Ocean, is an African nation by accident of geography only. It has no indigenous population, having been peopled by European settlers and their African slaves in the eighteenth century and later by indentured Indian workers for the sugar estates. It has now transformed itself into a manufacturing economy and is an embryonic Hong Kong.

Gabon and Botswana are both countries with small populations and mineral-based economies, dependent on oil and diamonds respectively. It would be easy to dismiss them, along with Mauritius, as special cases of no relevance to the rest of Africa. In the case of Botswana, particularly, this would be quite wrong. That country's recent history is pertinent to the rest of Africa, and demonstrates that it is possible to have successful development on the African mainland, whatever criterion of development is being used. Its story, which is described in greater detail in Appendix A, is one not just of mineral wealth, but also of successful political and economic management for development. It illustrates positively many of the themes which will be taken up in the following chapters, including the influence of pre-colonial history on subsequent political and economic developments. Most of all, it illustrates the dynamic nature of successful development. Success in politics, in economics and in human development have all supported and reinforced each other.

The picture in the rest of Africa is much more discouraging. Here, the interplay of different elements has often worked in a negative way. Poor economic performance in Africa cannot be explained without understanding the politics. The politics, in turn, have to be seen in a historical context. Thus, it is to the history of Africa that we turn next.

3 A Historical Survey

There is history in all men's lives,
Figuring the nature of the times deceas'd,
The which observ'd a man may prophesy,
With a near aim, of the main chance of things
As yet not come to life, which in their seeds
And weak beginnings lie intreasured.
(Shakespeare, *Henry IV, Part 2*, Act III, Scene i)

> Pre-colonial societies consisted of small, ethnically homogeneous groups, geographically dispersed and led by priests-kings. This basic social unit was strong and resilient. Yet there were few successful attempts at nation-building on a larger scale, though Islam tended to be a unifying force in much of West Africa. European slaving and the introduction of firearms massively destabilized the continent. Colonization later imposed a superficial order and, through indirect rule, encouraged a tribal structure which in reality was less strong than it seemed. Missionaries brought Christianity and education. With the latter, the people of Africa acquired the means to end colonialism, which actually lasted for little more than 70 years.

It has sometimes been said, most famously by Professor Hugh Trevor-Roper, that Africa has no history prior to the colonial period. There is certainly little written evidence, before the nineteenth century, of the sort of history that schoolboys learn, with kings and kingdoms and famous battles. This lack of a written history is a great handicap for the modern African. He has no Magna Carta, Declaration of Independence or Rights of Man with which to glorify his people's contribution to the making of the world. Thus, although the first and longest period of human history occurs in Africa, the written history which survives is mostly of recent times and recounts the story of the Europeans in Africa, largely seen through European eyes. It is mostly a history of oppression and, subsequently, of African 'civilization', 'modernization' or, to use the latest term, 'development' – all expressions with a pejorative ring, since the role of the African seems essentially passive.

African history does have an oral tradition, however. Being oral, it is essentially a private history, used to give explanation and meaning to the particular society concerned. It does not form part of the written corpus of international or world history. Yet with modern methods much can be and has been pieced together from oral and archaeological sources. In recent years, a number of dedicated scholars have tried to do so. There is more to be done.

In the meantime, it is not possible to understand modern Africa, or indeed any society, without some understanding of its antecedents. In particular, some knowledge of pre-colonial African history is important, especially since the colonial period was extraordinarily short – just three generations. Politically and socially, the colonial impact may have been much slighter than is commonly supposed.

First, some geography is needed, since, as in any other region of the world, geography has played an important part in history. The geography that matters in Africa is not so much one of rivers and mountains, but rather one of climatic zones which form bands across the continent. These are illustrated in Figure 3.1. The Sahara desert starts almost immediately behind the north coast and extends right across the continent. Immediately to the south is a semi-arid band known as the Sahel and, to the south again, is a tropical savanna zone, perhaps a thousand kilometres deep and stretching from the Atlantic Ocean in the west to the Ethiopian highlands in the east. This area is often referred to as the *sudan*, but should not be confused with the country Sudan, which sits at its easterly end. It is one of the most climatically hospitable regions of the continent and has seen much history. Further south again is the equatorial forest, which starts at the Gulf of Guinea, encompasses southern Cameroon and much of Zaire, and reaches almost across the continent. In the east a corridor of savanna passes right through the tropics, particularly along the cooler, higher ground of the East African Highlands – which extend from Ethiopia southwards. The Great Rift Valley, which gives rise to the huge, deep inland seas of Lake Tanganyika and Lake Malawi, runs in a parallel direction.

South of the Central African tropical forest, the same zones appear in reverse. Relatively fertile tropical savanna country extends from the west coast across Zambia to East Africa. This gives way to drier savanna further south in Botswana and South Africa, with a narrow

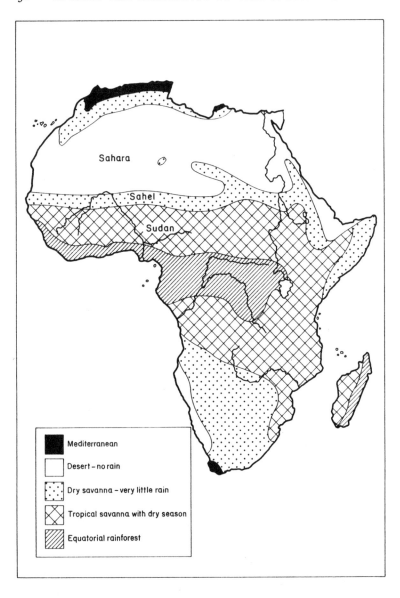

Figure 3.1 Climatic zones

band of real desert along the southern Atlantic coast of Namibia. Then, right on the very tip of the continent, a Mediterranean climate reappears in the Cape area. These climatic features have been determinant elements in history right up to modern times.

Pre-colonial History

Early Man

Archaeologists believe, from fossil evidence, that mankind originated in Africa. The earliest clear hominid remains, *Homo erectus*, dating from about one and a half million years ago, were found in East Africa. His precursors, *Homo habilis* and the *Australopithecenes*, have also been found only in East Africa and, in the case of the latter, date back about four million years. *Homo erectus* used simple stone tools but probably did not build any shelter. He lived by hunting the rich fauna of the East African savanna, prospered and spread northwards across the Sahara and eventually out of Africa into Asia. *Homo sapiens sapiens*, or modern man, only emerged about a hundred or two hundred thousand years ago, again first in Africa itself. By this time, stone tools had become a great deal more fashioned, varied and sophisticated, and fire was being used.

As humankind spread into different environments, different races emerged. From linguistic evidence, four different groups can be identified, although races and linguistic groups are not quite the same thing: Afro-Asians north of the Sahara and in near Asia; a Nilo-Saharan group in the Sahara itself; the Niger-Congo people south of the Sahara in the sudan; and the less well defined Khoisan group from the tropical forest zone southwards (Oliver, 1991: 38–50).

The next important development, occurring perhaps around ten thousand years ago, was the gradual transition from hunting and gathering to a more settled life based on food production – both cultivation and fishing. This change probably occurred independently, at different times and places, but most likely first in the sudan and the Sahara, facilitated by the local climate at that time being much wetter than it is today. Pastoralism came somewhat later and, unlike crop production, was probably introduced into Africa from the Near East.

About five thousand years ago, two great population expansions occurred. The tall, aquiline Afro-Asiatic group, probably mostly pastoral, moved to the east and west around the Nilo-Saharans and ended up occupying most of the northern and eastern part of the sudan region. The more agrarian Niger-Congo people, or more particularly the Bantu sub-group, expanded from around present-day Cameroon throughout the continent south of the Sahara. The Bantu were technologically more sophisticated than the Khoisan hunter-gatherers, who had previously been the only inhabitants of the southern part of Africa.

These movements of people should not be seen as conquests, since there must surely have been room for all, but rather the gradual expansion of one group relative to another. Except in the sudan, where trading possibilities allowed the creation of larger states, which we shall discuss further below, the maximum viable size of a community would be that of a village of a few hundred or a thousand inhabitants. As villages grew beyond their optimum size, a group, probably an extended family or an embryonic clan, would break away to settle in a new area. In addition, the whole village would probably move every decade or so, as the surrounding agricultural land became exhausted. Thus, low population density gave rise to a particular settlement pattern and type of social organization which has largely survived to the present day.

Egyptian Civilization

About three or four thousand years BC, the Sahara again returned to desert. At this point, the Nile becomes important. The longest and most important river in Africa, the Nile's annual flood washed fertility over the surrounding plain. Thus, the many people who now lived along the Nile were pushed closer to the floodplain itself and to each other. Such was the agricultural richness of their environment that an economic surplus emerged for the first time; not everybody had to spend their whole time engaged in food production. Exchange and trade became possible, with the river itself providing the major highway. More complicated forms of social organization, beyond merely that of the immediate group or band emerged. There was more permanent settlement. Quite suddenly, in about three thousand BC, the Pharaonic civilization emerged, with its belief in divine kings, who were surrounded by elaborate rituals of life and death, and with its pyramids and elaborate grave goods. It was an authoritarian, centralized bureaucratic state in which the central administration was able to tax away the economic surplus for its own ends, and in which social control was maintained partly through the spiritual powers of the king.

The Egyptian civilization lasted about three thousand years, starting to decline in the last millennium BC. The religious ideas and values it represented had by that time been adopted by another state higher up the Nile, the Nilo-Saharan kingdom of Kush, which at one stage was an Egyptian colony. The kingdom of Kush in its turn expanded further south again, possibly taking the new iron-smelting techniques with it. A new capital was established at Meroe, just north of present-day Khartoum. The Meroe civilization lasted until the early centuries AD. Thus, while the Egyptian civilization appeared to Europeans to be in decline, it was in fact replicating itself further south, breaking out of the Sahara altogether into the pasturelands of the sudan. The artistic heights and accomplishments of the Pharaohs were not to be repeated, but some elements of their culture and religion were adopted and adapted by other later African states to the south and especially in the sudan region.

West African States

The sudan was fertile and hospitable. It had useful mineral deposits, notably of gold, and it was bordered by the different climatic zones of desert to the north and tropical forest to the south, each supporting different species and crops. Thus, it was not surprising that the next important developments occurred there. The arrival of the camel in the Sahara in about the fifth century AD was the most important new element. Previously, the Sahara would have been an almost impenetrable obstacle – the Egyptian civilization, as we have seen, moved up the Nile rather than across the desert. However, with the camel the desert was transformed into a sea, capable of being traversed at will and in many directions. The camel truly was the ship of the desert. A fully loaded camel caravan could carry at least as much as a Mediterranean ship of that period. For the first time substantial trade became possible across the Sahara, between the North African, or Mediterranean civilizations and the people living in the sudan to the south. Traded goods included salt and dates going south, gold from the mines of West Africa, ivory and slaves from the African interior being taken north.

The traders themselves came from the north or were Berbers from the desert itself. They penetrated, influenced, and, to some extent, may even have governed the societies and states to the south. In due course, in about the ninth century, they brought Islam across the

desert. Although initially an alien belief of a separate trading and elite
community, Islam was a great unifying and civilizing force. It offered
the people living south of the Sahara a link with one of the great
religions and civilizations of the world, and incorporated them in a
greater world view. It introduced a common set of beliefs, values and,
for its followers, laws across a wider region. For the first time, it
brought a written culture. Timbuktu, for example, became a centre of
Islamic scholarship.

Thus, Islam fostered social and political stability, and provided a
framework for trans-Saharan trade. International trade, then as now,
encouraged prosperity and development. Thus, there followed one of
the great epochs of African history, with the establishment of a number
of great states or empires. The Ghanaian empire, which was situated
in present-day Mali, lasted from the beginning of the tenth until the
second half of the twelfth century AD. It was followed by the more
extensive, and more Islamic, Malian empire, from the mid-thirteenth
to the end of the fourteenth century. The Songhai empire, from the
mid-fifteenth to the end of the sixteenth century, was greater still,
extending more than a thousand kilometres, from the Niger river
across to Lake Chad.

These are perhaps just the better known or more successful of the
West African states of the time, and none of them survived more than
about a hundred and fifty years. They were in fact scarcely states in
the usual sense of the word. Rather, one particular clan would come
to dominate neighbouring clans and would be able to exact tribute
from them, or tax the trade passing through the region. There would
be little attempt at nation-building or at imposing a common system
of law or administration. The state boundaries were always fluid.
Whenever the power of the centre weakened, as it would for example
when a king died since there were no established succession rules,
those on the periphery would simply cease to pay their tribute or
would become subject to another local hegemony. Underneath the
superficial trappings of a centralized state, with its significant towns
and its trade goods and luxuries, society was still organized by clans.
Put another way, these African states did not succeed in creating a
bourgeoisie which would have its own stake in the political system
and an interest in its long-term stability and maintenance.

Nevertheless, the process of state formation continued and in due
course moved further south across the sudan. The southernmost
boundaries were initially determined by the northern limit of the

tropical forest. The forest zone itself was still thinly populated, mostly by Pygmies, who were a remnant from the Khoisan group of peoples, and cultivated agriculture had barely started there. We have to await the arrival of food crops, particularly root crops such as yams and cassava, from South-East Asia before much cultivation occurs in the forests. Moreover, the forests harboured tsetse fly, which carried disease vectors fatal to cattle, horses and camels. Thus transport had to be by human porterage, and trade possibilities were consequently limited. All in all, the forest zones represented a far greater barrier to trade and the transmission of cultural ideas than did the Sahara desert.

Nevertheless, in due course, probably from about the thirteenth century, a number of states did extend through the forest to the coast along the Gulf of Guinea. These included Bono, Banda, Ife, Benin and others, which together encompassed much of present-day Côte d'Ivoire, Ghana, Nigeria, Togo and Benin. The coastal region was rich in gold, ivory and kola nuts, a stimulant tolerated by Islam, and these were traded northwards for cloth and metal artefacts, many of which came from north of the Sahara. Thus, by the time the Portuguese sailors first arrived off the Gulf of Guinea, in the fifteenth century, they found a pre-existing urbanized civilization which was already extensively trading northwards.

Eastern and Southern Africa

To the east, the Ethiopian and East African highlands provide, as we have seen, a corridor of savanna around the tropical forests, linking up with the savanna region to the south. Islamic expansion in this direction was blocked by the ancient kingdoms of Axum and Nubia, in present-day Ethiopia and Sudan, which had been Christian from the earliest days of christendom and remained so, adhering to the Coptic Church. The Ethiopian kingdom was harassed and invaded by a pagan kingdom from the south in the tenth century, by Ottoman Turks coming from the Red Sea and the Arabian Peninsula in the sixteenth century, and by Italians in the nineteenth and twentieth centuries. Yet on each occasion it survived and recovered, making it, in one form or another, one of the longest-surviving states in the entire world.

Thus, the whole of eastern and southern Africa, broadly extending from present-day Ethiopia down to the Cape, was rather isolated from the trading and cultural influences coming across the Sahara. Nevertheless, the East African coast was a great deal more navigable than that of West Africa and thus had been known to the outside world from at least Roman times. From about the ninth century until the fifteenth, when the first Portuguese traders arrived, the main contact along the coast was with Arab, Persian and Indian traders and gave rise to considerable prosperity in the coastal region. Initially, the foreign traders tended to establish themselves on the offshore islands – Kilwa, Mafia, Zanzibar, Pemba and Mombasa. Later, the native people living along the coast, who came to be known as Swahili, intermingled with the foreigners, learnt how to sail, adopted Islam and took over much of the coastal traffic. The trade goods of interest from Africa were gold, ivory and slaves, which would be exchanged for various imported manufactures.

However, the impact of this coastal trading and external contact on the East African interior was very limited, and not at all comparable with the trade and exchange across the Sahara. The presence of tsetse fly along the coast excluded, as in the forest zone of West Africa, the use of any beasts of burden, so transport depended on human porterage. As a result, the hinterland retained a rather simple Iron Age economy with only scattered political organization. Society continued to be based around small clan groups, which shared a common kinship and lived in isolated villages. The world view of these people would not have extended much beyond their immediate village and family. There was little need for sophisticated political or economic structures, and the notion of tribes came much later, as we shall see.

However, a few states, generally smaller than those in the west, did gradually emerge in East Africa. One was Buganda, just north of Lake Victoria. It emerged from the earlier Bunyoro state to the north and lasted from the fifteenth century to the colonial period. Its external contact was probably with the north rather than the east. In Buganda, absolute authority was vested in the priest-king or Kabaka, who managed to assert authority over the various clans by including a wife from each in his harem. Consequently, the succession could pass from one clan to another. Further south, the Zimbabwe state, also a priest-kingdom, was responsible, in about the eleventh century, for the building of Great Zimbabwe, which still survives. Its prosperity lay in cattle rearing and in trading gold down the Zambezi valley to Arab merchants on the east coast. Later, the original dynasty was superseded by the Mwenemutapa state to the north, which was less advanced than its predecessor, and with which the Portuguese came into contact in about 1560.

Perhaps the most distinctive socio-economic change in East Africa occurred during the first millennium AD, as cattle passed along the cooler savanna corridor of the East African highlands into the savanna of southern Africa, south of the tropical forests. Here, joint agricultural-pastoral economies were established. Crop production was for food consumption; livestock was a source of wealth and carried quasi-religious totemic significance. The large village settlement pattern, characteristic of Zimbabwe southwards, also emerged as a consequence of this mixed economy. Anyone wishing to acquire wealth and power in this society would do so through accumulating large herds of cattle, rather than through trade. This was quite unlike West Africa, where cattle-rearing remained a specialist activity carried out by particular societies, especially the widely dispersed Fulani, and where wealth and power were to be had through trade and the accumulation of wives and children.

The Arrival of Europeans

Figure 3.2 summarizes the state of affairs in Africa at the beginning of the fifteenth century, when European influences begin to appear for the first time. The Portuguese had developed a new type of ship, the carvel, more seaworthy than previous designs and were beginning to learn how to beat up into the wind. They could become more adventurous. Early in the fifteenth century they discovered Madeira and the Azores, further out into the Atlantic than they had ever been before. However, to sail down the west coast of Africa seemed particularly hazardous, since the wind always seemed to blow from the north. How would it be possible to return? In 1434, the navigational problem was solved by tacking right out to sea. From that time on, the whole West African coast was explored, culminating in Bartholomeu Dias' rounding of the Cape of Good Hope in 1488. In 1497, Vasco da Gama went even further. He sailed around the Cape and then up the East African coast as far as Malindi and from there across to India, where he loaded up with spices and returned in 1499. Thus by the beginning of the sixteenth century the whole of the African coastline was known to Portuguese navigators.

Apart from reaching the East Indies, one motive for all of this exploration was the possibility of tapping into the gold trade, which was coming from south of the Sahara. In 1482 the Portuguese established the first European presence on the African continent, a coastal

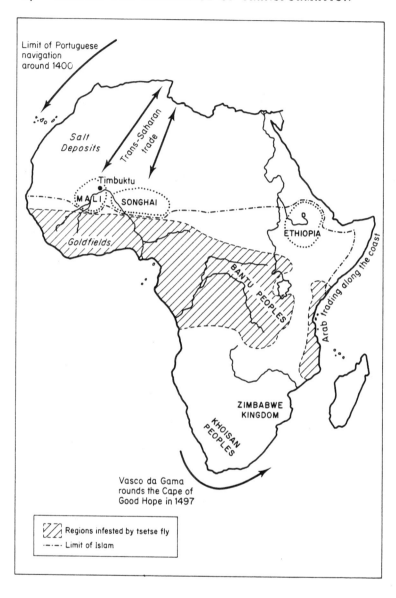

Figure 3.2 Africa in the fifteenth century

fort at Elmina in what is now Ghana. Later, trading enclaves were established at a number of other points down the West African coast. The most important of these was at the mouth of the Congo river, where the Kongo kingdom was extensive and surrounded by a number of vassal states. The Portuguese later moved around the Cape and up the East African coast, attempting to wrest the coastal and Indian Ocean spice trade from the Arabs. Their main eastern base was established at Sofala near the mouth of the Zambezi, where the Mwenemutapa kingdom reached down to the coast. Here there were also possibilities for trade in gold and ivory from the interior. From time to time excursions would be made further north, leading to the sacking of Mombasa in 1505 and 1528.

More than a century later, in 1652, the Dutch established a small colony at the Cape of Good Hope, in order to provide a base for resupplying their ships on their way to the East Indies. This was an area which was much less densely populated, though by no means empty, as the Afrikaners later claimed. It was principally occupied by the pre-Iron Age Khoi and San people, who, as we have seen, were of a different race from the Bantu peoples and who still inhabited the remoter parts of eastern and southern Africa. They were soon wiped out by the new settlers.

However, apart from the Dutch at the Cape, with its Mediterranean climate, there was no great European interest in actually settling on the African coast, still less in penetrating the interior. The climate was difficult, and the mortality rate from malaria and other diseases high. Tsetse was endemic around almost all of the coast, except at the Cape, so domesticated animals could not survive. The higher interior of East Africa, with its cooler climate, was still unknown to Europeans. Compared with other parts of the world, Africa had little to offer other than gold – no silk or spices such as could be had in India. The new European colonies then being founded across the Atlantic were much more promising and hospitable. They did, however, require labour for the plantations being established there and, since there was no one else to do the hard work, slave labour was indicated.

Slaving and the Slave Trade

Slavery and slaving had always been a feature of African society. If population density was low and if the strength of a society lay in its numbers, then it was more likely to go to war for slaves than for land

– as European societies did. Thus, slaving in African history corresponded to the no less brutal territorial wars in European history. Moreover, it was women, as workers and bearers of the next generation, together with their young children, that were wanted.

However, if one clan took prisoners from another what could it do with them? There was no way to lock them up permanently, and there were no material goods for which to exchange them. Male prisoners might as well be killed and often were, but to kill females would be to destroy wealth and the potential for future prosperity. Try and keep them and they would soon drift back to their original clan. The only solution was to send them far away, in exchange for slaves captured in other remote wars – hence the origins of the internal slave trade.

The external slave trade, prior to the introduction of firearms, was a by-product of this internal market, though there would be some export demand for males slaves as well as females. Thus the presence of slave-traders on the coast did not, initially, necessitate the creation of special slaving expeditions into the interior. It was sufficient to tap into the existing internal trade. Moreover, before the sixteenth century the total export of slaves, most of whom went to the Arab world, was relatively modest, perhaps one or two thousand a year (McEvedy, 1980: 80).

The original Portuguese interest had been in exporting gold; around 1510 they turned their attention to slaves. This was not quite the beginning of the West African slave trade. The Portuguese had been importing a few slaves into Spain and Portugal itself since 1443 to work on sugar plantations on the Iberian peninsula. So, the idea of slave trading was already well-established. However, the new colonies in the West Indies and Brazil greatly increased demand. Since the Kongo kings of West Africa were unable or unwilling to supply all the slaves now being sought, the Portuguese proceeded to provide some native groups with firearms, enabling them to make slave raids into the interior. The trade passed into increasingly disreputable hands, outside the immediate control of the Portuguese government – had they wished to control it. Moreover, once the slave trade became established, it was so brutalizing that it became practically impossible for Europe to have any other sort of simultaneous contact with Africa – be it commercial or religious. The early efforts at evangelization of the few missionaries who had arrived with the Portuguese were thus completely frustrated.

By the end of the sixteenth century, perhaps five thousand slaves a year were being exported from Africa across the Atlantic, mostly by the Portuguese to Brazil and the West Indies. By the seventeenth century, other European nations had also taken up the trade to serve their colonies, initially the Dutch and then the French and English. In the end, the role of the Portuguese came to be rather minor. The slave trade doubled, at least in number, in the seventeenth century, while, at its peak in the eighteenth century, probably around a hundred thousand slaves a year were being exported from Africa. By that time, Britain was responsible for about half of the total. Trade on this scale was no longer an incidental by-product of internal war but a serious, brutal business.

At least 80 per cent of the exported slaves crossed the Atlantic from West Africa, which was well populated. The Dutch and the British established their bases off the Gold Coast of the Gulf of Guinea. Behind was a well-populated hinterland. The main base of the French was further around the coast at the mouth of the Senegal river. Indeed, in contrast to the British and the Dutch, who stuck firmly to the coast, the French penetrated some way up the river, which is navigable for some distance. However, it was not necessary for the Europeans to go in search of slaves themselves. They merely had to arm a coastal warlord, thereby giving him overwhelming military superiority over the clans and groups in the interior.

The introduction of firearms in this way was thus a major destabilizing element in African society, comparable perhaps in its own way to the uncontrolled proliferation of modern weapons in our own time. It changed the balance of power between those on the coast and those in the interior and thus led to the breakdown of the pattern of society, which by then had existed across the sudan region south of the Sahara for several hundred years. In due course, new West African states emerged, notably Ashanti, Dahomey and Oyo, which looked more to trade with the European ships arriving off the coast of the Gulf of Guinea than with merchants coming overland from the north. The importance of the trans-Saharan trade declined.

Similarly, in both central and eastern Africa, firearms increased the relative strength of groups and clans living near the coast and having access to European traders, at the expense of those living in the interior, who were increasingly at the mercy of arbitrary raids from coastal bandits and warlords. Indeed, the impact of the slave trade and the introduction of firearms in East Africa, which was rather thinly populated and less politically developed than West Africa, may have been a great deal more socially devastating, even though the number of slaves involved was much smaller.

The eventual abolition of the slave trade came about as a result of both humanitarian and commercial interests. Radical Christians had long campaigned in Britain for the abolition of the slave trade, but it was only when British colonists in the West Indies tried to bring their slaves back to England that the British people, with a long civil rights tradition behind them, began to appreciate the enormity of what they were doing. Eventually, in 1807 and 1811, two Acts of Parliament outlawed the British slave trade, more than a hundred years after it had started.

Having thus cut themselves out of the most profitable of African trade, the British were not going to let other European powers continue, and they applied a mixture of commercial and political pressure on the other European slave trading nations. This was not pure altruism. As long as the slave trade continued, any more normal commerce in which the British would hope to participate was impossible. By about 1840, the trade had been made illegal in all European countries and Britain, having the most powerful navy at the time, together with France and the United States, patrolled the Atlantic, trying to enforce its abolition. However, it was not until the end of the nineteenth century that the African slave trade died out for good.

Missionaries and Explorers

The nineteenth century was important for a growing awareness in Europe of the geography and culture of Africa, and, within Africa itself, of Europeans other than those who sold firearms and bought slaves. It was also the beginning of Christian influence in Africa, the most important cultural import since the arrival of Islam in North Africa about a thousand years earlier. Missionary interest in Africa started very slowly from the end of the eighteenth century, but, as the slave trade declined, it expanded steadily throughout the whole of the nineteenth century, even before the sudden burst of European political interest in its closing years.

A number of Anglican and Protestant missionary societies, of British origin, started to operate in Africa from the beginning of the nineteenth century. These included the Anglican Church Missionary Society and the independent London Missionary Society, to which Livingstone belonged. In the Catholic Church, the French were most active, the foundation of the White Fathers in 1868 being a significant event. The lives and work of the early missionaries must have often seemed like failures. Their condemnation of witchcraft, of practices such as female circumcision and, most of all, of polygyny cannot have been easy for their hearers to accept. Indeed, Livingstone's interest in exploration may well have been stimulated by his lack of missionary success. Yet, in the end, taking a historical perspective, the southern half of the continent was Christianized with astonishing speed, which is one impact of European contact that will endure. The Christian gospel of salvation for the poor and oppressed was a message which appealed to African people, whatever the ineptitudes and personal failings of individual missionaries themselves.

Their impact on what we would now call development was also important. Missionaries set about, with great patience, to learn the local languages and in some cases to write them down. The main purpose was to translate the Bible, and to train catechists who would then preach the gospel more widely. Indeed, in the end, most Christians heard the gospel from other Africans rather than from missionaries. Nevertheless, the effect was to introduce education and a written culture to the southern half of Africa for the first time.

At the same time as the missionaries were spreading through the continent, the explorers were mapping its interior. West Africa was explored first, notably by Mungo Park, who explored the Niger river basin in 1795-97. It was not until 1830, however, that its outlet to the sea, lost among the maze of mangrove swamps which line much of the West African coast, was finally established. Exploration of central and eastern Africa came much later, and a significant contribution was made by German explorers. Nachtigal, for example, explored the Sahel region between Lake Chad and the Nile in 1870-74. Livingstone's celebrated journeys in eastern and central Africa were made over two decades between 1853 and 1873, exploring the Zambezi river and putting Victoria Falls and Lake Malawi on the map for the first time.

Increasing External Pressure

Hitherto, European governments had shown little or no interest in colonizing the African continent. True, the Dutch colony on the Cape had been established for nearly two hundred years but the Boers, as the colonists came to be known, had from the beginning always demonstrated a fierce independence from their original homeland.

Otherwise, the continent was so unpromising that the attitude of the European powers was to allow the missionaries and the traders to pursue their respective concerns but to provide them with no more support or protection than could be achieved with a few enclaves scattered along the coast.

For the British, the longest and best established of these enclaves was at Freetown in Sierra Leone, where freed slaves from ships captured by British naval patrols were released. The people of Freetown, having been torn up from their roots, were probably the first black Africans to take to Christianity and to assimilate Western culture. For the French, Libreville, in what is now Gabon, served a similar purpose, though on a smaller scale. The British also had a number of forts along the Gold Coast, now Ghana, protecting trade from that region and harrying slaving ships. However, they had an uneasy relationship with the Ashanti kingdom, which was just inland and was probably the most advanced African power at the time. In 1824 the dispute flared up into warfare – the first major war between a European and an African state. As time went on, British enclaves and authority spread further along the coast towards the delta of the Niger river basin, where a profitable trade in palm oil was developing. Meanwhile, the French continued their somewhat less profitable occupation of the mouth and lower part of the Senegal river. Further down the coast, the Portuguese held the coast of what is now Angola, from which they continued to export slaves to Brazil until about the middle of the nineteenth century.

In the south the British had taken over the Cape colony from the Dutch in 1806. But the long-established Boers, Africa's white tribe descended from the original Dutch immigrants, were already seeking new pastures further east away from British control. This brought them up against the Bantu people living between the coast of what is now Natal and the Drakensburg mountains, leading to clashes with the strong Zulu kingdom, with its celebrated leaders Shaka and Dingane, between about 1810 and 1825. Later the Boers, still short of land in which to expand and still dissatisfied with their British overlords in the Cape, began trekking northwards. They established two republics beyond British influence, namely the Orange Free State and the Transvaal, the independence of which the British recognized in 1852 and 1854.

On the east coast the Portuguese maintained their presence along what is now Mozambique and up the Zambezi river and continued to range far inland, selling firearms and buying ivory and slaves. The coastline further north was still the purview of Arab powers, in particular the sultanate of Oman, which was ruled by Seyyid Said for the whole of the first half of the nineteenth century. Zanzibar, an island off the East African coast, grew to be the centre of this empire, and became a major producer and exporter of cloves. More importantly, it was the base for the East African slave trade, which ranged as far inland as Uganda, where other Arab slavers operating out of Khartoum and trading north along the Nile were also active. It was only in 1873, under naval pressure from Britain, where concern had been greatly aroused by the writings of Livingstone, that the slave market in Zanzibar was finally closed. Similarly, the British were attempting, through the Khedive of Egypt, to close off the northern slave trade, an attempt which led in due course to the siege of Khartoum, held at the time by a British force under General Gordon, but overrun by the forces of the Mahdi.

These external pressures along the whole East African Coast, from the Boers in the south to the Arab slavers operating out of Zanzibar further north, devastated the interior of East Africa. Although the numbers of slaves were smaller, the impact seems to have been far greater than in West Africa, where the process of state formation was more advanced and therefore more resistant to outside pressure. By the nineteenth century, the whole of East African society was destabilized, and vast movements of people were taking place. Underlying these movements may have been land and food shortages and a desire to move away from the external pressures. The more proximate cause was a sudden military expansion of the Zulu kingdom in the 1820s. This set in train a whole series of consequential migrations, principally of Nguni tribes moving from the south to the north. In this way the Matabele kingdom in Zimbabwe was established, as were the Tswana, Sotho and Swazi kingdoms.

The Scramble for Africa

Matters might have continued in this way for some time if the Belgian King Leopold II had not raised the stakes among the European powers. Resentful that his country had established no colonial presence elsewhere in the world, he was determined to establish a personal colony – somewhere, anywhere. He eventually decided on the basin of the Congo river in Africa, which had recently been explored by

Stanley, who in 1879 had entered Leopold's employ. As a result of Stanley's exploration and of Leopold's skilful diplomacy in Europe, the Congo basin fell under his influence – at least as far as the European powers were concerned.

It was Germany under Bismarck that really catalysed the scramble to partition Africa between the European powers, even though Germany hitherto had had no significant presence in Africa and no particular desire to be a colonial power. Bismarck's motives appeared to be to preoccupy Britain and France, by setting them against each other in another part of the world. The ostensible purpose of the conference of Berlin in 1884–85, which Bismarck convened, was to settle the matter of what sort of European sovereignty there should be in the Congo basin, but the very raising of such an issue immediately provoked issues of sovereignty throughout the whole African continent. Consequently, following the Berlin Conference, each European power began to push its influence and control inwards from the coastal enclaves towards the interior, with a view to having its occupation of territory eventually recognized by the other European powers. The Germans themselves had taken the precaution of setting up some coastal enclaves of their own just prior to the conference – on the coasts of what are now Togo, Cameroon, Namibia and Tanzania.

The French moved inland from Senegal in West Africa, in effect going around the hinterland of the British coastal enclaves on the Gold Coast, at Lagos and Freetown, and at the mouth of the Gambia river. Britain, however, was more interested in Egypt, where it enjoyed an effective but precarious suzerainty. From this command of the lower reaches of the Nile, it laid claim to the whole Nile basin, from Egypt to Uganda and across through Kenya to the East African coast.

At the same time, the British South Africa Company of Cecil Rhodes also pushed up strongly from South Africa, through what is now Botswana to Matabeleland in Zimbabwe, and then onwards into present-day Zambia. His ambitions were not greatly supported by the British government. Nevertheless, Rhodes, who had made a fortune in the Kimberley diamond mine in the Cape Colony, where he was also prime minister, was an ambitious man, and hoped for an eventual British presence right up the middle of the continent, from the Cape to Cairo. Expansion to the East was constrained by the still independent Boer Republics and by the Portuguese in Mozambique, while to the west the Germans were in occupation of South West Africa, now Namibia, most of which consisted of inhospitable desert.

In the meantime there was simmering hostility between the British interests in the Cape and the two Boer republics, particularly the Transvaal, where large gold deposits had been found. In 1896, Rhodes attempted to interfere with the Transvaal government in the so-called Jameson raid on Johannesburg. This was unsuccessful in its aims and only served to exacerbate a situation that was already delicate. Eventually, in 1899, war erupted and the British government became directly involved. At the end of the war, in 1902, the whole of South Africa came under British control. In 1909, the Union of South Africa was formed as a self-governing dominion in the Commonwealth.

However, most of the various European occupations of the continent were initially achieved not through warfare but by entering into so-called treaties with African chiefs. Sometimes, the colonial power was not directly involved but was represented by private commercial companies, such as the British South Africa Company and the Chartered East Africa Company, which were looking for land for settlement and mining rights. By and large the chiefs, with whom they negotiated, probably had little idea of what they were giving away. In a society and economy where land had never been in short supply, where there was not the same territorial hunger as in Europe, where there was a tradition of hospitality, and where written contracts were unknown, signing away some land cannot have seemed a very serious matter. It was these bogus treaties, however, which demonstrated the establishment of a colonial presence, under the framework established by the Berlin conference and as far as Europeans were concerned.

By 1891, most of the rival claims to the African continent were settled between the European powers. Since very little was actually known about much of the land which was being seized and of the societies being dominated, lines of latitude and longitude were heavily relied on to define borders, particularly in the interior. Nevertheless, some matters remained outstanding. One was who was to occupy the Sudan, a question which almost led to war when the army of the British General Kitchener met a French expeditionary force at Fashoda in southern Sudan, forcing the French to back down. The Sudan became a joint Anglo-Egyptian condominium, although in reality it was a British colony since Britain was effectively running Egypt at the time. A second loose end was the extent of British suzerainty behind the Gold Coast, which was resolved by a British invasion of Ashanti. The only territory south of the Sahara which remained independent was that of Ethiopia, which, under King Menelek, defeated an Italian invading force in 1896. Italy had to content itself, for the time being, with the coastal territories of Eritrea and Somalia, although Mussolini's forces did invade Ethiopia in 1936 and held it until 1941.

Thus, the expression 'scramble for Africa' is apt. In the last two decades of the nineteenth century, the European powers occupied a whole continent which previously had been of negligible importance to them and which was many times larger than Europe itself. The question then arose: 'what to do next?'

Colonial History

Having partitioned Africa, the colonial powers ceased to have much interest in it. Their main concern was that the new African colonies should not be a burden on the European treasuries. Several consequences followed from this.

Indirect Rule

The first was that, once the skirmishing with disgruntled African societies was over, the resources deployed in colonial administration were very few indeed. For example, Johnston was expected to start a colonial administration in Nyasaland, now Malawi, with an annual budget of £10,000, which was sufficient to pay for 70 Indian soldiers and two British officers (Oliver and Fage, 1988: 173). This was typical of the situation across the continent. Such limited resources in money and manpower could not possibly exert more than a skeletal authority across the vast tracts of country which now supposedly came under European rule. The only option was to govern through, or with the consent of, the established authorities, as far as they could be identified. This system of indirect rule, which was formulated by Lugard, who took possession of Uganda for the British East Africa Company and was later High Commissioner for Northern Nigeria, came to be the guiding principle throughout the British and German colonies.

The theory of indirect rule was that the pre-colonial rulers, or chiefs, would continue to exercise authority over their people in accordance with customary law. The colonial power, often represented in each locality by no more than a single district officer, would interfere with established customs and procedures as little as possible, as long as there was no inter-tribal warfare. The principle may have worked better wherever there already existed larger African states. Such was the case for example in much of West Africa and in the fertile kingdom of Buganda in Uganda, under its powerful Kabaka.

Elsewhere in East Africa, society was a great deal less structured and organized. True, there were many hundreds of mini-states, each with a few thousand people and their own king, who would also be a spiritual leader. Beyond these mini-states, the predominant pattern would be for a society to be based around the village and structured by clans. They would be in contact with other neighbouring groups who spoke the same language. If they acknowledged any authority at all to a chief or a king outside their immediate society, it would as likely be as a tribute to a more powerful group rather than a willing act of allegiance.

Indirect rule interfered with the established political pattern within and between African societies. The colonial authorities would seek out a manageable number of chiefs through whom they could govern. Those local chiefs or headman who were prepared to cooperate came to be preferred to those who were not. The implicit feudal model of authority, which was probably unconsciously used by the Europeans, was inappropriate for African society, where there was little hierarchy between different states and communities. Thus, colonialism conferred on some pre-colonial African leaders a greater authority than their popular legitimacy warranted, while others lost out. Those leaders who cooperated too closely with the colonial authorities would be suspect in African eyes, not necessarily for the fact of collaboration itself, but rather because they acquired excessive power within their own society and over neighbouring societies which may not previously have owed them any allegiance at all. In this sense the tribal basis of African society was, if not exactly invented by the colonialists, certainly greatly reinforced. It gave the appearance to outsiders of a society more much hierarchically structured and monolithic than it appeared to be to Africans themselves.

Before we leave the topic of indirect rule, it should be said that the French approach was somewhat different. Whereas the British built their administration on the backs of local society and institutions, even if they distorted the underlying political structure in the process, the French philosophy was that, given time and sufficient education, all could eventually be assimilated into French civilization. There was, thus, less interest in preserving supposedly pre-existing hierarchies and social structures, and many of the more powerful chiefs and kings in the French colonies were deposed. It was an approach that was both more intolerant of African society and yet less racist than that of the British, who were more inclined to doubt whether Africans could ever reach their own levels of civilization.

Taxation and Revenue

A second consequence of the parsimony of the colonial powers was the need to raise some revenue from the colonies, in order to contribute towards, and preferably to cover, the costs of running them. For a few territories this cannot have presented too serious a problem. In the Oil Rivers Protectorate in eastern Nigeria, palm oil production, which had started in the nineteenth century, provided a ready source of tax revenue. Most of the newly acquired territories, however, were pure subsistence economies, where the use of money was practically unknown. Consequently, it was necessary to create, even on a modest scale, some exportable production, either cash crops or mineral extraction. Thus, in East Africa coffee was planted on the slopes of Mount Kilimanjaro, Africa's snow-capped highest mountain, where the local Chagga people soon learnt how to cultivate it. In the Sudan, the smallholders on the vast Gezira irrigation scheme came to be among the most important cotton-growers in the world, though many were actually employers of migrant labour or absentee landowners. Similarly, cocoa was introduced to the Gold Coast, though not as it happened by the colonial government, and taken up with remarkable enthusiasm by the Ashanti farmers, who also proved adept at land speculation, employment, and other notions supposedly associated with advanced economies (Hill, 1986). However, the introduction of new crops and economic activities was not always as smooth or successful as these few examples suggest.

To service this new productive activity, transport was required, particularly railways. Practically the whole African railway network, as it exists today, had been built by the 1920s. Regrettably, except in southern Africa, the railway system was scarcely interconnected. It served the needs of the times, to bring crops or minerals from a few hundred miles inland to the African coast, but did not form the basis for an integrated continent-wide transport system.

The building of the railways and other construction activity posed considerable labour problems to the colonial authorities. Having little need of money, African men were not inclined to take up labouring – it was women's or slaves' work. Different solutions were adopted in different places and circumstances. The first was to impose a tax on the local people, in the form of a poll or hut tax. This was a new and alien imposition, and was deeply resented. It forced men to find paid work, or to commute their tax in exchange for a period of work on the government's projects. This requirement to provide labour for the projects of an alien power was probably the most important and most degrading impact of colonization on ordinary African society. Where the tax incentive was insufficient, as would often be the case, there was frequent resort to forced labour, not necessarily directly by the colonial government but perhaps indirectly through the local chief or headman. In the Congo under King Leopold, who was having more and more difficultly financing his personal colony, forced labour was widespread. Eventually, in 1908, the Belgian state took over the Congo from its financially exhausted king. Forced labour was also used in the Portuguese colonies of Angola and Mozambique.

The levying of labour was not always feasible or successful. Consequently, in East Africa, where the local population was rather sparse, indentured labourers were brought in from India, particularly to build the East African railways. This led to a great expansion in the Asian community in that part of the continent, though its origins go back to the days of trading by Arabs and Indians all along the East African coast.

Bit by bit, the colonial governments consolidated their position and the territorial economies expanded. Effective government slowly extended outwards from the capital city, almost invariably on the coast except in land-locked countries, towards the centre of the continent. The investments in infrastructure began to pay a return. Export crop production increased. Domestic revenues expanded to a point where, by the time of the First World War, most colonial administrations had become self-supporting, no longer dependent on an annual grant from the metropolis.

Throughout this early part of the colonial period, indeed almost up to the Second World War, the colonial presence in Africa was characterized by a *laissez-faire* administration and by a minimizing of expenditure. All that was required was to govern territory that had been acquired almost unthinkingly at the end of the nineteenth century. There was no objective of eventually assimilating the colonies into the metropolitan country, as later came to be the French and

---

The 1905 Maji-Maji uprising in Tanzania was one of the most violent episodes in colonial domination. As an oral account shows, it arose over the question of tax and forced labour:

Then when the European arrived he asked, 'Why did you not answer the call by drum to pay tax?' And they said, 'We do not owe you anything. We have no debt to you. If you as a stranger want to stay in this country, you will have to ask us. Then we will ask of you an offering to propitiate the gods. You will offer something and we will propitiate the gods on your behalf; we will give you land and you will get a place to stay in. But it is not for us as hosts to give you the offering. That is quite impossible.' Another eye witness says: 'This was why the people became furious and angry. The work was astonishingly hard and full of grave suffering, but its wages were the whip on one's back and buttocks. And yet he (the German) still wanted us to pay him tax. Were we not human beings?' In the end there was a widespread revolt, encouraged by a spirit medium's promise that the Germans' bullets would turn to water. But: 'Oh so many people died that day! For they had not known what a machine gun was.' To pacify the area the Germans resorted to a scorched earth policy. It is estimated that two hundred thousand people died in the subsequent famine (Gwassa and Iliffe, 1967).

Portuguese aim, nor, on the other hand, was it intended that the colonies should eventually emerge as independent African countries. Indeed, there were no long-term objectives at all.

As far as African education was concerned, the missionary initiative in this direction seemed sufficient for the need. Missionary education was of course primarily directed at evangelism but it also reflected the Christian view that, since all people were equal before God, they had equal potential. When, half a century later, newly created African countries hurtled towards independence at a rate no European colonizer had ever anticipated, they mostly found their politicians and rulers from among those who had originally been educated in the mission schools. However, the numbers of Africans with an advanced education were very few, measuring only in the dozens or the hundreds in each country. This shortage of local human capital was one of the biggest handicaps faced by the newly independent African countries.

Colonialism between the Wars

The First World War changed perceptions in a number of ways. After the war, the German empire in Africa was broken up and made the responsibility of the newly created League of Nations. This body in turn mandated other colonial powers to administer these territories – Britain for Tanganyika, Britain and France for the West African sections, including Cameroon, and South Africa for South West Africa, now Namibia. The new element was that the mandates were seen as temporary, albeit long-term, trusteeships over the colonies concerned, which would be governed in the ultimate interests of the indigenous peoples, who would be educated and encouraged to develop – to use present-day jargon. Similar views began to permeate British and French policy towards their own colonies. They were formulated in France by Sarraut, who was the minister responsible, and in Britain by Lugard in his book *Dual Mandate in British Tropical Africa* and later in two reports, in 1924 and 1926 for East and West Africa, respectively, by Ormsby-Gore.

As a result, government-sponsored and -financed schools were established for the first time. In British Africa the focus was on primary education, especially in the less remote areas, with a few children then going on to secondary school. In the French colonies, the effort was more concentrated on a full education for a tiny elite of Africans who would, and indeed did, become fully integrated into French society. In both cases, a handful of Africans began to be incorporated into the colonial political structures: in the British colonies, usually as nominated members of the governor's advisory Council; in French Africa, as members of the French Parliament. In the end, the growing number of educated Africans would come to be the most important force for political change.

At the same time, a number of colonies prospered, especially in West Africa. Foremost among these were Nigeria and the Gold Coast, where income per head was not far behind that of South Africa, with its large white population (Oliver and Fage, 1988: 199), and, among the French colonies, Côte d'Ivoire and Guinea. In East Africa, Uganda, with its fertile soils and climate, was particularly prosperous. Some European investment was also going into mining ventures in Africa –

for copper in the Katanga region in the south of the Belgian Congo and in Northern Rhodesia, and for a number of minerals in Southern Rhodesia. However, these mining ventures only really began to be profitable after the end of the depression in the 1930s and with the outbreak of the Second World War, which greatly increased demand for metals. They were always dwarfed by the much greater investment in the South African diamond and gold mining industries.

The Settler Societies

At this point, a divergence occurs between most of colonial Africa and those parts of the continent where European settlement was envisaged. In West Africa, this was practically excluded – the climate was inhospitable – and indeed the British and Belgian colonial administrations discouraged permanent European settlement. In Eastern and Southern Africa the picture was quite different. The greatest settlement actually occurred in the Portuguese colonies of Angola and Mozambique. Among the British colonies, Kenya and Southern Rhodesia had both originally been claimed by chartered companies with European settlement very much in mind. In both countries, white settlers expropriated land from the local people – in fact pastoral land rather than crop land and, in Kenya, as much from the Masai and Nandi peoples as from the more vociferous Kikuyu. There was indeed some alienation of land for estates and plantations throughout the continent. It did not necessarily mean forcible eviction of settled peoples, but more often the appropriation of what farmers would regard as reserve land in their more or less regular cycle of shifting cultivation, or what pastoralists would consider as part of their legitimate grazing area.

The new colonial doctrine of, albeit slow, African advancement placed the settler societies, which lived on privilege and monopolies (Leys, 1975), on a collision course with Britain and with the local Africans. In Kenya, the issue was effectively settled in favour of the indigenous population as early as 1923 when the British government stated that the interests of the local people would be its prime consideration, a position which was repeated in a 1930 declaration. This did not prevent the later Mau Mau troubles, which were as much concerned with issues within Kikuyu society as directed against the white settlers.

In Southern Rhodesia, the situation was quite different. Its origin was, as we have seen, as an offshoot of another colony, the Cape, rather than as the result of direct British intervention. Accordingly the European, mostly British, settlers expected the colony to follow a similar political evolution to South Africa's. Thus in 1923, Southern Rhodesia became, like the Cape, a largely independent self-governing colony, though with African or native interests still the responsibility of the British government. The white settlers, however, were becoming increasingly segregationist. Many were relatively unskilled emigrants from Britain, who had come to seek 'the good life' in Africa and who now perceived that their privileged economic position in the country would be rapidly eroded if they had to compete with Africans in a single labour market.

The white Rhodesians had long considered that their best hope for the future lay in a federation with the neighbouring colonies of Northern Rhodesia and Nyasaland, now Zambia and Malawi respectively. In economic terms they may well have been right; the economies of most independent African countries are far too small to prosper alone. But the other two colonies only had small white communities, apart from in the Northern Rhodesian copper mining belt, and neither the British government nor the Africans themselves were convinced that such a federation was in the interests of the African people of the territories concerned. However, in 1953 the Rhodesian settlers eventually got their way, and the Central African Federation came into being. It was to be short-lived. Africans in Northern Rhodesia and Nyasaland, led by Kaunda and Banda respectively, were dissatisfied with the rather weak constitutional provisions to protect their interests and continued to oppose the federation. Their voices finally prevailed. The two territories were allowed to secede from the federation and move towards independence, which came in 1964.

After the break-up of the federation, the settler government in Southern Rhodesia became more determined to resist the pressure for African political advancement. It made a unilateral declaration of independence from Britain in 1965. There followed a period of economic and political isolation, resulting from the imposition of international sanctions and growing internal African protest, which eventually led to war. The settler community, never larger than about a quarter of a million, was eventually exhausted and overthrown by the nationalist armies in 1980. We return to this below.

Post-war Political Change

For the rest of the continent, prior to the Second World War any idea of self-government, still less independence, could only be envisaged on a time scale measured in centuries rather than years. The war had a profound effect on colonialism in Africa. To Africans, the European powers suddenly appeared more venal and vulnerable than ever before. They had been roundly defeated by the Japanese, a non-white race, and forced to abandon Singapore and Hong Kong. Many Africans were recruited into the armed forces, though they did not normally serve in the front line. There they witnessed the vulnerability and fragility of European powers, which in Africa itself seemed so dominant. The thin white line of the colonial administration was seen for the first time as just that.

At the same time, the British government was coming under pressure from the Americans. The 1941 Atlantic Charter proclaimed the 'right of all people to choose the form of government under which they should live' and, although Churchill claimed that this had never been meant to apply to African people, it set the mood for the post-war settlement. Similar principles were enunciated, under American influence, in the creation of the United Nations. Such political pressures might have been resisted if their African colonies had been of great economic importance to either Britain or France at that time, but the evidence suggests that they were not (Fieldhouse, 1986: 3–24).

Thus, by the end of the war it was clear that things were going to have to change in Africa. As far as British policy was concerned, African countries would begin to be prepared for eventual independence. By 1943, eventual self-government for African colonies had become official British policy. By 1947, indeed, it was thought that perhaps one country, probably the Gold Coast, would become independent before another generation had passed. However, that was looking rather far ahead. The immediate implications were that indirect rule would have to be replaced by a more representative system of African government in which, bit by bit, Africans could play a greater role. This new policy was imposed by the post-war Labour government on the reluctant colonial governors, principally by sacking them and bringing in new men.

In France, Portugal and Belgium, the long-term objective was to incorporate their colonies into the metropolitan power rather than to offer independence. The post-war French constitution established a French Union in which the African and other colonies were merely overseas territories. As a result, the activity of francophone African nationalists became involved with domestic French politics to a point where Houphouët-Boigny, one of those Africans who had acquired a thorough French education and culture and who was later President of Côte d'Ivoire, actually became a French government minister in 1956. In this capacity he was instrumental in formulating a *loi cadre*, a framework under which self-governing status could be accorded to French colonies, but strictly within the unity of France.

At the same time, African nationalist movements, whose origins went back to before the war, were becoming more vocal and strong. Their leaders came from the small group of Africans whose education had started in mission schools and had ended up in British or French universities. They were extra-parliamentary – staying outside the consultative structure now being set up by the colonial administrations – and opposed to the traditional African chiefs and elders, whom they regarded as representative of the old order and who had compromised with the colonizers for short-term gain. Otherwise, they drew on as wide a support base as they could, extending as far as possible beyond the kinship and ethnic groups which had hitherto formed the basis of indigenous African organization. They implicitly accepted the European notion of a nation state, which went beyond pre-colonial political structures and asserted the right to govern their own nation states. There was also a pan-African element. The Fifth Pan-African Congress, held in Manchester in 1945, demanded self-government for the British African colonies. Among its participants were many who would eventually emerge as African leaders, including Kwame Nkrumah, Jomo Kenyatta and Hastings Banda.

Many of the nationalist leaders had been inspired by Gandhi's preaching of non-violence. Thus, the pressure on the colonial governments, although relentless and increasing, was not particularly violent. Under this pressure, the timetable for moving towards independence got ever shorter – envisaged in centuries before the Second World War, in generations immediately after it, then in decades and finally in the 1950s in a matter of just a few years. As often before, the Gold Coast, where Nkrumah's Convention People's Party (CPP) was particularly strong and effective and where African education and advancement were ahead of the rest of the continent, led the way. Shortly after the war, the Gold Coast had received a new constitution under which, for the first time, Africans commanded a legislative majority. This was not enough. In 1948, a small demonstration in Accra blew up into a riot in which 13 people lost their lives. The governor proposed drawing up a new constitution, but this did not satisfy Nkrumah and his CPP, who had campaigned for 'self-government now'. In 1951, the CPP won the election which was called under the new constitution, whereupon Nkrumah was released from jail, where his campaigning had led him, to play a part in the new administration. From that point on, it was only a few years before the Gold Coast acquired full independence as Ghana in 1957.

Once this pattern had been established it could only be repeated in the other British West African colonies. Nigeria became independent in 1960, with a federal constitution, Sierra Leone in 1961, and Gambia, a country with few economic resources, in 1965.

A similar process was occurring in French Africa, where the principal nationalist leaders, apart from Houphouët-Boigny, were Senghor, a literary figure and poet from Senegal, and Sekou Touré in Guinea. In 1958, the French President de Gaulle, following his success in dealing with the Algerian problem, offered French West Africa a choice between immediate and complete political independence and a measure of self-governing autonomy within a wider French Community, a choice which was to be decided by referendum. All of the territories voted for the latter, more limited option, except for Guinea. Consequently, France immediately withdrew completely from Guinea without further preparation, leaving an economic and political mess, from which it took years to recover. However, the other French territories soon also reverted to the view that complete independence was better, after all. The French government's first intention was that these territories should become independent as two large federated states, covering western and central Africa respectively. In this, they were supported by the Pan-Africanists, such as Léopold Sédar Senghor of Senegal. The richer territories, notably the Côte d'Ivoire, however, resisted this proposal and, by the end of 1960, all had been granted separate independence.

Countries in eastern and central Africa were just a few years behind those in West Africa. In the Congo, the Belgians had long since established a benign but autocratic administration which gave no place for the political aspirations of the local people. In 1958 and 1959, these began to boil over. The Belgian reaction was to draw up hastily an independence constitution and withdraw, which they did in 1960, leaving Patrice Lumumba, the only nationalist leader of any standing in the country, as prime minister. As we shall see, he did not last long.

Independence for the East African countries came in quick succession. Tanganyika, with few internal tensions and no settler population, underwent the easiest transition and became independent in 1961, with Julius Nyerere as prime minister, later president. In Uganda, there was a conflict between the dominant Buganda and other peoples from the north of the country. However, a coalition of interests was formed, allowing Uganda to become independent in 1962 under Milton Obote. Rwanda and Burundi became independent in the same year. Kenya followed a year later. There, the political skills of Kenyatta, who only ten years before had been given a seven-year jail sentence, persuaded the white settler community to cooperate with the tide of history and the march to political independence.

Of the other important countries in sub-Saharan Africa, Ethiopia had already been liberated from the Italians in the Second World War. Sudan gained independence as a single country in 1956, although the southern Christian part would have preferred to be separate from the dominant Muslim north. Somalia was formed in 1960 by merging the old British Somaliland Protectorate and the former Italian Somaliland colony. The British Southern African Protectorates, Bechuanaland, Basutoland and Swaziland, were finally released from the threat of incorporation into South Africa by the latter's departure from the Commonwealth in 1961 and its adoption of an apartheid constitution. They became independent as Botswana, Lesotho and Swaziland in 1966, 1966 and 1968, respectively. In the latter year, Spain also gave up its two tropical African colonies, which were combined to form Equatorial Guinea, but it held on to the Western Sahara until 1976.

The Liberation Wars

There were just five mainland countries still to be liberated – Southern Rhodesia, South West Africa, now Namibia, which was still a UN Trust Territory mandated to South Africa, and the four Portuguese colonies of Angola, Mozambique, Guinea-Bissau and the Cape Verde islands. In all of these countries an armed struggle was necessary to dislodge finally the colonial power.

In Angola, Mozambique and Guinea-Bissau nationalist movements emerged in the late 1950s, much as they had in other African colonial territories. However, the Salazar regime in Portugal, out of touch with the rest of the world, was totally unwilling to cede sovereignty over these territories. After all, Portugal had pioneered the European contact with Africa, and the African connection was now Portugal's single surviving claim to be a European power of some consequence. Therefore, the option of opposing the nationalists by military means was chosen. In all three countries, a bloody war was fought for more than ten years with major casualties on both sides. It was only with the collapse of the Salazar dictatorship in 1974 and the subsequent political turmoil in Portugal itself that independence finally came in 1975 to these three countries, but without any of the constitutional and political preparation which Britain and France had tried to offer their former colonies.

The most successful of the guerrilla movements was that in Guinea-Bissau. Here, the PAIGC, under the outstanding leadership of Amilcar Cabral, had succeeded by the early 1970s in taking over much of the country except the capital Bissau. Thus, it readily assumed power once Portugal had withdrawn, though Cabral himself did not live to see his triumph, having been assassinated by Portuguese agents in 1973. The PAIGC was also responsible for the liberation of the Cape Verde islands, though the two territories did not, as originally expected, come together as one state.

In Angola, there were three nationalist movements – MPLA, UNITA and FNLA. In principle, power was to be shared between them after independence. The FNLA, however, was crushed soon afterwards, and there was great dissension and discord between the other two. The MPLA came to be backed by the Soviet Union, and Cuban troops were brought into the country to support it. Consequently, UNITA was supported by the United States and by South Africa. The MPLA, which controlled the capital, Luanda, and the country's oil resources, was officially recognized as the government by most countries, while UNITA retreated to the bush from which it carried on a protracted civil war with supplies mostly coming through Zaire or South West Africa. With the collapse of the Soviet Union and the withdrawal of the Cuban troops, the MPLA lost its external support. At the same time, in December 1990 the United States officially withdrew its assistance to UNITA. Thus, the two main protagonists were forced to the negotiating table, and elections were eventually held in 1992. In reality, the elections did not resolve the underlying conflict, and the country was again plunged into civil war.

In Mozambique the various nationalist movements had combined in 1962 to form Frelimo, which then waged guerrilla war against the Portuguese. By the time the Portuguese withdrew, Frelimo already occupied about a third of the country. The policies of the one-party state that emerged were initially Marxist but in the 1980s became progressively more market-oriented during the 1980s, as the government leaned more towards the Western powers. In the meantime, however, the Rhodesian- and later South African-backed Renamo movement waged a guerrilla war to destabilize the Mozambique government. Renamo was never much more than externally organized banditry, but it was probably able to draw on some initial popular support as a result of the original socialist excesses of the Frelimo government. By the end of the 1980s, the destabilization and devastation was so great that the whole country, apart from a small area around the capital city of Maputo and along the railway line between the port of Beira and the Zimbabwe border, was in complete chaos. Renamo bandits roamed the countryside, indiscriminately harassing the population, looting and raping, and eventually searching for food. The result was mass starvation, and more than a million refugees crossed the border into Malawi and Zimbabwe. By late 1992, with a million people dead, a peace agreement had been announced. It was agreed that an election would be held under UN supervision, which it was hoped would be stronger and more effective than it had been in Angola.

The fall of the Salazar regime also led, indirectly, to the liberation of Southern Rhodesia, now Zimbabwe. The main liberation movements ZANU and ZAPU were founded in the early 1960s. They had their origins in previous organizations which had campaigned for black rights in Southern Rhodesia but which had been banned and driven underground by the white settler government, as white attitudes steadily hardened. The liberation war started in 1966, but the change of power in Mozambique in the mid-1970s left the government of Rhodesia particularly exposed on its eastern flank. As a result, ZANLA, ZANU's military wing, was able to consolidate its bases in Mozambique and from there to direct an increasingly effective campaign into Zimbabwe itself. At the same time, ZAPU forces operated out of Zambia, though rather less effectively. Finally, exhausted by war and the cumulative effects of economic sanctions, the white Rhodesian government was forced to the negotiating table. The 1979 Lancaster House Agreement provided for a new multi-party constitution with certain safeguards for the white minority. Robert Mugabe, the ZANU leader, won the subsequent election and became Zimbabwe's first prime minister and later president.

Namibia, formerly known as South West Africa, had been a German colony and became a League of Nations Trust Territory after the First World War. South Africa was given the mandate to govern it. From the 1950s, South Africa began to introduce apartheid policies in the territory and, in effect, to make it virtually a province of South Africa. In the meantime, local opposition mounted, with the South West Africa People's Organization (SWAPO) being set up in 1960. The United Nations withdrew its mandate in 1966 but this made no practical difference to South African control. At around the same time, SWAPO began a guerrilla war.

The situation did not really begin to change until the end of the 1980s. South Africa refused to give Namibia independence as long as Cuban troops remained in Angola, supporting the MPLA regime there. However, by 1989 agreements had been reached for the Cubans to withdraw, and South Africa, under pressure from the United States, allowed a UN-supervised election to take place in Namibia. This was decisively won by SWAPO, and the last African colony became independent in March 1990.

Lessons from History

The Colonial Legacy

What is the balance sheet of the colonial period in Africa? First, the worst excesses of European influence and intervention in Africa, with the international slave trade and the introduction of firearms, which were responsible for the destabilization of fragile African societies in the eighteenth and nineteenth centuries, actually occurred before colonization. The colonial invasion itself ushered in a period of political stability. Colonialism has of course become a pejorative word. However, it is difficult to argue that mainstream colonial rule, once established, was excessively harsh or oppressive. With hindsight, we can also see that the much-maligned colonials were responsible for a great deal of social progress, particularly in the establishment of a rule of law and reasonably impartial government, in the creation of a number of modern institutions and in the introduction of new technologies and crops. This judgement on the colonial period is made notwithstanding human rights abuses by all the colonial powers at one time or another.

Second, it seems fair to say that Africans at the time accepted colonial rule, even if they did not consent to it. The thin white line of colonial officers and small garrisons, mostly made up of African soldiers, was far too weak to govern through systematic and continuous repression, though they were helped by creating an illusion of greater force behind the local administration than there really was. Certainly, the British Empire could never have contained a simultaneous rebellion in several of its far-flung colonies. It was the Second World War that revealed the illusion.

Third, apart from the political stability it brought, the colonial occupation, particularly in the later years, laid the economic foundations of independent Africa – the building of roads and other infrastructure and the establishment of export crops or mines. According to the 1969 Pearson Commission Report, economic growth in Africa between 1950 and 1967 averaged 4 per cent a year (Pearson et al., 1969: 358). This suggests that, allowing for the lower population growth rate at the time, average living standards were rising at much the same rate as in the post-colonial period. Of course, these were colonial economies – in other words, dependent on raw material exports – but it is difficult to see what economic alternative there was both at the time and now.

Finally, the colonial period of African history, originally expected to last for hundreds of years, proved to be extremely short, no more than three generations. However, two great influences were left behind which changed Africa for good. One was Christianity which, with its ideals of the equality of all men, has affected man's deepest views about himself and his place in the world – notwithstanding the parallel survival of much African religion. The second is education, which even though it was very patchily provided, has been the door to knowledge and the bridge to the modern world. It is a subject to which we shall return later.

Pre-colonial Influences

None of this is to argue that colonialism was actually necessary. Some African states, especially in West Africa, were more complex and stable than outsiders realized or than history has yet given them credit for. It is possible that some states, for example the Ashanti kingdom in what is now Ghana, would have emerged into the modern world without having been occupied first, much as Japan did, though it is idle to speculate on what might have been. However, since the history of colonialism has, so far, been largely written from the perspective of Europeans, the African story itself seems to have been ignored during this period. It is as if the river of indigenous African history froze for a time, though in fact it was continuing to flow under the superficial stability of European domination. As the colonial period receded, the ice broke up and the flow of the river became apparent again.

Thus, to understand Africa today we have to discern the features of pre-colonial African history that remain important and significant. What are they? First, society was not organized into nation states with recognized bureaucratic forms of government and fixed geographical boundaries. *'Omwami tafuga ttaka; afuga bantu'* runs a Buganda proverb: 'A chief does not rule land; he rules people' (Fallers, 1964). The organizing principle was that of social relationships grouping families and larger clans. As a result, the dominant pattern of social and political organization was that of mini-states, with populations numbered only in tens of thousands, and held together by common kinship with a chief or king, who also had a religious role. Relations with some neighbouring states would be closer than with others by virtue of sharing a similar language, perhaps some common habits and customs and occasional intermarriage. In this sense it can be said that they belonged to a common *tribe*, as long as it is understood that this is a fluid concept with no clear definition or boundaries and, unlike feudal Europe, no very strong or permanent hierarchical structure. Relations with other neighbours would probably be in a state of neither permanent war nor peace.

Nevertheless, there were continual efforts, in West Africa especially, to build up larger states. These would be coalitions of clans, often achieved through intermarriage and polygyny, or by one clan managing to exert dominance over others and exact tribute from them. This was probably easier in West Africa because of the higher population density and the presence of long-distance trade across the Sahara, which could be taxed. As Cockcroft has pointed out in his book *Africa's Way*, such larger efforts at state-building were unstable. He argues that political systems throughout sub-Saharan Africa have been beset by three problems: that of succession, since there was no established rule of primogeniture; that of authoritarianism; and the concentration of power into small kinship groups. These tendencies persist to the present day and still contribute to political behaviour and instability across the continent (Cockcroft, 1990: 2). In other words, the larger pre-colonial African states, with their uncertain boundaries, could only hold together for as long as the centre could continue to exert a dominance over and exact tribute from those on the periphery. Take that away, and they immediately disintegrated. There was little or no sense of building a nation in the European manner. In the words of Professor Oliver:

> It becomes ever plainer that the largest states of pre-colonial Africa tended to have the fragility of card-houses: one unexpected challenge, and they would disintegrate into their component particles. By contrast, the minuscule states of ten or fifteen thousand people seem often to have had greater cohesion and durability. They could be annexed into large formations and yet retain their individuality (Oliver, 1991: 158).

The strength of a particular clan or society would be determined, not so much by the territory it controlled, but by its size, including the numbers of its slaves. Women were particularly important, not so much in themselves, but as part of this wealth and as the means by which it could be multiplied. Thus, both polygyny and slaving, particularly of women and children, were crucial social institutions. The more powerful and important a man, the greater the number of his wives and children, but each wife and her children would be an independent, self-sufficient unit. Other men were expendable. In some societies there was probably a high ratio of females to males – as was reported, for example, by the early visitors to the kingdom of Buganda.

Such societies were, by and large, not governed by well-defined and impartial codes of laws. Rather, people were dependent on the patronage and protection of the local king, chief, or headman. As with any other autocracy, these kings would sometimes be arbitrary and tyrannical and sometimes just. We should note, too, that in at least some African societies, for example the Ashanti in West Africa and the Tswana in the south, the king ruled only with the consent of his people who ultimately could overthrow him. In the economic sphere the king would also have the right to retain much of the economic surplus, which would mostly consist of food reserves, but also a duty to redistribute it at times of shortage or to those in need.

Meanwhile, with no national boundaries or particular geographical constraints, there was a constant moving and intermingling of peoples – like different species of fish in a sea. People would travel, perhaps as individual traders, perhaps as migrating societies, perhaps as slaves, from one area to another and with little conflict over the use of the abundant land. Pastoralists and agriculturalists would live together, making use of the land in different ways. In this way, different ideas and traditions would be exchanged and passed on from one group to another. This custom of accommodation and hospitality to new arrivals no doubt facilitated European settlement in East and Southern Africa, before African societies appreciated the threat and understood that what Europeans were after were exclusive rights to land.

In the long span of history, two of the most important historical events were the introduction of Islam to the northern half of the continent and later of Christianity to the southern half. Islam introduced, for the first time, a written tradition based on original, unchanging texts. This other African religions did not have. They were consequently limited in their geographical scope and in their ability to survive external influences. By contrast, a sense of Islamic solidarity could be created across vast areas, permitting Africans to travel throughout the Islamic world and thereby opening them to the wider world. It also greatly facilitated the trans-Saharan trade.

More recently, Christianity has swept through Africa like a bush fire, despite the initial lack of success of the early missionaries. Christianity would have appealed first to those who in some way did not fit easily into their own society, but it also gave its converts education and, with this, a window into the wider world. With this knowledge eventually came real power, sufficient to cause the European colonial forces to retreat. Christianity also, like Islam before it, brought a written culture. However, the Christian missionaries did not just bring new texts in an alien language but painstakingly learnt and wrote down the languages spoken by Africans themselves. This undertaking must have greatly contributed to an awareness of common language as a basis for a wider society going beyond proximate kin, or, in other words, a growing sense of tribe.

Finally, the prosperous societies in African history appear to have been those which were in trading contact with the rest of the world. The link between trade and prosperity is not unusual in world history, but it is a lesson which, as later chapters show, independent Africa was inclined to forget.

4 Political Africa – the First Generation

Dictators ride to and fro upon tigers which they dare
not dismount. And the tigers are getting hungry.
(Churchill, *While England Slept*)

The first priority of the leaders of independent Africa was to hold the new nation states together. This led to the abandonment of democratic constitutions, in many countries to a military takeover, and eventually almost invariably to some form of personal rule. With no effective restraints on government behaviour, corruption and human rights abuses became widespread as politicians increasingly pursued the narrow interests of a small group. Economic and social development was the main legitimizing ideology of the new nations, but this too was corrupted and misdirected. At the end of the 1980s, the people of Africa, increasingly sophisticated and educated, began to rebel against dictatorship and corruption. The second African revolution had started.

Much commentary on independent Africa, by outsiders looking in, concerns nation states and the personalities and power plays of national politicians. Nation states do, after all, present Africa's face to the world; they are the mediators with those outside. They and their governments are institutions with which we are familiar, at least we believe ourselves to be, even when governments actually behave in unfamiliar ways. Yet much of what is influencing and changing African society is occurring, as it has always done, not in national politics, but in smaller groups and societies and in the minds and hearts of individuals resolving day-by-day the tension between 'modernity' and older local values and beliefs. By comparison the nation state itself is still an immature institution, less powerful and embracing than it

93

appears or would like to be. Nevertheless, in searching for an under-standing of Africa today, national politics cannot be ignored.

The first part of this chapter discusses the central place which nation-building and the search for legitimacy by African governments has had in the political agenda of independent Africa's first generation. The following section analyses political trends over the last 30 years, as the formal written constitutions left by the colonial powers to the new nation states proved quite incapable of containing the various forces at work. Notwithstanding the number and variety of countries on the continent, political developments have been remarkably similar. One such trend has been the erosion of human rights across the continent, which is the subject of a further section. We then turn briefly to the topic of warfare in Africa. Unlike many other political events which barely touch people's lives directly, warfare, which Clausewitz described as the 'continuation of politics by other means', brutally affects ordinary lives without always resolving the underlying tensions and conflicts which cause it. The chapter concludes with a discussion of the new turn of events in political Africa since the end of the 1980s.

The Building of Nation States

A Presidential Fantasy

African politicians rarely get a good press these days, and this book does not set out to be an exception. Nevertheless, they deserve some sympathy. Imagine oneself in the early 1960s as president of a newly independent African country. In a short ceremony, the colonial flag has been pulled down; a new flag raised; a new national anthem sung. The former governor has departed and you have moved into his residence. What do you do next?

You have probably achieved power by putting together coalitions of interests across the country, tribal leaders, trade union leaders, a few intellectuals perhaps, and have organized passive resistance and street demonstrations. If yours was a British colony, in all probability you will, like Nkrumah and Kenyatta, have spent a period in jail or detention or, like Seretse Khama, in exile. If it was a French colony, on the other hand, you might, like Houphouët-Boigny, have been a minister in the French government. More recently, since you won a pre-independence election, the colonial administration has been careful to court you and is now leaving behind all the trappings and bureaucracy of a functioning government. Ultimately, the colonial state depended on force, and all the instruments of a coercive state – including an effective and disciplined police force – have been bequeathed to you. Just as well perhaps. In addition, many of the former colonial civil servants now work for you. Of course, they will have to go before too long, but very few of your own people have yet acquired the same skills and certainly do not have the administrative experience. There are also the new foreign advisers, some of whom supported your nationalist struggle.

You realize that making the government work is going to be greatly more difficult than it was for your predecessors. For a start, they were outsiders, aloof representatives of an alien power, people of some mystery who expected, and got, respect and deference from the people they ruled. True, much of the mystique of the colonial power had been wearing thin since the end of the Second World War and you, having been at university in England or Scotland, know that the colonials are very ordinary when they are at home. However, you, for all your success at mobilizing crowds and popular demonstrations, do not earn this automatic respect. People know who you are and where you have come from. Where you have been during all those years spent abroad studying in cold climates actually means very little to them.

Of course, the people have enjoyed the celebrations of the last few days, since any celebration is a relief from the boredom of village life, but they are really rather indifferent to the political changes. They know the British or the French have gone and have heard that life should now be better; but they do not really understand this nation thing which has come instead. Their own lives in their own small communities will be rather little affected. You have talked about national self-determination, the right of people to govern themselves. You see yourself as the embodiment of this new nation. Yet the people are not really interested. The nation is made up of many groups and societies; some have been hostile to each other for a long time, the remains of pre-colonial ethnic conflict. People still look to the elders of their own clan or to their chiefs for guidance and direction. Some of these leaders are not even part of this new nation but live over the border in another equally artificial new nation. One thing is abundantly clear – these ethnic leaders represent a threat. They may not be a very modern or educated bunch of men but they represent a dangerous focus for alternative loyalties and dissent. Their influence will have to be destroyed or at least emasculated if the nation is to hold together. After all, through indirect rule they have effectively collaborated with the colonial power.

In the meantime, who can be trusted? The group immediately around you is a motley crowd. As far as possible, you have tried to incorporate representatives of all societies into your nationalist movement, but some can scarcely be relied on, while others clearly see the departure of the colonials as merely a prelude to your own demise. They all expect some instant gratification from political independence – power, a seat in the cabinet perhaps, or at least wealth. The fact of the matter is that you only feel really comfortable with those from your own society, your brothers, those with whom you can share a joke in your own vernacular.

It is clear that this new nation is far too fragile, and your own hold on power far too tenuous, to allow for any argument or dissent. Why should anyone want to dissent? You were chosen by the people, after all. This paradox of Her Majesty's Loyal Opposition may be all right for the British, whose sense of nationhood is deep and quite taken for granted, but it is utter nonsense here. Of course, the colonials really knew this; they only allowed party politics to emerge once it was clear that their own days were numbered. This country will only hold together if everyone works together as one people. Disloyalty is national treason.

You do, however, have international legitimacy. The people may not believe much in, or understand, this nation thing, but when you go abroad people know who you are. It is ironic to have this greater sense of legitimacy outside your country than at home. This belonging to a community of nations has almost come as a surprise. For the first time your people have a voice in international affairs and diplomacy and that voice is yours. You could go to the United Nations in New York and make speeches on matters of international politics. You can become involved in world affairs. Some countries are already beating a path to your door, including both the United States and the Soviet Union. You must avoid Nkrumah's mistake, though, of being toppled by a coup at home while he was abroad in China trying to mediate a peace agreement in the Vietnam war (in 1966).

Within Africa, the new Organization of African Unity (OAU), set up in 1963, will be a useful forum to discuss common problems with other new presidents. You were not convinced by Nkrumah and Senghor about the Unity bit – after all, why give up power once you have got it? Nevertheless, the emerging mutual understanding not to interfere in each others' countries nor to engage in border disputes is very welcome. The borders left by the colonials to Africa are totally illogical and arbitrary, but equally no politically logical way exists to adjust or rearrange them. There are no pre-colonial borders to fall back on. People had managed without frontiers at all in those times. Fortunately, your brother presidents seem to see things in the same way. There are enough potential troubles at home.

Actually, people do not seem to take much notice of borders even now. That is a worrying sign. The farmers are supposed to sell their produce to the official crop marketing board, which your predecessors thoughtfully established, but some still goes straight over the border. You cannot allow too much smuggling; your government needs the revenue, of which taxes raised through the board are a major component. Of course, the old colonial power may help out with the budget deficit for a while but it will not do so for ever.

The Search for Legitimacy

Thus, the problem of building the nation state and its legitimacy in the eyes of its citizens was at the very centre of politics in post independence Africa. Independence was in fact an African revolution – let us call it the First African Revolution, since the second comes later – which attempted to superimpose a completely new form of political organization on the old. Some revolutions in history, such as the American Revolution of 1776, were carried out by drawing selectively on the traditions, values and constitution of the previous order and interpreting them in a new way. The outcome may have been an imperfect compromise of what the revolutionaries wanted, but by virtue of the continuity with the past it was more readily accepted by the people as a whole. Other revolutions, such as the French Revolution, so totally rejected what went before that it took time and a period of political instability, even repression, before new institutions and practices emerged and even longer before they were endorsed and internalized by those concerned.

Africa's independence revolution was more of the latter type than the former. The new nation states, with their values of impartial bureaucratic government, their electoral procedures for determining who should rule, their fixed geographical boundaries, and their codified systems of law, were utterly different from previous forms of African

Country name changes include: Gold Coast to Ghana; Dahomey to Benin; Upper Volta to Burkina Faso; Congo to Zaire; Tanganyika to Tanzania, which also incorporated Zanzibar; Nyasaland to Malawi; Northern Rhodesia to Zambia; Rhodesia to Zimbabwe; Bechuanaland to Botswana; Basutoland to Lesotho.

domestic political organization. Many of these practices and forms – the bureaucratic administration, the systems of law and the agencies for its enforcement – had of course been used by the colonial powers and were therefore more or less familiar. However, since this was an anti-colonial revolution there was always a distinct ambivalence in referring to colonial practice and procedures to legitimate and justify the new administration. Whatever may have happened in practice, no nationalist politician could ever say: 'Things must be done this way because that is what the colonial administration did'. At the same time, the discontinuity with pre-colonial political organization was almost total. African chiefs and kings and other traditional leaders of society represented the counter-revolutionary forces of reaction to the new nationalist regimes. They may have been drawn into the anti-colonial nationalist struggle which sought support from as many people as possible, but, almost invariably, once independence came, these traditional structures of authority were outlawed and suppressed by the national governments, while the spiritual/religious basis on which traditional authority often rested was also ridiculed and denounced.

In short, there was very little continuity with the past on which the new governments could draw in support of the new politics and political organization. Nevertheless, there were frequent attempts to re-invent or re-interpret traditions in order precisely to convey some sense of continuity. Thus, a number of African presidents tried to surround themselves with a mystical aura, rather reminiscent of the priest-kings of earlier African societies. The grotesque antics of Emperor Bokassa of the Central African Republic between 1966 and 1979, including a ridiculous and extravagant coronation in 1977 which cost the equivalent of a whole year's revenue, are perhaps the most extreme example. The 1972 *authenticité* decree in Zaire, forbidding the use of all non-African names, served a similar purpose, as did the frequent renaming of the new states – rejecting the colonial name and using instead that of a more ancient kingdom. Other examples include

Tanzania's deliberately imposed use of Swahili as a national language in place of English. While in Zambia supposedly ancient tribal customs and festivities were revived and officially sponsored by the state, though more as folklore than as an expression of traditional authority.

Developmentalism

Governments were also helped by having some form of legitimizing ideology – a story that could be told about why those who held and exercised power were entitled to do so. In established Western countries such an explanation could draw on historical precedent accepted by the society as a whole. In Islamic states, it was to be found in religion and God's order of things. The new African states had neither of these things, but they did make the important claim to be the only political organization able to deliver economic and social development, or more broadly modernization, to the people as a whole. The much more fluid and local pre-colonial society had not been able to do this, while the colonial regime had offered development to the few, certainly not to society as a whole.

Thus, this ideology of developmentalism was presented as the essential justification for having a nation and, as we shall see later, for the growing centralization of power in the national government. Much of the rhetoric and the speechifying of African politicians revolves around the aim of economic development and the nation state as its champion. African newspapers, almost invariably government-owned, are full of reports of one politician or another exhorting different groups to work hard and productively and, in so doing, to build the nation. Enemies of the state are those who wreck this agenda of national development, including of course foreign interests and multinational companies, which are merely concerned to exploit and rape the resources of the continent.

The point is that the political agenda actually put nation-building first and development second – and only to the extent to which it supported the first. Indeed, as we shall see in Chapter 5, much economic policy was actually hostile to economic development. Further, the political regimes in some states have used the rhetoric of development as a thin disguise for their real purpose which was to deliver power and wealth to a small group – just as in the later years of the Soviet Union, Marxist-Leninist ideology disguised a regime increasingly concerned with the privileges of a small *nomenklatura*. Hiding behind the rhetoric of development in this way is referred to as developmentalism.

Nevertheless, developmentalism, like Marxism, travelled well. External development agencies, on which African governments have come increasingly to depend (Chapter 6), could feel comfortable offering assistance to governments which appeared to make development their central concern – even to the point of overlooking other, less attractive features of these regimes. It was easy to confuse this apparent emphasis on development with reality and to disregard the fact that economic development has been very much a second priority in the minds of African politicians.

Political Trends

It is not particularly useful to describe all the political changes that occurred in the first generation of independent Africa. Some of them, and the characters involved, deserve no more than a footnote in history. Clearly, the multi-party democratic constitutions which had been bequeathed by the departing colonial powers were not going to survive long. Indeed, several of these constitutions had attempted to reconcile great internal tensions, such as the dominant Buganda kingdom with the numerous smaller societies which were also incorporated into independent Uganda. As we saw in the previous chapter, independence in Sudan was conferred even while a civil war was being fought, and in the Congo, now Zaire, there was so little preparation that the ensuing civil war was almost inevitable.

However, at the risk of oversimplification, two general patterns can be discerned between the 1960s and the end of the 1980s. In one group of countries, the multi-party constitutions were abandoned at an early stage in favour of single-party government. The second pattern is that of a cycle of military coup followed by civilian government followed by a further military coup and so on in a series of short-lived unstable regimes.

Figure 4.1 illustrates the two dominant processes. Interestingly, most countries fell into one side or the other from quite an early stage. After about 1970, there were rather few first military coups, that is in countries which had not previously had one, though there continued to be many second or third coups in those countries which had fallen into a cycle of short, unstable governments.

Ultimately, the two patterns appear to converge in the diagram –

at least up until the 1990s. In the single-party state the president comes to dominate the state and rules almost unchallenged for a long period. In the unstable states, which are subject to military coups, one man frequently emerges as a dominant strong leader and consolidates his power.

Single-party States

The left-hand side of Figure 4.1 groups those countries which quickly abandoned their multi-party constitutions and established one-party systems. Among the major African countries, Kenya, Tanzania, Malawi and Zambia fall into this group from anglophone East Africa, and Côte d'Ivoire, Cameroon and Gabon are to be found in francophone West Africa. Thus, the emergence of this pattern cannot obviously be attributed either to a particular colonial heritage or to pre-colonial differences between West and East Africa.

The creation of single-party states was a particular attempt at nation-building. In many cases the pre-independence election had effectively returned only one party, anyway – that which represented the most effective nationalist movement. For example, TANU in Tanganyika, later Tanzania, had won all the parliamentary seats except one. There was in effect no parliamentary opposition, and no other party of any significance. President Nyerere of Tanzania was in fact one of the most articulate and persuasive protagonists of the one-party state. In 1965 he said:

Since 1958 in election after election, the overwhelming national support of TANU has been increasingly demonstrated ... only one independent candidate has ever been elected to this House in opposition to TANU ... In consequence of this a candidate supported by Tanu is automatically elected; the people want a TANU representative. Yet because we have been operating in the context of a multi-party system the people have no choice as to which TANU candidate. This means that our procedures are, in practice, endangering both democracy and unity; if the people always acquiesce in the TANU candidate who is submitted to them by the Party machinery they are losing their effective power over their representative and his actions. If they oppose him they are in danger of giving sustenance to the enemies of our national unity and bringing into jeopardy the future of the principles which they wish to defend' (Nyerere, 1968: 36).

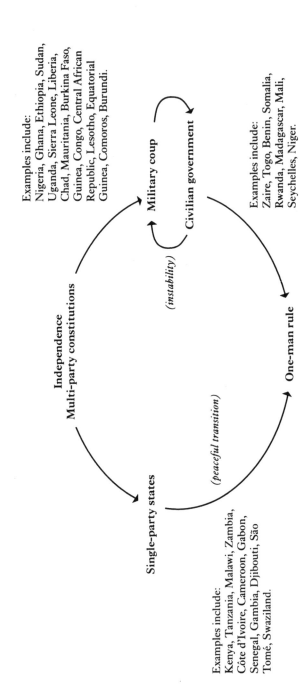

Examples include:
Nigeria, Ghana, Ethiopia, Sudan, Uganda, Sierra Leone, Liberia, Chad, Mauritania, Burkina Faso, Guinea, Congo, Central African Republic, Lesotho, Equatorial Guinea, Comoros, Burundi.

Examples include:
Zaire, Togo, Benin, Somalia, Rwanda, Madagascar, Mali, Seychelles, Niger.

Military coup

Civilian government

(instability)

Independence
Multi-party constitutions

One-man rule

(peaceful transition)

Single-party states

Examples include:
Kenya, Tanzania, Malawi, Zambia, Côte d'Ivoire, Cameroon, Gabon, Senegal, Gambia, Djibouti, São Tomé, Swaziland.

Excluded are: multi-party democracies – Botswana, Gambia, Mauritius.
liberated states – Mozambique, Angola, Guinea-Bissau, Zimbabwe, Namibia.

Figure 4.1 Political change, 1960–90

He also claimed that multi-partyism was unnecessarily divisive and wasteful of scarce educated talent, whereas the single-party state allowed regional and other differences to be balanced within one overall and controlling framework. Moreover, it was a recovery of pre-colonial African tradition in which the elders of a society would meet and thrash out a problem endlessly until a solution had been devised. Under this traditional African democracy, there was genuine debate and discussion but the overall social framework was not allowed to be compromised. This was perhaps a rather rose-tinted view of pre-colonial African society, but it did offer a legitimizing ideology for the one-party state.

At the same time, the party itself was intended to become a unifying force for the nation as a whole. In many countries it was meant to be all-embracing, penetrating all layers of society – rather like a Marxist party. In Tanzania there was a cell structure reaching right down to village level. This, it was claimed, enabled the people to be consulted on important issues. At the national level, the party effectively usurped the constitutional position of the National Assembly, which henceforth merely rubber-stamped decisions taken by the party.

In many respects, these single-party states have to be considered a success, at least in their early years. There was political stability, albeit often achieved with some political repression. As we saw in Chapter 2, political stability has, in its turn, been associated with greater economic and social development (see Figures 2.6 and 2.8). Most observers would consider Kenya, Côte d'Ivoire, Cameroon, Gabon, Malawi and Swaziland to be among the more economically successful of Africa's countries up to the early 1980s. All six were stable, single-party states. All have had political disturbances at one time or another but none has been ravaged by civil war or serious secession movements. In other countries of this group – Tanzania comes particularly to mind and perhaps Zambia, too – the one-party state does seem to have created a strong sense of national identity even if economic success has been elusive.

However, as time went on the weaknesses of the system became apparent. First, since there was no political opposition, the local-level party structure tended to wither away, and rural life was increasingly subject to government by bureaucrats rather than by representative politicians. In some countries, the inter-ethnic balance of the single political party was lost, and it fell into the hands of one ethnic group, the Beti in Cameroon, for example.

Finally, and almost invariably, the party became a personal fiefdom of the president, who in effect instigated personal rule – Moi in Kenya, Nyerere in Tanzania, Kaunda in Zambia, Banda in Malawi, Houphouët-Boigny in Côte d'Ivoire, Bongo in Gabon and so on. Senegal, which is a very restricted multi-party state, can also be fitted into this pattern.

Military Regimes

The second major pattern of political events, shown in Figure 4.1, is the cycle between military coup and counter-coup, sometimes interspersed with a period of civilian rule. The initial military coup is normally justified by its perpetrators on the grounds that the civilian politicians have failed to resolve their differences, causing political instability, or because of some unmanageable secessionist movement. Part of the legitimizing rhetoric of the military coup is that it is a temporary measure to clean up the government and restore some order to a situation which is out of control, after which new elections will bring back a civilian administration. Thus, in a number of countries, for example Nigeria, Ghana, Burkina Faso or Sudan, there have been attempts – sometimes more than one – to return to civilian politics. As often as not, however, the innate contradictions which undermined civilian rule in the first place continue. So, since the second time is much easier than the first, a second coup follows. Thereafter, the cycle continues.

In some countries, however, such as Zaire, Togo, Benin, Somalia, Madagascar, Mali and Rwanda, the cycle between coup, counter-coup and occasional civilian government was fairly decisively broken with the emergence of a strong leader who then established personal rule. Normally, at this stage the constitution would be rewritten in order to provide a figleaf of legitimacy. Thus, this group of countries frequently merged with the previous one – the one-party states – which, as we have seen, also evolved towards personal one-man rule.

Before considering the consequences of personal rule, it is instructive to compare again all of the countries on the right-hand side of Figure 4.1 with their development record, which was discussed in Chapter 2. Of them only Congo and Lesotho, both small countries, can be considered to have been particularly successful in economic and social development over the 25-year period considered. Moreover, with one or two exceptions, perhaps including Nigeria, Ghana and

Personal rulers in Africa have included: Traoré in Mali; Senghor followed by Diouf in Senegal; Touré in Guinea until his death in 1984; Houphouët-Boigny in Côte d'Ivoire; Rawlings in Ghana; Eyadéma in Togo; Kerekou in Benin; Ahidjo in Cameroon until his resignation in 1982; Macias in Equatorial Guinea until his overthrow in 1979; Mengistu in Ethiopia until the military defeat by the EPLA; Barre in Somalia until his overthrow in 1991; Kenyatta followed by Moi in Kenya; Nyerere in Tanzania until his resignation in 1985; Mobutu in Zaire; Bongo in Gabon; Kaunda in Zambia; Banda in Malawi; King Sobhuza II in Swaziland until his death in 1982; Jonathan in Lesotho, until he was overthrown in 1986; Ratsirika in Madagascar.

Uganda, it would be difficult to argue that they have been any more successful at nation-building. By and large, force has brought their leaders to power and force holds the state together, but it has not created a fertile environment for national consolidation or for economic development.

Personal Rule

Thus, the most important political trend in post-colonial Africa has been the journey, by one route or the other, to government by the personal rule of one man and his immediate coterie. In this there are echoes, though on a much larger scale, of the priest-kings who governed so many pre-colonial societies. By the end of the 1980s, at least half of all sub-Saharan African countries had arrived at this destination, though it is obviously a matter of judgement as to at what point the consolidation of personal power can be said to have been achieved. These regimes may have all the appearances of strong autocratic government but are in reality much weaker than they appear. The man who emerges on top will have done so merely by a greater political skill at playing off his rivals against each other, often together with a willingness to use torture and assassination when it suits him. It is most unlikely that he will have acquired any real popular support or legitimacy, notwithstanding an election in which he will have stood as the only candidate.

Political scientists call this type of government neo-patrimonial. Its characteristic is that the formal bureaucratic organization of a modern nation state is captured by an individual who then uses, or interferes with, the powers and functions of government in order to distribute patrimony – for example, in the award of government contracts, in the appointment of people to public office and in the creation of business monopolies, exclusive import permits and the like for relatives and associates. This distribution of patronage, helped by his control over the state instruments for law and order, notably the police and army, enables the president and his small coterie to remain in power.

One of the convenient myths of such political regimes, which is not confined to Africa, is that the president himself is an upright man who is surrounded by corrupt relatives and advisers. In some countries, it is the president's wife who is cast as the villain of the piece. From time to time, the president will make a show of clearing up the corruption around him. The advantage of the myth is that it encourages citizens in the belief that they are governed by an honest man who has their interests at heart, and enables outsiders, such as aid agencies, to delude themselves that they are dealing with an essentially legitimate and honest state. However, a few of these political leaders have become so confident of their hold on power, and of the support of the West for their regime, that they no longer find it necessary to promulgate the myth of personal honesty.

Inevitably, a neo-patrimonial state behaves in ways that appear irrational. Behind every decision lurks a hidden agenda. The normal procedures of government are distorted. Regulations and contracts are determined by personal considerations rather than by rational arguments and then cannot be enforced in the courts. Those who would like to make the system operate according to rational, modern standards, and there are many, are frustrated in their attempts to do so. The economy suffers, as we shall see in the next chapter.

Human Rights

The breakdown of constitutional government and the rise of the neo-patrimonial state in Africa have been accompanied by an erosion of human rights across the continent. In most countries, the denial of the rights of citizenship to Africans by their governments – in other words the loss of democracy and of political rights and freedoms – was followed by a more fundamental abuse of basic human rights – for example, the right not to be detained without trial or not to be tortured. Freedom of speech, an independent press and freedom of association, including the right to establish independent trade unions, were all early casualties. Legislative assemblies became rubber-stamping bodies aping the political slogans of the time. Judiciaries lost their independence and stopped dispensing justice – at least where the affairs of state were concerned.

Westerners are inclined to view the human rights of individuals as being self-evident. Have not the essential principles been endorsed by the whole world in the UN Charter and the Universal Declaration of Human Rights? However, these documents, although claiming universality, were essentially drawn up by Western powers in their period of shame following the episode of Hitlerite fascism in Europe. Their assertion of Western, individualistic, liberal values may not be as self-evident in other cultural traditions, or at least may appear to be rather one-sided.

One criticism of Westernism is that, since the individual only finds status and meaning in belonging to a particular group or society, the rights of the group should be at least on a par with those of the individual, or even take precedence. Thus, Shivji, a Tanzanian, writes: 'African traditional society is based on a collectivity (community) rather than on an individual. And therefore the notion of individual rights is foreign to African ethnophilosophy' (Shivji, 1989: 23).

A second criticism of the Western attitude is that the right to private property is so deeply embedded in Western values that it is too often allowed to override other rights or essential human needs, for example, that everyone should have enough food and the basic means to survive. The Westerner is inclined to consider that an unequal distribution of wealth and economic power, while perhaps being regrettable, is part of the natural order of things. However, those with an empty belly, it is argued, are not interested in abstract notions of human rights. What they really want is food and shelter, which the Western emphasis on the exclusiveness of private property denies them. Put another way, there is a collective right to development. According to this line of argument, Western liberalism is a rich man's excuse for the continued existence of poverty.

The argument can be taken further and applied to international relations: that the West uses its belief in property rights as a justification for an international economic system of unequal exchange which maintains poor countries in their poverty. We come back to this point in the next chapter.

There is much justification in all of these complaints and criticisms. The problem, in practice, is that they can too easily be turned into a pretext for suspending human rights in the supposedly wider interests of society, the nation or some other collectivity, or of development, or of the anti-imperialist struggle or whatever the excuse may be; and they very often have been. Further, those who decide to suspend human rights on these grounds are often the very people or governments against whom the human rights principles are intended to provide protection.

The African Charter on Human and People's Rights

The human rights debate, as well as specific criticism of human rights abuses in Africa, led the African states to proclaim their own African Charter on Human and People's Rights. This was drawn up at the end of the 1970s and adopted in June 1981 by the OAU General Assembly. It has subsequently been ratified by most OAU member countries.

In detail, the African Charter is a defective document in many ways, and not just because it reflects rather different priorities from those of the UN Charter and Declaration. First, it asserts the rights of peoples rather than of individuals, thus opening up the possibility that the rights of individuals may be subordinated to the perceived rights of the group. Moreover, a careful reading of the text of the Charter indicates that 'peoples' essentially means nation states; its framework does not allow for the possibility of individuals opposing the state. In other words, self-determination was all very well for the original nationalist movements, but it is not to be tolerated for any ethnic minority groups which may now want to break away from the established African states. Second, the African Charter sits firmly in the developmentalist framework. It argues that all peoples have a right to development. As a rejection of imperialism and of exploitation of the poor by the rich, this argument is acceptable. The problem is that the developmentalist tradition can easily turn the right to development into a right by the state to dictate what is good for its subjects, or to restrict their rights to free speech, to free association, to democracy and so on, on the grounds that these undermine development. Third, the African Charter is unique in also imposing duties on peoples, notably the duty not to compromise the security of the state, and to pay taxes. As Shivji comments:

Read as a whole, and taking into account the notorious authoritarian practices of African states, it is clear that what is demanded of the African people in this catalogue of duties is absolute allegiance to the existing State and the institution of the family – both of which respectively represent, politically and historically, retrogression. To dramatise a bit, these provisions read like Mobutu's authenticity or Banda's traditionalism on the pan-African level and probably bearing the same rationale (Shivji, 1989: 99).

Finally, the provisions for enforcement of the charter are weak. In principle aggrieved parties can complain, subject to a number of highly restrictive conditions, to the African Commission set up for the purpose. The commission's deliberations are secret, being publicized only if the African governments agree. Up until now, no individual cases have been made public.

It is easy to see this document as a cynical product of a political system which has been captured by a small elite and manipulated in its own interests. However, it does constitute a basis on which an African human rights tradition can begin to be built. Increasingly African non-government organizations and human rights pressure groups are using the charter to pursue their aims. In the end, this is the most important development. Human rights for Africans will not be achieved by making declarations or by philosophical arguments concerning what are traditional African rights and what are Western cultural imports. Rather, they will emerge from the struggle by Africans, singly and collectively, to assert those rights over and against their own rulers. International organizations, such as Amnesty International, the Minority Rights Group, and the International Commission of Jurists, can help and be supportive of the process, but the suffering and the courage will have to come from Africans themselves.

Inter-country Comparisons

How bad is the African human rights record? Comparing human rights abuses between one country and another is fraught with philosophical and methodological difficulties. Some would argue with Ralf Dahrendorf that:

> Human rights are not part of a balance sheet which one can draw up about countries and where you can say, 'Well, there is a little more of this and a little less of that,' and somehow it adds up to an acceptable mixture. They are not negotiable (Dahrendorf, 1990).

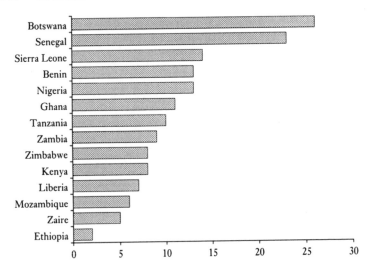

Figure 4.2 Human freedom index, 1985

Nevertheless, we do carry some notion that some regimes are worse than others, which it may not be totally illegitimate to try and measure. The UNDP attempted this type of measurement in its 1991 *Human Development Report*, where it drew up a human freedom index (UNDP, 1991). It is based on Humana's *World Human Rights Guide* (Humana, 1986) and scores 40 different types of right or freedom – thus, 40 is the maximum possible score. A number of countries were examined, using data for the year 1985. Fourteen of them were in sub-Saharan Africa. Figure 4.2 illustrates the result. Botswana and Senegal, with indices of 26 and 23, respectively, come close to values of Western democracies, which all fall in the range of 30–40. The indices for the other African countries examined were all below 15. Clearly, in the matter of human rights the continent has some way to go.

Warfare

Warfare is the worst abuse of human rights. Apart from the liberation wars described at the end of the previous chapter, several major wars have been fought in Africa since the 1960s. Most have been wars of secession, which are discussed briefly below. There have been few wars of invasion – one nation state against another. One exception was Tanzania's overthrow of the Amin regime in Uganda in 1978–79, though this war was started by Uganda. It was a surprising move, since everyone had rather assumed that Nyerere was a peaceful man who would not go against the OAU doctrine of non-interference in other African countries. A second was Somalia's unsuccessful invasion of the Ogaden region of Ethiopia, to which it laid claim, in 1977–78.

Wars of Secession

Given the geographical arbitrariness of most of the new nation states, it was inevitable that some regions would try to secede from the centre. The first case was that of the Belgian Congo, now Zaire, which almost broke apart in 1960 on the very morrow of independence itself. Zaire is a vast state of mostly tropical forest, hard to hold together, in which the huge Congo river provides the main means of internal transport and communication, though not very effectively since goods have to be trans-shipped several times between river and rail or vice versa in order to get around unnavigable stretches. Since there is so little geographical cohesion to the country, and since it had in no way been prepared for independence, it is unsurprising that it immediately began to fall apart. The Katanga province, where the mineral wealth is to be found, declared separate independence under Moïse Tshombe. There followed a period of struggle in which UN troops were brought in, while various outsiders interfered either in support of the principle of a unitary state or in favour of a more federal structure, depending on their own particular interests in the matter. Eventually, in 1965 the army commander General Mobutu Sese Seko took power over the whole country, he has ruled ever since.

This early experience in the Congo warned African politicians of the dangers of allowing their new countries to disintegrate. Nigeria's civil war, or the Biafran war, contained the same lesson. As with Zaire, the war was prompted by a dispute over how the revenue from these natural resources should be shared out between the nation as a whole and the particular region.

Nigeria is sub-Saharan Africa's most populous country, with about ninety million people. It came to independence in 1960 with a constitution which joined the three principal regions of the country – north, south-east, and south-west, broadly corresponding to the Hausa, Ibo and Yoruba societies, respectively – into a federal state.

This did not work well – the national political parties divided along regional lines and the political process became increasingly corrupt and violent. Law and order began to break down. In 1966, there was a military coup against the federal government. The military government itself was increasingly dominated by northerners, and there were anti-Ibo riots in the north of the country. This prompted the eastern region, where the country's oil resources are to be found, to attempt to secede from Nigeria in May 1967, declaring itself the independent country of Biafra. The ensuing war lasted two and a half years. As with the Congo uprising, outside powers took a stand in support of one side or the other: Britain for Nigeria, while France, Portugal and South Africa supported Biafra. Eventually, Biafra was crushed, slowly squeezed by the Federal Nigerian Army. It is estimated that two million people died in the war, mostly from starvation.

What followed was one of those remarkable African gestures of forgiveness. General Yakubu Gowon, who was the Nigerian president at the time, refused to allow reprisals against the Biafran people and set in train a process of national reconciliation. Many believe that, notwithstanding the social and ethnic tensions which continue to beset this, the most important country in black Africa, Nigeria as a whole was strengthened by its baptism of fire, perhaps as the USA one hundred years earlier had also emerged strengthened from its own civil war.

Sudan, the largest African country, has also experienced a long civil war which is still (1994) unresolved and which has caused the deaths of perhaps a million people. Although there are oil deposits in southern Sudan, mineral wealth has not been as prominent an issue as it was in the Congo or in Nigeria. The tensions arose more between a politically powerful Islamic north and a more Christian or animist south. Sudan had been ruled as an Anglo-Egyptian condominium until 1956, when, after a certain amount of squabbling between the Egyptians and the British, it became independent as a single state with a parliamentary democracy. However, the southern Christian Sudanese, fearing political domination by the Muslim northerners, had long campaigned for a separate state, or at least for a federal state. Indeed, the civil war between the two parts of the country had already started in the year before independence.

In 1958, the parliamentary constitution was overthrown by a military coup. Eventually, in 1971, Gafaar Nimeiri came to power, and the following year he reached an accommodation with the southerners which gave them a degree of political autonomy and temporarily halted the civil war. Nimeiri's administration, however, became more and more uncompromising and influenced by Islamic fundamentalists, and in due course the war resumed. Nimeiri himself was overthrown in 1985. There followed a short period of civilian government under Sadiq al-Mahdi, a descendant of General Gordon's adversary. A further military coup brought to power Omar al-Bashir, whose government has been even more fundamentalist. On the other side, the southern rebel leaders are divided among themselves, with a large element of banditry among them – having an army makes cattle raiding easier, for example.

Sudan is an example, in the early 1990s, of a country engaged in civil war, but which has been largely abandoned and ignored by the outside world, other than occasional attempts by relief agencies to get food to southern areas and to resettle refugees. Very often these efforts are deliberately frustrated by the Sudanese government or by the rebel groups. The situation is an archetypal challenge to the international doctrine of non-interference in the internal affairs of other countries, a matter to which we return in the last chapter.

The case of Eritrea is also important. It had been part of the original Italian colony which extended along the east coast of Africa from Sudan to Kenya, and included much of present-day Somalia. After the Second World War, the United Nations decided that Eritrea should be incorporated into the Ethiopian empire from 1951. Ethiopia itself had never been colonized, though it had been briefly occupied by the Italians between 1936 and 1941. It was indeed an empire in its own right, in which the dominant Amharic Christians ruled over other surrounding societies. It is one of the world's poorest nations, yet its people, certainly the elite, have a remarkable self-confidence which must surely come from two thousand years of history and civilization.

However, the high-handed Ethiopian rule, including the imposition of the Amharic language in Eritrea and the adjacent province of Tigré, was never accepted by the Eritreans, and a secessionist struggle commenced almost immediately. After Emperor Haile Selassie was overthrown in 1975 the war intensified, with the new Marxist military government being supplied by the Soviet Union. Eventually the cost of the war, which was absorbing about half of government expenditure, exhausted the Ethiopian economy, and external support fell away with the collapse of the Soviet Union. The highly disciplined rebel forces,

Tigrean and Eritrean, captured Addis Ababa in 1991, formed an interim Ethiopian government and gave Eritrea independence, thus ending the world's longest-running civil war of recent times.

Endemic Wars

Apart from these set-piece affairs with a beginning, an end and some resolution to the underlying problem, a great many small-scale wars on the continent flare up and die down from time to time without anything ever being settled. Among the long-running, but minor, civil wars have been those of Uganda, Rwanda, Burundi, Chad, and more recently Somalia, where, since 1990, old clan rivalries have erupted again. The ultimate origins of all of these go back a very long way, and they are only minor in the sense of being almost completely unimportant in geo-political terms. The local impact, in terms of death, starvation and social breakdown, is anything but minor, and the economic costs of this low-level endemic warfare on the African continent are enormous, both in terms of lost production and in the diversion to military expenditure of resources which could be used for human and economic development, even in countries which are not actually engaged in war.

Much of this endemic warfare is little more than banditry. Indeed, some observers see it as a continuation of a pre-colonial military tradition in which involvement in warfare was part of a youth's in-itiation into manhood. Certainly, the outcome resembles the relations of the neither-war-nor-peace condition which probably existed between many of Africa's pre-colonial mini-states. A local warlord will gather some men around him, acquire a few weapons, which are freely avail-able and not expensive, and use them to terrorize local populations or to skirmish with the official army of a government with whom he is in disagreement. Often the official armies themselves are indistinguish-able in their behaviour and their origins from the bandits.

Many of the political changes which have occurred in Africa, and which were summarized on the right hand side of Figure 4.1, have been the result of such adventures, but, because they happen to affect the official machinery of a nation state, they are afforded the dignity of being considered a change of government. The successful bandit is then graced with international recognition and diplomatic fawning and is free to address the United Nations on world peace and similar topics.

The New Democratic Challenge

Political corruption, human rights abuses and warfare added up to a very gloomy picture of Africa at the end of the 1980s when, all of a sudden, the established regimes began to be challenged. There was a remarkable outburst of disaffection of African people with their governments. It began in 1990 with Cape Verde, the first country to restore multi-partyism (though arguably Senegal preceded it in 1974 (Wiseman, 1990:168)) and Benin, and spread first through francophone Africa before finally engulfing more than half the continent.

One never knows why a dam bursts at a particular moment, but the collapse of communism in Eastern Europe and the former Soviet Union was certainly a factor which affected African politics in three ways. First, and least important, there was no longer a socialist economic model for African governments to emulate. Second, Soviet assistance for client regimes in Africa, notably in Ethiopia and Angola, collapsed. This in turn reduced the need for Western countries to support their own favourite regimes, such as those of Moi in Kenya, Mobutu in Zaire, as well as a number in francophone Africa, where France has made it clear that it will no longer automatically support African governments which come under domestic political pressure. Third, and most importantly, the peoples of Africa perceived that repression and exploitation did not have to be tolerated.

Pressure from external aid and development agencies also played a part. In this, the 1989 World Bank study, *Sub-Saharan Africa: from Crisis to Sustainable Growth* (IBRD 1989), was seminal. It argued that, as long as corruption was rampant, people were excluded from full participation in the economy and polity, and civil and legal codes were unenforceable, then it would not be possible to establish a reasonably efficient economy. For the first time the political issues which have been holding back development in Africa, and which had previously always been discussed *sotto voce* by the development agencies, came out in the open. Of course, a World Bank study like that mentioned above does not directly affect popular opinion, but the old-style, neo-patrimonial African governments began to realize that they could no longer automatically rely on external support. This impression was reinforced by public statements from European politicians, even though aid agencies have been rather slow to turn such statements into policy decisions actually to withdraw aid. We return to political conditionality of aid in the final chapter.

> *In 1990 President Mitterrand spelt out France's attitude to aid and democracy:*
> This traditional aid will be more tepid for regimes that behave in an authoritarian manner, without accepting the evolution toward democracy, and more enthusiastic for those who can take this step bravely and go as far as they can.
>
> *Douglas Hurd, the British Foreign Secretary, spoke in a similar vein:*
> Countries which tend towards pluralism, public accountability, respect for the rule of law, human rights and market principles should be encouraged. Governments which persist with repressive policies, corrupt management and wasteful, discredited economic systems should not expect us to support their folly with scarce aid resources which could be used better elsewhere (*Economist*, 1992b).

Patterns of Events

In a rapidly changing situation it is not particularly useful to describe the outcome in individual countries. Indeed, in few cases, at the time of writing, was it at all definitive. Nonetheless, a number of patterns do emerge. Almost invariably, the first reaction of the established politicians and presidents to the pressure for change was to deny its existence, to repress it and to retreat into their bunkers. However, in most countries this refusal soon ceased to be sustainable, and tactics then switched to one of three other possibilities.

The first was to cut the ground from under the feet of the embryonic opposition. Some regimes, of which Côte d'Ivoire and Burkina Faso provide examples, accepted the need for multi-partyism, rapidly changed the constitution and called an election. All this happened before the opposition, which up until then had been suppressed, had time to get organized. In the electoral process itself, the existing regime would use its privileged access to the media, to the security forces and to the contents of the ballot boxes to assist its re-election. As a result, the previous administration would be returned to power – for the time being. By late 1993 this had been the outcome in around ten countries.

The second was for the government to appear to go along with the calls for democratic change while in practice being obstructive and causing delay. This seems to have been the tactic of the Babangida regime in Nigeria. A common pattern in francophone Africa has been for a national constitutional conference to be called, supposedly bringing together all the interested parties, but which the established politicians then pack with their own supporters or attempt to intimidate and influence in their favour. Such has been the case in Zaire. Interestingly, in these constitutional conferences the local Catholic Church, often the one nationwide movement which commands a certain degree of popular support, has frequently emerged as a major force and a focus for anti-government opposition. This tactic of prevarication has been adopted in about fifteen countries.

The third response is that of more or less gracious acceptance of the changing situation by the government and politicians in power. Kaunda in Zambia did so, though perhaps he never believed he would lose an election. Sassou-Nguesso of the Congo also retired gracefully from the political scene in 1992. In some cases, the existing president initially tried to put himself above the fray, arguing that there should be a democratically elected government but that he would remain as ultimate arbiter and constitutional figurehead. Kerekou of Benin attempted this but without success. You cannot at one moment be an autocratic personal ruler and at the next a constitutional figurehead.

By the end of 1993, 12 countries had actually thrown out their old rulers in this way. Since these are the countries where the return to democracy has moved furthest, they are worth listing: Cape Verde, Mali, Niger, Benin, São Tomé e Principe, Central African Republic, Congo, Burundi, Zambia, Lesotho, Madagascar and Comoros. Interestingly, most are from West Africa, and eight of the 12 are francophone. Did the French colonial tradition lay a better foundation for democracy than other colonial powers, or is perhaps the longer history of state formation in West Africa over that in eastern and southern Africa now assisting its adjustment to the modern world?

A critical element in the process of democratic change is the way the opposition has been organized. In only a few countries, for example Zambia, did a single powerful opposition party emerge, sufficient to unseat the previous government, which generally had almost exclusive access to the media and controlled the police and security forces. But, like the nationalist movements a generation earlier, a successful opposition party has to represent a coalition of interests, some more unsavoury than others, with the single uniting purpose of overthrowing the entrenched regime. Once that has been achieved often very little else of a political programme exists to hold them together. Hence, not all of the countries listed above have managed to achieve stable government following their elections.

In other countries, the opposition has been divided into a multitude of small parties, none of which are strong enough to secure an absolute electoral majority – at least in a first past the post electoral system. In the case of Senegal, for example, which has claims to be an established multi-party democracy, the ruling party, the Union Progressiste Sénégalaise, has long been successful at fragmenting opposition parties and undermining their support. In Kenya too a divided opposition proved unable to unseat President Moi in the first multi-party elections in two decades.

Overall, therefore, popular pressure had by 1993 forced the majority of sub-Saharan African states to adopt multi-party constitutions or to begin to move in that direction and, in several of those which had not done so, the political system had largely broken down into civil war. Throughout this process, multi-partyism has been seen as the keystone of genuine democracy. In fact, the acid test for democracy is not so much multi-partyism but whether people can actually change their rulers without going outside the constitution. It may well be that other democratic forms have still to be evolved which would be more suited to the culture and history of the continent. For example, in Uganda the single-party National Resistance Movement claims to have achieved some measure of sucess in creating a democratic process in which a pyramid of group consensus is built from the village level upwards. However, it is too early to say whether this represents a real alternative African political system or is merely an *ad hoc* means of maintaining a regime in power, as the old single-party governments were.

The Second African Revolution?

These recent political changes are qualitatively different from anything which has gone before in independent Africa. The previous cycles of change between civilian governments and military regimes, or between one military regime and another, which were summarized in Figure 4.1, have had the characteristics of palace coups. Of course, they may have drawn some inspiration from real differences in society as a whole but they were scarcely the result of mass movements. By contrast, the new democratic movements appear to grow from a real, popular demand for political change and to command the support of huge numbers of people, particularly townspeople, who are much better informed than ever before. Superficially, they resemble the nationalist movements of colonial times, but with a crucial difference. The early nationalist leaders rallied their people, with speeches and slogans, and called for self-determination, whereas the mass movements of the 1990s seem to have emerged spontaneously, independently of any charismatic leadership. It is as if the essentially modern belief that popular sovereignty is ultimately the only legitimate basis for government has finally and dramatically been absorbed in the African polity as it has in much of the rest of the world, religious fundamentalist states apart. This is perhaps the beginning of a Second African Revolution.

One consequence will be a great deal more political instability than in the recent past. The democratic genie, once having been released, will not go back in its bottle. Outsiders will have to be much more circumspect in their relationships with particular African governments. They should be wary of drawing too close to a regime which carries no popular support and which may at any time be overthrown by popular pressure.

Recent developments may also mark the end of the nation-building phase of African history. If, as we have argued, nation-building was the major priority of the first generation of African national leaders, before they succumbed to the lucrative temptations of personal rule, now is the moment when their achievements will be tested. There are no national politicians left with the personal stature and support consciously to take on the task of nation-building, as our prototype president was able to do at the beginning of this chapter. At this point, the nation either exists, in the sense of being conceptualized by Africans as a natural and proper way of organizing society, in which case it will eventually be consolidated in some way, or, if it does not exist in the minds and hearts of ordinary people, then ethnic and tribal forces may yet tear it apart. The outcome is likely to be different in different countries, and the implications for outsiders, such as aid and development agencies, will also vary from one country to another. We return to these matters in the last two chapters.

5 Economic Debates and Development

> And he gave it for his opinion, that whoever could make two ears
> of corn or two blades of grass to grow upon a spot of ground
> where only one grew before, would deserve better of mankind,
> and do more essential service to his country than the whole race
> of politicians put together.
> (Swift, *Gulliver's Travels*, 'A Voyage to Brobdingnag')

In the 1960s, the era of African independence, theories of
economic development envisaged a central role for the state,
not only in planning and regulating economic activity, but also
in owning factories and enterprises. Excessive emphasis was
also placed on industrial development and the needs of the
towns. These theories played into the hands of the increasingly
corrupt and patrimonial governments. The interests of ordinary
rural people and of the agricultural sector, still the backbone of
most African economies, were increasingly neglected. Eventually,
economic problems piled up, and external debt accumulated.
In the 1980s most African governments, under external pressure, adopted programes of economic adjustment which,
although open to criticism, may be beginning to bear fruit.

Theories of Development

The Starting Point

As previous chapters have shown, most African countries came to
independence in the 1960s, with seemingly precipitate haste, under
very similar historical and political circumstances. There were common
elements of culture and history across the continent, though with
some variation between West Africa and eastern and southern Africa,
and a shared colonial experience; only Ethiopia and Liberia had es-
caped colonial rule.

African economies were also similar. The colonial powers, French, British, Portuguese or Belgian, had not been particularly interested in developing their African colonies, at least not until after the Second World War. Their interest had rather been to maintain basic law and order at minimal cost to the metropolitan power. The economic development that did occur was essentially colonial – intended to extract a few primary commodities, agricultural or mineral, from the interior for export to the metropole. Infrastructure was built for the limited needs of the administration or for transporting raw materials to the coast. Only in the countries of southern Africa, where there was a major mining sector and a settler population, had an integrated rail network been developed. In the rest of Africa, the railway lines ran from the coast just a short way into the interior but without interconnections. They were not intended to promote internal economic integration.

Most people's lives had been little changed. They still had to till the soil to grow their own food, even if some cash crops were now also grown. Poverty remained the normal condition. Few people were educated; although the missions had, for a long time, been providing some basic education to Africans, there was little secondary or higher education. Less than 4 per cent of the children of the appropriate age were enrolled in secondary schools, and less than half of one per cent were at university (ODI, 1992). Thus, all of the new countries were desperately short of skilled manpower.

From this common starting point, the course and outcome of economic policy have been similar across the African continent for most of the last 30 years. As discussed in the previous chapter, there was the common political consensus on developmentalism, the philosophy which in many ways legitimized the new nations and gave them purpose. Development seemed to require strong states and active intervention in the workings of the economy, so policy differences between one country and another were more superficial than real. Thus, for example, Kenya was a supposedly capitalist country, while neighbouring Tanzania introduced, with the 1967 Arusha Declaration, a version of soft African socialism with which it was then cursed for the next two decades. Yet, the Kenyan government also actively intervened in the workings of the economy. Moreover, interventionism reflected the prevailing wisdom of development economists at the time.

Outside Influences

In the 1950s and 1960s development thinking was dominated by big ideas and big theories. The great Soviet socialist experiment, which had started before the Second World War, had been extended, forcibly, to other countries in Eastern Europe, and to other parts of the world. The debate between capitalism and communism was fully engaged, and the first full flowering of sociology gave it utterance and jargon. In retrospect, much of this literature now seems extraordinarily pompous and sterile. It certainly did not foreshadow the future pattern of events. Few of the advocates of one theory or another were able to back up their ideas with detailed empirical studies. The discussion proceeded by assertion and by selection of examples which happened to suit the case being argued.

For African nationalist movements and later for newly independent countries, however, these were exciting times, full of heady ideas. The new national leaders, although African by culture and background, had been educated in Europe and exposed to European ideas and expectations – some, indeed, on the communist side of the Iron Curtain. Faced with the problem of turning an independence movement into a national ethic, the debate seemed particularly pertinent. Which model offered the greater opportunities for economic and social development?

Determinants of Economic Growth

At the same time, economic development theory was influenced by other strands of thought which were probably more important than the theoretical debates between socialists and capitalists. Many economic ideas were influential precisely because they were not debated but were rather pervasive and taken for granted. One was the overwhelming importance of capital investment as the key to economic growth and thereby to development. The Marshall Aid loan programme for the reconstruction of Western Europe's devastated capital stock after the war had proved extraordinarily successful, or at least so it appeared; in fact, Marshall Aid never represented more than a rather small proportion of European capital investment. Perhaps the same success could be achieved in the so called under-developed, former colonial countries. If post-war European reconstruction was any guide, the trick seemed to be the injection of sufficiently large capital flows from outside the country. Assuming that this capital was invested wisely, and there was no reason why it should not be, it would generate sufficient income both to repay the original loan and to raise living standards in the recipient country. Further, the softer the initial loan the greater would be the proceeds of the investment that would remain in the receiving country.

Behind this was an economic literature on what drove economic growth. Physical capital, in the form of buildings and machinery, was certainly an important element, as was labour. However, labour, at that time, tended to be seen as a lump of rather undifferentiated workers, rather than as a group of people with differing education, skills and experiences and having different cultural backgrounds. But just supplying capital and labour would not produce economic growth. There was a third element, not very well defined, which was to do with technology or technical change. One reason why it was not well defined is that technology can be incorporated into either capital or labour. Replacing old machines with new is an injection of new capital, but it may also be the introduction of new technology embedded in the machine. Equally, much technical knowledge and expertise is in fact held in the minds and skills of particular workers – be they farmers, engineers or managers.

The debate about what drives economic growth is important, because much of the changing view about development actually reflects a shift in the perceived relative importance of these three elements. However, in the 1950s and 1960s, capital shortage was rather mechanistically seen as the key constraint to economic development. Several influential books, of which perhaps Hirschmann's *The Strategy of Economic Development* and Rostow's *The Stages of Economic Growth* were among the most influential, seemed to support this view, though in reality these authors' ideas were not quite as simplistic as they came to be interpreted. Development aid, seen essentially as capital aid, came into being to overcome this capital constraint.

Industrialization

A second idea largely shared by both capitalists and socialists was that industrialization was the key to economic development, indeed for some it was practically synonymous with development. This had certainly been the historical experience of the richer countries. In Europe, in the eighteenth and nineteenth centuries, advances in agricultural technology first released workers for the factories being established in the towns and cities. Thereafter, it was industry that led the further economic advance and embodied advances in science and technology, while agriculture remained a relatively backward and conservative sector. The same process was being imitated and forced behind the Iron Curtain in the twentieth century.

The industrial base in African countries before independence was practically non-existent. Indeed, the lack of such an industrial base is the most obvious economic characteristic of underdeveloped economies. Most countries were highly dependent on the export of a few unprocessed raw materials or commodities, either agricultural – coffee, tea, cocoa, cotton, groundnuts – or, in a few countries, minerals – copper, phosphates, iron ore and later oil. Some, such as Zambia, obtained around 90 per cent of their export earnings from a single commodity and still do. How could these small, agriculturally-based, raw material exporting economies be industrialized?

There were other considerations driving the debate. Research results at that time suggested that the international prices for Africa's exports of raw materials, although varying from one year to another, were nevertheless tending to decline relative to the international price of manufactured goods. This meant that the African countries could import fewer and fewer manufactured goods for the same quantity of their own exports or, in economic jargon, their terms of trade were deteriorating. This cycle had to be broken.

Whether this apparent trend continued over the long term is somewhat debatable. A few years later, in the late 1960s and early 1970s, coinciding with the early years of African independence, the prices of raw materials that African countries export were actually rising – counter to the previously observed trend. Indeed, towards the end of that period, there were growing fears of an eventual worldwide shortage of raw materials, notably expressed in the influential Club of Rome report, *Limits to Growth* (Meadows et al., 1972). This perhaps encouraged false hopes and unrealistic dreams in the newly independent countries. Later again, the 1980s saw a reversal back to the previously observed trend as these prices deteriorated once more. Instability in prices for its exports has been a major cause of Africa's problems. We return to this topic below.

If industrialization was the key to breaking dependence on raw material export prices, how could it be achieved? It was obviously not happening spontaneously in the underdeveloped countries, and attempts to build a domestic industrial base in the poorer countries ran up against the difficulty of competing with manufactured imports from the industrial countries, which benefited from economies of scale and from years of accumulated industrial experience. There was only one conclusion. A domestic manufacturing sector in the developing countries could only be born and nurtured if it were protected against competition from imports. This was the so-called 'infant industry' argument. Protection would be achieved by imposing high import duties on imported manufactured goods or by restricting what could be imported.

Much of this theory was developed in the context of Latin America and initially applied there (Baer, 1961). Latin America was very different from Africa in that there were no obvious social impediments to industrialization and to the introduction of an industrial culture. The native peoples in Latin America had long been exterminated, or forced onto the margins of society, and much of the population was consequently of European descent, with broadly Western values, though not necessarily the Protestant work ethic which drove northern Europe and North America.

In Africa, there were greater barriers to industrialization – most notably the shortage of entrepreneurs with the relevant skills to run modern manufacturing enterprises. Many African countries had only a handful of university graduates at the time of their independence, and, outside South Africa, experience with the impersonal discipline of industrial culture was very limited. In such circumstances the newly independent state would itself have to promote and establish infant industries and, at least until they had grown up, nurture and protect them from outside competition.

In his book *Development Economics in Action*, Killick vividly portrays this process at work in Ghana, the most promising of African countries in the early 1960s (Killick, 1978). President Nkrumah had well absorbed the conventional wisdom of the need for protected industrialization, and his grandiose plans were aided and abetted by expatriate advisers – not to mention by foreign machinery suppliers eager to sell their products.

Savings, Investment and the State

A third belief concerning the process of development was that peasants, practising traditional farming methods, were conservative and resistant to change. Moreover, the peasantry was also feckless, or, as economists put it, their rate of saving was extremely low. This was a rather depressing view of three-quarters or more of the African population. However, since capital investment was essential for development and was obviously in short supply and since the peasant farmer would not voluntarily save sufficiently, there was no alternative but for the government to tax rural incomes heavily enough to generate the necessary resources for state-sponsored investment.

Other investment capital would have to come from overseas, mostly from external aid. This would require coordination at a national level. Any major productive investment – a mine, factory or plantation – would almost invariably require large complementary investments – a new road or railway, the expansion of a power station, a new dam, as well as housing, schools and hospitals. There was no choice but to plan and coordinate all such decisions at the national level. Even those countries which did not formally avow socialism, such as Kenya or Côte d'Ivoire, considered that national planning and control of the economy were required.

All of these arguments concerning the promotion of industries and the need to attract external aid combined to give the state an essential role in economic development, not only in industrial production, but indeed in all aspects of the economy. In essence, the argument was that market mechanisms alone would not deliver development. This was particularly so in small, weak economies, such as those of Africa, still lacking many of the supporting and regulatory institutions which, as discussed in Chapter 2, a modern market economy requires.

Another consideration pointed in the same direction. It was widely perceived that African economies had been exploited by the colonial system, either by foreign firms or by foreign minority groups, including white settlers. The independence movements had aimed to break this foreign domination and to take control over their own societies and economies. As they were transformed into national governments, they attempted to put this into practice. As the Pearson Report commented in 1969:

> Of course, in looking at the role of private capital in Africa one must remember that, since the days of early contact with Europe, commercial interests have caused, directly or indirectly, some of the most disturbing political upheavals on the continent. Thus, it is not surprising that many new African governments see imported enterprises and foreign ownership of crucial sectors, such as plantation agriculture, timber extraction,

mining, transport, and communications, as a perpetuation of policies and practices prejudicial to African interests and aspirations or as an undue influence of the private sector on the general orientation of development (Pearson et al., 1969: 265).

All of this fitted neatly with the widespread socialist rhetoric of the time, since socialism is concerned above all with ensuring a fair allocation of goods, wealth and power among the population.

A final consideration was that, since skilled manpower for managing the economy was in such short supply, it was more efficient to concentrate it in a small central unit in central government, where all the key economic decisions would be made, and, in most countries, a small number of expatriate advisers held extraordinary influence. Many of these were people who were engaged in the big ideas debates of the time, often holding leftist views.

Explaining Development Performance

Chapter 2 examined the development record and found that, on almost every measurable indicator, Africa had been falling behind other developing regions of the world. Explanations for this are various. Some have blamed external circumstances, including the colonial past and the structure of international trade. Others emphasize internal factors, focusing on the common political elements across the continent, the tendency to centralization of all powers in the state and in many cases the capture of the state by a single man and his immediate cronies – matters that were considered in the previous chapter. Africans themselves increasingly endorse such internal explanations but without accepting that these are simple problems amenable to simple solutions.

The Vicious Circle of Underdevelopment

The reality is that most of these explanations contain some element of truth, but no single explanation is adequate. Rather, the various handicaps faced by Africa combine into a vicious circle of underdevelopment. To illustrate this and to provide some framework for the discussion that follows, Figure 5.1 sets out some of the key economic elements underlying the poor development performance and shows how they are related.

Any such diagram is inevitably arbitrary and subjective. The terms used are not precisely defined. For example, at the bottom of the

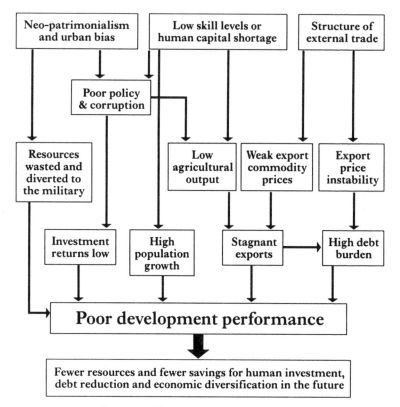

Figure 5.1 Explaining underdevelopment

diagram is the notion of poor development performance. This can be taken to include low rates of economic growth, widespread poverty and disease, limited education and limited human rights and freedoms – elements which, as discussed in Chapter 2, go towards the idea of human progress but do not encompass it. Moreover, the sketch shows links and relationships between various elements. These links are not all the same in nature and may operate over very different periods. For example, Africa's current high rate of population growth makes for a steady drain on economic and social resources, but it does not necessarily present itself either to the people concerned or to their governments as an immediate crisis. It will take two or three generations to eliminate, even if there were to be a rapid fall in fertility levels. By contrast, the debt problem, whose immediate impact is very obvious and severe, is more amenable to rapid solutions.

However, the main purpose of the figure is to emphasize the complexity and interrelatedness of the factors that contribute to the African economic crisis. There are no simple solutions to be had – a point to bear in mind when the discussion turns to the unleashing of market forces in Africa. More market-driven economies will no doubt help, but there is much more to development than that.

One of the most important links is not actually shown on the figure. The top of the diagram represents the starting conditions, while the bottom shows the outcome. There is a link between the bottom and the top: the outcome in one period creates the starting conditions for the next. A consequence of the outcome of poor development performance is that limited resources are available next time around to ameliorate the starting conditions.

Let us illustrate this point with five obvious examples. First, to reduce dependence on a few raw materials whose prices are uncertain, economies have to be diversified, but economic diversification actually occurs by new sectors growing much faster than old ones. In other words, diversification always requires resources for new investment and new skills. Second, to break the constraints imposed by skill shortages in the economy, there has to be major investment over a long period of time in education and training, but some degree of economic progress is necessary in order to have the resources for this long-term investment in human capital. The following chapter argues that external aid is particularly suited for this purpose but that in practice it has become too bogged down in matters of short-term economic management. Third, the fragility of political constitutions and the ease with which African countries have fallen prey to a few rapacious individuals and to corruption can only be countered in the long term by a more educated, better-informed citizenry. That again requires investment in people. Fourth, a reduction in payments on external debt would release resources for future investment. Finally, an equally important way of finding additional resources for investment in the future would be to reduce military expenditure, which in Africa as a whole is of the same order of magnitude as debt service or as the investment now being made in people.

The following pages examine in turn different parts of Figure 5.1, considering the arguments and tracing through the relationships in more detail. From there, the discussion moves on to the recent attempts which have been made to break out of the vicious cycle of stagnating development by means of so-called structural or economic adjustment.

The three boxes at the top of the diagram represent the starting point. Thus the box *Neo-patrimonialism and urban bias* is a shorthand summary of the whole political discussion in the previous chapter. The box *Low skill levels* encapsulates the importance of the shortage of human capital as an impediment to development in Africa. The last of the three starting boxes is the *Structure of external trade*. This is where we shall begin our examination of the processes at work.

Trends in External Trade

A major problem for Africa has been the nature and structure of its external trade. All African countries, with the exception now of Mauritius and to a lesser extent Zimbabwe, depend on a few raw materials, largely unprocessed, for their export earnings. Moreover, most are heavily dependent on just one or two commodities. This is illustrated in Figure 5.2, which shows, for a number of countries, the proportion of total export earnings which come from the two most important exports. In about half of the countries, they account for 70 per cent or more of the total. In a few countries, such as Nigeria, Zambia, Congo or Uganda, a single export accounts for more than 80 per cent of total exports (IBRD, 1991a). In all of these cases, there are enormous variations in export earnings from one year to another as a result of price changes in the international markets or of fluctuations in production, caused perhaps by drought or disease, or unforeseen problems in a particular mine. We come later to the peculiar difficulties which this instability in export revenues creates for economic management.

As discussed previously, the development strategy adopted was largely based on the belief that international prices for raw materials of the sort exported by African countries were in decline. However, this was taking a very long-term view. In the comparatively short period since independence, commodity prices have actually swung up and down from one year to the next. For example, a few countries – notably Nigeria, Gabon, Cameroon and Congo – are oil exporters, so they have benefited at times of high oil prices when other African countries have suffered. In general, however, prices of commodities exported by Africa tended to rise during the 1970s and to decline during the 1980s. For the poorer countries in particular, which are mostly dependent on agricultural rather than mineral exports, the trend has been for export prices to decline (after taking into account

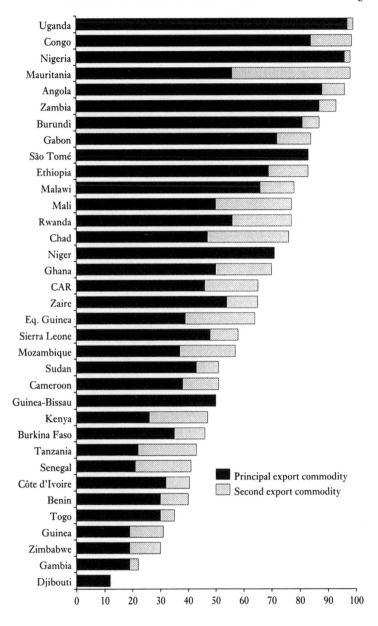

Figure 5.2 Main exports as a percentage of total exports, 1990

the general level of inflation) more or less continuously ever since independence (IBRD, 1989: 24).

This decline in commodity prices is not a complete explanation of Africa's poor export performance. Even for the commodities which it does export, Africa has lost its previous share of the international market. Its share of total world trade fell from 2.4 per cent in 1970 to 1.7 per cent in 1985 (IBRD, 1989: 19). Thus, other parts of the world, often developing countries in Asia, have coped better with declining prices. Indeed, in doing so, they have often exacerbated Africa's difficulties – the expansion of Malaysian palm oil production is a good example. This decline in market share may seem small but is actually rather important. If African countries had only maintained their share of world commodity exports, excluding oil, between 1970 and 1985, their export earnings would at the end have been up to US$ 10 billion a year higher. For comparison, this is the same the amount as was then being paid out on servicing Africa's external debt (IBRD, 1989: 19).

Unfairness in Trade?

Some see the whole international trading environment as being in some sense unfair to developing countries. They consider perhaps that international trade should be managed in some way so that rich consumers pay more for the tea, coffee, cocoa, etc. they import from developing countries in order to support their economies. This would be a dangerous path to follow. Higher prices would tend to discourage consumption of these products in the West, although not by very much. More importantly, they would encourage greater production in the countries concerned. Stocks of unsold commodities would build up. In the end, prices might crash catastrophically, causing small farmers to lose their livelihoods. Thus, it is unlikely that high prices of primary commodities could be maintained over the long term. The workings of the international commodity markets may be unfortunate but this is one area in which market forces have to be allowed to work, though there may be an argument for price stabilization, to which we return below.

The better solution in the long term is the more difficult one of economic diversification in such a way as to reduce dependence on a few primary commodity exports. That indeed is one of the main economic challenges of development. Unfortunately, unlike other developing regions, Africa has seen very little diversification of its exports away from primary commodities.

Nevertheless, there certainly are elements of unfairness in inter-national trade. Protective barriers to imports by the industrial world have discriminated against developing countries in areas where they might be expected to have some comparative advantage – agricultural commodities, for example, or light manufactures, such as textiles. The Multi-fibre Agreement, which limits textile imports into Western countries, is an example, but does not greatly affect Africa, whose manufactured exports are negligible. Indeed, in general, such pro-tective discrimination has not been a major problem for Africa. All sub-Saharan African countries except South Africa are now signatories of successive Lomé Conventions – currently the fourth – which are aid and trade agreements between the 12 member states of the Euro-pean Community and currently 69 developing countries in Africa and the Caribbean and Pacific areas – hence the term ACP group of countries. The agreement gives duty-free access for goods manufac-tured in the ACP and exported to the EC. However, in Africa, only Mauritius has exploited this possibility in any substantial way. Thus, even where trade barriers to manufactured exports have been sub-stantially removed, African countries have been unable to take much advantage of the new trading possibilities.

Another form of manipulation of international trade is the sub-sidizing by the EC and the USA of their agricultural output and the dumping of surplus agricultural produce on the world market. This drives down the international price of agricultural products which developing countries may also wish to export and in which indeed they may have a comparative advantage. On the whole, however, for African countries, this has been as much an advantage as a disad-vantage since they have generally been importers rather than exporters of the temperate agricultural products, notably wheat and dairy pro-duce, in question (Killick, 1992; Page et al., 1991). The one import-ant exception is probably sugar, for which African production and exports could almost certainly expand were it not for the highly artificial protection given by the EC and the United States to their own, less efficient sugar producers.

To summarize, it is being argued that while international trade distortions against Africa and other developing countries should be removed, it would be equally undesirable to rig international trade in the opposite direction, so as to give artificial protection to developing country exports. It might work for a while but would run the risk of being dangerously fragile in the long run and of eventually imposing

Mauritius is one of Africa's few success stories. Up until the 1970s, the economy was based on sugar, but the prospects for the sugar industry were limited and, with a million people on a small island, there was growing unemployment. So the government decided to establish export processing zones (EPZ), where investors could set up manufacturing industries free from taxation and much government regulation. A great many textiles companies were established. Wages in the EPZ were low, but by 1990 the unemployment rate in Mauritius had fallen to only one per cent. Businessmen began to complain about labour shortages and to invest in more sophisticated technology. In the end this will lead to higher wages for all. The 'Made in Mauritius' label is now well known, particularly on knitwear.

even greater costs on the developing countries. The moral obligation of the rich world to assist the poor should be worked out through aid relationships, albeit much improved on the present aid structures, as proposed in the next chapter, and through undistorted international trade relationships. This is what occurs within a national economy: poorer regions are not given preferential trading terms over the richer regions of the country but they are generally supported with a host of subsidies and transfer payments, including of course direct income support through social security systems. Unfortunately, the global political economy has not yet reached the point where such automatic resource transfer mechanisms from richer regions to poorer come into play.

That being said, fair or undistorted trade between countries will not occur spontaneously. Any trading relationship involves painstaking negotiation, and Africa's capacity to negotiate the best deals, for example over mineral concessions and sales or the prices for its exports, is still extremely weak. Botswana's success has partly resulted from a willingness to used 'hired guns', that is outside advisers, in its negotiations with other parties.

Price Instability

Experience has shown that stability in commodity prices is at least as important to developing countries as the absolute price level, and

The multinational company, De Beers, controls the international diamond market and stabilizes the price of diamonds. It does so by a monopolistic control over information, a willingness so commit enormous resources to buying up diamonds in the market if the price threatens to fall, refusal to deal with those who do not play its game and active promotion of the market. It is a private-sector operation and the only successful example of sustained commodity price stabilization in the world. It is difficult to imagine a public international commodity price agreement working in the same way or with such effectiveness. The operation has not always been so smooth: difficulties were emerging again in 1992.

Botswana, now one of the most important diamond producers, has always seen its interest to lie in cooperating with De Beers rather than confronting it. Indeed, in the 1980s the Botswana government became an important shareholder in De Beers and acquired a seat on its board of directors.

they would certainly benefit if primary commodity prices could be stabilized – which is not the same as maintaining them at an artificially high level. Some economists believe that, with well run and financed international commodity agreements, greater price stability could be achieved. Indeed the United Nations Conference on Trade and Development (UNCTAD) held in Nairobi in 1976 introduced such a scheme, the Integrated Programme for Commodities. However, it has never been financed sufficiently to be effective. Moreover, the various international agreements for specific commodities – cocoa, coffee and tin, for example – have collapsed, one by one, demonstrating both that in practice commodity price stabilization is extremely difficult, and also that such interventionist ideas became distinctly unfashionable during the 1980s.

Without some stability in export earnings, an economy is very hard to manage. It is not always appreciated that the magnitude of economic changes from one year to another with which African governments, and their people, have had to cope is far greater than the small, one or two percentage point, changes experienced in the Western industrial economies, which all have a wide range of export possibilities. For example, Nigeria's merchandise terms of trade, that is the ratio between the price of its exports and the price of its imports, fell by no less than 60 per cent during the 1980s. Madagascar's terms of trade fell by more than 70 per cent over the same period. The pattern has been repeated in many other countries.

When commodity prices or export earnings fall then a country becomes short of foreign exchange, economic activity is reduced and governments lose revenue. The International Monetary Fund (IMF) can help to cope with these problems by offering a short-term loan, in effect an overdraft facility, to the country concerned. Similarly, the European Community's Lomé Convention offers some compensation to African countries whose export earnings fall. Such measures can only be short-term palliatives. If the price fall persists for some time then the country has to take greater or lesser steps, depending on the size of the problem, to balance its accounts.

Sudden upswings in prices are generally sharper than downswings. Paradoxically, they can be even more damaging. When export earnings and corresponding tax revenues rise, governments tend to increase their expenditure, take on new staff, or start new programmes. These then become very difficult to cut back later when prices fall again, as they invariably do, and, consequently, the budget deficit – the excess of government expenditure over income – increases.

In fact, when prices rise in this way it would be far better for the government simply to pass on the benefits to the people, for example to the coffee farmers in Kenya when the price of coffee rose in 1976–79. Studies have shown that on the whole ordinary farmers are better at saving these windfall profits and putting them to good use than are their governments (Bevan et al., 1991).

External Debt

For these reasons, Figure 5.1 showed a link between the instability of export prices and the external debt problem, but it was the sudden upswings in prices that caused the problem. The origins of Africa's external debt crisis actually lie in the commodity boom of the 1970s rather than in the subsequent slump. When commodity prices rose many African governments quickly spent their windfall revenues, thereby ratcheting up the level of government expenditure. Some made matters worse by also borrowing on the strength of their increased earnings, urged on by the Western lending institutions. Thus, government expenditure, already rising on the back of increased export revenue, was geared up even further by means of external borrowing. When export prices faltered towards the end of the decade, there was a tendency to make the convenient assumption that this was a temporary downturn which could be bridged by yet more borrowing. Adjustment to the changed outlook was postponed, so the subsequent price downturn left them not just back where they had started but in an even worse position, with a heavy external debt to repay. In most cases, the proceeds of the borrowing had not been well invested.

In this way, the African oil-producing countries – Nigeria, Gabon and the Congo – got into difficulties as a result of the 1979 increase in oil prices. The most notorious example was that of Nigeria, though the Congo's mismanagement was relatively worse. Other non-oil producers also enjoyed commodity booms at various times – Kenya with coffee, Zambia with copper, Togo with phosphates – and almost all had a similar experience. A few countries, notably Cameroon and Botswana, did attempt to hold over some of their windfall gains for a rainy day, the latter with more success than the former.

Thus, instability in export earnings has been a major cause of Africa's external debt. It should be added, however, that the 1970s was also a period of considerable international liquidity, when real interest rates were negative, and both official lending agencies and commercial banks were willing to lend. Indeed, the banks, which were flush with petro-dollars at the time, were partly to blame for pushing loans on African and other Third World countries without making adequate assessments of their economic strength and creditworthiness (Griffith-Jones, 1991).

By 1990, Africa's external debt was more than US$ 170 billion, a sum which is greater than its total annual production (i.e. its GDP) (IBRD, 1992). African debt, relative to the size of the African economies, is far greater than that of Latin America ever was, although the absolute numbers were larger in the latter case. However, unlike in Latin America, most of the debt is owed to the so-called official agencies – industrial country governments, aid organizations, export credit agencies, or what are called the multilateral institutions, such as the World Bank, the IMF and the African Development Bank (ADB). In contrast, debt owed to private commercial banks represents less than a quarter of the total and is concentrated in a few countries, notably Nigeria and the Côte d'Ivoire.

However, the debt problem does vary considerably from one country to another, as Figure 5.3 illustrates. It shows the external debt of

34 countries, excluding very small countries, as a proportion of their annual income (or GDP). About a half have external debt equivalent to 50–100 per cent of GDP. A further third have even greater debt burdens, and, in Mozambique's case, its debt is nearly four times its annual income, though the GDP figures are particularly suspect here. At the other extreme, some countries have managed to keep their borrowing at a manageable level.

Although the origins of the debt problem are to be found in the 1970s, the crisis did not appear until the early 1980s, when international recession set in, prices for commodities fell, and real interest rates rose to unprecedented levels. Grace periods on loans taken out a few years earlier began to expire and repayments became due. In the case of many of the poorer African countries, they had taken out long-term development loans at very low interest rates from the various aid agencies, which now had to begin to be repaid. However, the development they were supposed to have fostered had simply not materialized. Although new borrowing was very much reduced, the debt problem continued to deepen. Foreign exchange coming in was not growing at the same pace as the requirement to pay out interest and principal on external loans – known as debt service.

In several countries, the theoretical ratio of debt service to foreign exchange earnings rose to over 100 per cent. This means that, if these countries were actually meeting their debt obligations in full, their debt service outflows would have been greater than the foreign exchange being earned. There would have been nothing left, apart from aid inflows, to pay for imports. Clearly, under such circumstances, many countries in practice limited their actual debt service to about 25 per cent to 30 per cent of exports. Payments due over and above this were simply postponed as arrears. For the continent as a whole, debt service has in fact stabilized at around US$ 10 billion a year since the mid-1980s.

Finally, towards the end of the 1980s, international efforts to manage the crisis began. These efforts have a number of elements. First, a very small proportion, around 10 per cent of the total and consisting mostly of highly concessional development loans, has been simply cancelled. This gave some industrial countries a great deal of publicity but contributed very little towards solving the problem. Second, following the 1988 Toronto Agreement among major Western countries, a more coordinated approach was taken to other official debt in low-income countries, of which most are in Africa. By 1991, this new

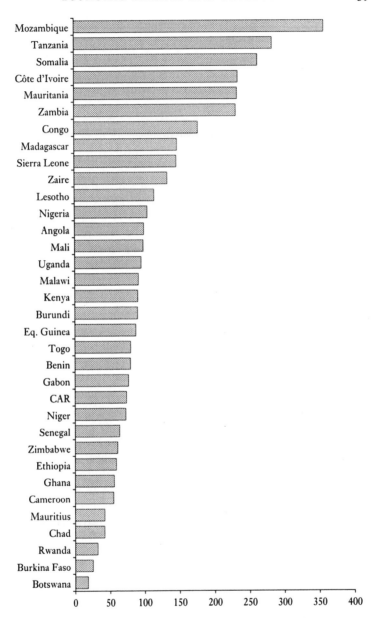

Figure 5.3 External debt as percentage of GDP, 1990

approach enabled up to half of this category of debt to be cancelled but only after detailed negotiation with the debtor country concerned. Only a few countries have benefited from the most favourable possibilities. They include Tanzania, Uganda and Zambia, following the latter's return to multi-party democracy. Third, the commercial banks have rescheduled or written off some outstanding debt but, as noted above, only a few African countries borrowed substantial sums from the commercial banks in the first place.

This leaves the debt provided by the multilateral agencies, such as the IMF, the World Bank and the ADB, whose loans together now represent nearly 30 per cent of the amount outstanding, as a largely unresolved problem. These agencies have carried on lending to African countries, by and large on softer terms than in the past, but their previous loans have not been cancelled or rescheduled. It is easy to say, as many do, that these institutions should take a more flexible line on debt repayments, but in reality they are merely instruments of the international community as a whole. It is the wealthy industrial countries, which stand behind, indeed hide behind, the World Bank and the IMF, who have shown an unwillingness to face up to the magnitude of the problem posed by multilateral debt.

It has been estimated (Palanza, 1989) that all of the present efforts at dealing with the African debt problem, if applied to the maximum extent and if sustained, might just permit the countries concerned to grow out of their difficulties. However, the balance is extremely precarious, and the impact of the various relief measures on different countries is uneven. Most see a wall of debt being pushed ahead of them and fear that any improvement in their circumstances will merely allow their creditors to take a larger bite of the cake. Moreover, the immediate prospects for more rapid economic growth do not seem promising. Thus, the external debt issue threatens to loom over the continent for at least the rest of the decade.

However, this view may be too pessimistic, as the situation continues to evolve. The reality is that a major part of African debt is not being serviced and will never be repaid. External lenders are coming to appreciate this. Indeed, it can be shown that the lenders would eventually recover more if they wrote off much of the outstanding debt than if they did not (*Economist*, 1991). Confidence would rise and this would encourage economic recovery and therefore the ability to repay what was left. The real problem is that there are no agreed rules for the game of international debt forgiveness. Why, it is argued, should the profligate countries, which have run up huge external debts, be rewarded by debt forgiveness, when the more prudent countries have so little to forgive? Moreover, a lender forgiving some or all of his debt may merely be improving the situation for other creditors who do not do so. What is therefore needed is the international equivalent of domestic bankruptcy laws, which would enable a debtor country to start again on a new footing (perhaps after a free election) and provide an orderly framework for sorting out the competing claims of the creditors. Nevertheless, unlike many of Africa's intractable problems, its debt crisis can be solved by political means if the political will can be found.

In the meantime, because much of the debt is not actually being serviced, the immediate financial impact of the debt crisis is less severe than it is often made out to be. Yet there are also huge hidden costs which may be as great as the debt service itself. Normal trade is hampered because of the difficulty of getting commercial trade credit, so imports become expensive. Anecdotal evidence suggests that a country such as Zambia, which has one of the most intractable debt problems, has been paying up to double for its imports compared with international prices, as a result of its uncreditworthiness. This is one of the most important reasons why, one day, the slate will have to be wiped clean.

To complete this discussion of the debt crisis, it should be stressed that external borrowing is not in itself undesirable. A growing economy will generally borrow abroad in order to be able to import capital goods for investment purposes. No problem arises if the investment then yields an adequate return. This has not been the case in Africa, where the issue has been not so much excessive borrowing as poor investment or, even worse, the use of the proceeds of borrowing for consumption or military expenditure.

Low Investment Returns

At the beginning of this chapter, it was pointed out that much early thinking about development focused on capital investment, and particularly on physical investment, in a rather mechanical way. As long as the rate of investment in an economy was high enough, and as long as there was an adequate return on this investment, then economic growth was bound to occur. The provision of external aid or foreign borrowing would maintain a high rate of capital investment in poor countries which could not generate sufficient internal savings, or, put another way, which faced a shortage of foreign exchange with which to buy investment goods.

Further, it was believed that projects would be carefully selected and objectively appraised by dispassionate platonic guardians in government or donor administrations who would make decisions in the interests of the public good. In retrospect, the approach appears naive. There were no platonic guardians, and rational project analysis was spitting in the political wind which, as we have seen, was blowing in a completely different direction. As a result, investment returns in Africa have been extremely low and falling, even for investment financed by external agencies who were believed to be the experts in project appraisal. According to World Bank calculations, the return on investment in Africa fell from 31 per cent in 1961–73 to 13 per cent in 1973–80, to a miserable 3 per cent in 1980–87. Over the same periods, the return on investment in South Asia rose slightly (IBRD, 1989: 26). The numbers themselves probably do not mean very much, but the downwards trend is significant and coincides with the steady shift away from rational politics in independent Africa towards states which have become personal fiefdoms, driven by corruption and by patron–client relations. This link between poor policy and corruption and low investment returns was shown in Figure 5.1 at the beginning of this chapter and has certainly contributed to poor economic performance.

Even without corruption, investment returns have still been low. Many investment projects were drawn up and appraised by outsiders, external aid agencies, equipment suppliers and consultants, who had little knowledge of local circumstances and no direct interest in the outcome. Weak or venal governments went along with this. Moreover, there was a pervasive assumption of sustained economic growth and expanding domestic demand in the economy concerned. It might be said that everyone was taken in by the developmentalist propaganda. Certainly, there was much optimism abroad, up until about the end of the 1970s. Forecasts of the outlook for export prices of major commodities, coming notably from the World Bank, have been consistently over-optimistic. In reality, such long-term forecasting is simply impossible, and it might have been better if it had never been attempted, thereby forcing project analysts to consider the outlook for their projects under a wider range of possible futures.

Indeed, many projects can survive major changes from their starting assumptions if they are well managed and if the managers are able to adapt to changing circumstances. However, in circumstances where management is weak, where entrepreneurship is discouraged and where trained and skilled workers are in short supply, all of which are characteristics of an economy with limited human capital (see Figure 5.1), the prognosis is not good.

Those who might have provided such skills and those who had substantial private resources to invest in Africa, whether they be Africans or foreigners, have, for a long time, been moving their skills and capital to other parts of the world. It is estimated that the total amount of capital which has left the continent and has been invested elsewhere or is held in anonymous Swiss bank accounts is equivalent to around 80 per cent of the continent's GDP (IBRD, 1993: 24). In other words, the total amount is not much less than the amount of official external debt. Of course, some of this may eventually return if economic conditions become more attractive, as Ghana may be beginning to find. In the meantime, however, this outflow of domestic capital is not being offset by any significant inflow of foreign investment, other than aid and other forms of public-sector finance. Indeed, flows of foreign private equity investment into Africa are declining (Bennell, 1990). In 1980, Africa attracted about 4.5 per cent of worldwide foreign investment. By 1990, it was attracting less than one per cent (*Financial Times*, 1993).

This decrease in investment is a most unfortunate development. If the modern sector in Africa is to expand and diversify, someone has to be prepared to invest in productive, risky, but also potentially profitable projects which bring in new technology and ideas and contribute to economic growth. What the continent has actually ended up with is the flight of domestic private capital, a reluctance to invest on the part of foreign private investors and an excessive inflow of foreign official loans to the public sector. These loans bring little associated technology and are, at least in principle, supposed to be repaid according to a fixed schedule, regardless of the success or failure of the project concerned. Hence, we come back again to one of the causes of the debt crisis – the failure of aid and other foreign loans to stimulate economic growth.

Parastatals and Urban Bias

Since private investment in the modern sector has always been limited in Africa, and since the original view of the development process was that state intervention would be required, a large number of government-owned public enterprises were created. These came to be known as parastatals. There were about three thousand of them throughout the continent (Knight, 1990); Tanzania alone accounted for 400. Almost invariably, they were highly protected enterprises and enjoyed domestic monopolies. They were essentially urban and modern-sector institutions favoured by subsidies and privileges at the expense of the rural agricultural sector, where two-thirds of Africa's people are still to be found.

Typically, for example, a parastatal agricultural marketing board might be established which would have the exclusive right to purchase a particular export crop from the farmers. The board would then pay out only a small fraction of the actual export price for a crop to the farmers who produced it. The difference would be retained by the board for its own operations, which were usually inefficient, or would be creamed off by government as an easy form of rural taxation. Unfortunately, this was a pattern repeated over and over again throughout the continent.

Moreover, as time went on the parastatals played a key role in the distribution of political patronage, not least because in most countries they were major employers and thus could be used to provide jobs to the relatives or cronies of the politicians. Much of their expenditure was justified merely in political terms. Those who made investment decisions in the public sector did not, by and large, have to live by them. No one was held responsible for white elephants. Government officials and parastatal managers were well protected from the consequences of their actions. The same, it has to be said, applied to the officials of the donor agencies which provided much of the investment capital. Finally, as one-man rule emerged as the dominant pattern of state government, decisions were increasingly influenced by the hidden kickbacks for particular individuals.

Similar distortions occurred in the private sector. The high levels of trade protection, originally intended to stimulate infant industries, offered abundant opportunities for profiteering, legally and illegally, in manufacturing and commerce. The general shortage of foreign exchange and its distribution by administrative decision, rather than through the market, had the same effect. The easy way to make money in Africa has been to corner the domestic market for some imported good which is in limited supply, or to set up an infant industry and then, in the name of development, insist, through one's relatives in government, on a high level of protection against competing imports. In other words, much of the urban, modern sector is engaged in activities which are not directly productive. All in all, the centralized regulation of so many aspects of economic life offered many opportunities for petty corruption, not to mention the predations of the super-kleptocrats.

Further, townspeople were able, by virtue of their geographical concentration, to exert far more political pressure on the government than the more dispersed rural dwellers. So urban wages and salary levels rose, prompting in turn an accelerated drift of people to the towns. Higher urban living standards were effectively paid for by heavy taxation of farmers and the agricultural sector. As we saw above, this was often achieved by obliging farmers to sell their produce to parastatal marketing boards, which then did not pay a fair price.

Foreign exchange controls, administered by the government or the Central Bank, encourage the value of African domestic currencies to appreciate beyond what they would be worth in an open market. The effect of this is to make imported goods appear cheap in local currency terms. Simultaneously, those who produce exports earn relatively little local currency for doing so. In Africa, imported goods are mostly consumed by townspeople, while exports, being largely agricultural, are mostly produced by country people. Thus, an overvalued currency again favours urban people at the expense of country people.

This phenomenon of urban bias has occurred throughout the continent, but curiously has been greater in the more socialist economies than in the capitalist ones. Thus, Côte d'Ivoire, Kenya, Malawi and Botswana, among the more capitalist of African countries, have all been exceptions to some degree. In each case, the ruling group in the country had a significant stake in agricultural production. In Botswana, of course, there was also a rural electorate to consider. In Malawi, an unusually strong and influential commercial agricultural sector, which included President Banda himself, exerted pressure on the government to keep wage rates down throughout the country – in urban and rural areas alike. As a result, Malawi remains among the least urbanized of African countries. By contrast, the decision-makers and parastatal managers in socialist countries such as Tanzania had little personal stake in agricultural production and output.

All of this was shown in Figure 5.1 as *poor policy and corruption*. This short phrase encapsulates the dominance of the public sector in the economy, the capturing of investment resources by the public sector, bad and corrupt investment decisions, overvalued exchange rates, the tilting of the economy against the rural areas and in favour of the towns, and excessive government control over: imports, foreign exchange allocations, prices, trade, hiring and firing of workers and so on. The details vary from country to country; the pattern of excessive state interference has been universal.

Agriculture and Food Production

Thus, for most of the last 30 years, African agriculture, on which the majority of people still depend, has laboured under the influence of wrong-headed policies and political discrimination. Right at the beginning of this book, we referred to Tanzania's disastrous experiment in forcing millions of people to move into larger villages. It was not alone in this; the Mengistu regime in Ethiopia, for example, did something similar. Nonetheless, even apart from these extreme cases, lesser distortion and discrimination against the agricultural sector – concerning crop pricing and marketing and inadequate technical and infrastructure support – pervaded the whole continent.

As a result, overall agricultural production in Africa has grown at only 2 per cent a year since the mid-1960s, despite a population increase of around 3 per cent a year over the same period. We have already seen the consequence, in terms of declining per capita food consumption (Figure 2.4), notwithstanding an increase in food imports to the continent, including food aid, to 10 million tonnes a year by 1990 – or 20 kg per person per year (IBRD, 1992). In the last few years, the trend may have changed; it is still too early to say. The matter is important since, the occasional city state apart, there are few examples in history of countries which have achieved sustained growth and development without first securing adequate domestic food supplies. For this reason, the box entitled *low agricultural output* stands in a central position in Figure 5.1.

Unfortunately, the country people, farmers and small entrepreneurs, having been marginalized from the political process, were in no position to resist urban bias in its various forms. Farmers had been excluded from the determination of agricultural strategies and were often labelled ignorant or worse if they appeared to have views of their own. Fortunately, they could and still did sell their produce on black markets and sometimes smuggled exports into a neighbouring country, if the economic environment there was more favourable. Such informal inter-country trade continues on an enormous scale, particularly in West Africa, with its long trading tradition.

Farmers could also opt out of the monetary economy and revert to subsistence production. Contrary to earlier beliefs, it turned out that the African farmer was just like everyone else. If she (or he) was not adequately rewarded for her work, and received only a fraction of the real value of her produce, she would not expand production.

Equally, if the supply of all essential goods – textiles, soap, matches, cooking oil, etc. – is preempted by urban dwellers and they do not reach the rural shops there is little incentive to earn money. The lack of basic supplies in African capitals is frequently observed and commented on – how much more often it must occur in the remote countryside. Across vast tracts of the continent, particularly in the more socialist economies, such as Tanzania, Mozambique, Ghana and Madagascar, where private trade was outlawed or discouraged, basic goods are simply not available outside the towns. A study by Berthelemy and Morrisson on the availability of manufactured goods in the rural areas comments as follows:

> All observers note that it is the essential commodities which are missing … Although these findings are similar from one country to the next, the picture nowhere parallels the poverty and despair of Mozambique. The universal view is that, even if farmers can produce a surplus, they abandon the idea or let the opportunity go by as they can obtain nothing either by purchase or barter. A 1986 report describes a situation of total deprivation in these terms: there is nothing in the shops, not even matches or candles or the fizzy drinks found in all tropical countries. The point has been reached where money no longer has any use. If you give someone a dollar tip, it is returned with a request for two cigarettes instead (Berthelemy and Morrisson, 1989).

They conclude that: 'If consumer goods are not available, farmers reduce their production for the market as they see no point in increasing unusable cash holdings' (Berthelemy and Morrisson, 1989: 9). In consequence, many rural people appear to have abandoned cash crop production, partly explaining why the volume of Africa's agricultural exports fell from the early 1970s until at least the mid-1980s (IBRD, 1989: 19).

Yet at the same time there was growing evidence, not just from Africa, that farmers are indeed prepared to experiment, to try new crops or techniques and to invest in their farms, if they are given the financial incentive of fair prices for their production. Pradervand (1989) quotes one former rural extension worker as follows:

> We were told during our training (late 1960s, early 1970s) that the farmers did not have any initiative, that they knew nothing, and that we had to teach them everything. In our view of things we knew everything and the farmers knew nothing. This was a widespread attitude among the rural extension workers ... We ourselves did not understand the vicious mechanism that we were part of, and that is why there were so many problems when, in 1985, the Senegalese government decided to liberalize the economy and deregulate the rural sector. People were not used to handling their own affairs. So what today's peasant organisations are teaching the farmers in terms of self-reliance represents a real revolution.

Moreover, on closer examination it turned out that the return to on-farm investment was in practice rather higher than was being achieved in the modern industrial sectors, where, in Africa at least, there was a series of disasters and white elephants (Lipton, 1977). Thus, one of the main premises of early development theory, that it was better to invest in the modern industrial sector, was simply wrong. A great deal of productive potential still remains to be exploited in the African agricultural sector.

This may seem a surprising conclusion in view of the numerous failed rural and agricultural development schemes, mostly donor-financed, throughout the continent. What is really needed is not large-scale agricultural projects but millions of small investments, often consisting of no more than the acquisition of better hand-tools, but which would be decided on by the farmer herself or himself. To some degree, poverty is caused by poverty. In other words, farmers who have more land, better tools or the resources to invest in erosion control or improved water supplies do indeed achieve higher crop production, as do farmers who are healthier or have more education (Collier et al., 1990). This offers hope, since it implies that, if only the vicious circle of poverty could be broken, there is still great potential for economic growth without waiting for the intervention of new technology or the development of new varieties of crops.

Nevertheless, there are unsolved technical difficulties as well. African agriculture has not experienced Asia's Green Revolution. African staple foods are root crops, such as cassava, and the coarse grains – maize, millet and sorghum. The latter are mostly grown under dryland farming conditions, rather than under irrigation; in other words, they are subject to the very uncertain African rainfall. By contrast, the research that led to the Green Revolution concentrated on rice and wheat grown under irrigation. Only about 3 per cent of the crop area in Africa is irrigated, and most irrigation schemes have been over-engineered, under-managed failures. There has been little similar research on African staple foods grown under dryland conditions, and it tends to have been erratically funded and poorly coordinated, with few important technical breakthroughs so far.

This is not to say that there has been no progress at all. Improved varieties of sorghum and millet, better adapted to the uncertain African climate, are becoming available, and hybrid maize is increasingly being grown in Kenya, Zimbabwe and Malawi. However, the presently available types of hybrid maize may be less drought-resistant than the traditional varieties, a factor which may have exacerbated the impact of the 1991/92 drought in southern Africa.

Basic agricultural research is one contribution to future development which should not be left to market forces. Public funds are and will continue to be required for research into new varieties of African staple food crops. Since external aid funds do not have to produce a financial rate of return, they are particularly appropriate here. By and large, however, one can be confident that when the scientists and technologists do have something new to offer, the African farmer will be no slower than her or his Asian counterpart in taking it up.

Industry and Small Businesses

In the end, African economies will also have to diversify. The world does not have enough demand for cocoa, coffee and similar products for these to remain the sole basis for economic growth, and the old arguments about declining terms of trade for countries which only export raw materials still retain some validity. What are the prospects for industry and manufacturing?

Manufacturing represents about 10 per cent of GDP in most African countries, and the sector produces consumer goods principally, of which foods and drinks, especially beer, and textiles and garments normally constitute the major part. Almost all production is for the domestic markets concerned, all of which are minuscule by international standards. Costs are too high and the quality is too low for the output to be exportable. Much industrial plant is owned by parastatal corporations and is now technologically outdated and poorly maintained. Very little of this publicly owned plant is worth salvaging.

Formal trading of manufactured goods between one African country and another is tiny, though Zimbabwe is an important supplier for a number of southern African countries and even more so for South Africa. Nevertheless, much informal trading continues as it always has done, particularly in West Africa. For example, it is estimated that up to 40 per cent of Nigeria's textile production is exported unofficially to other countries in the region; however, textile exports scarcely appear in Nigeria's official statistics.

Twenty years ago there might have been a chance of attracting foreign investment to build a substantial African manufacturing-for-export sector. At that time, international industrial location decisions were heavily influenced by labour costs, and, although African labour costs were not the lowest in the world, some foreign investors might have been persuaded to locate on the continent. Unfortunately, that was the period when African governments were at their most xeno-phobic and fearful of multinational corporations, so investors went to Asian countries instead. To attract them back now, even though gov-ernment policies have officially changed and become more receptive, will be much more difficult. Moreover, labour costs are becoming a less important factor in industrial location decisions, since, for almost all products, they represent a declining proportion of total production costs. International investors are today far more influenced by the proximity to major markets, to a supply of skilled labour and to where support services are readily obtainable. On all counts Africa is ex-cluded. In modern technology-based production, success increasingly breeds and follows success (Arthur, 1990).

Thus, in this sector the continent will have to fall back on its own resources and create a class of local entrepreneurs. Africa does have entrepreneurs, but, in many countries, the entrepreneurial class has consisted of political outcasts, Asians in East Africa, and the Lebanese in the West. Throughout East Africa, the Asian community was either barred or discouraged from industrial and commercial enterprise. In Tanzania, many productive activities were reserved for state para-statals. In Uganda, the Amin regime expelled the Asian community and expropriated their property. In Kenya, they were pushed out of commerce. In Malawi, where the modern sector was dominated by Press Holdings, President Banda's own company, Asians were allowed only limited access to credit or to markets.

A further difficulty is that many of these entrepreneurs are engaged in commerce rather than manufacturing. Many have become adept at extracting an economic rent in some way or another from the maze of regulations, interferences and patronage of the state – for example, getting an exclusive import quota for something which is in short supply and then selling it at an exaggerated price. A few are engaged in genuinely productive activities, but they have been hampered by the privileges accorded to public sector enterprises, by the absence of a stable business environment and by the difficulties of obtaining suitable finance.

However the future may not be quite as gloomy as the past. As in so many features of the contemporary African scene, there are encouraging signs just below the surface. A real African entrepreneurial class may be about to emerge. A 1990 study published by the International Finance Corporation (IFC), an affiliate of the World Bank, concluded that: 'although the statistical coverage is far from complete, sufficient evidence is available to demonstrate a layer of modern African entrepreneurs lying between the informal sector on the one hand and large foreign-owned or state-owned enterprises on the other' (Marsden, 1990: 6). Moreover, case studies of individual entrepreneurs show that, like African farmers, they are no different in their motivations and behaviour from entrepreneurs elsewhere in the world.

The Human Dimension

Skill Levels and Productivity

This brings us finally to the human factor in development – the millions of individuals, whether they be peasant farmers, small entrepreneurs, industrial managers or government officials, using their own skills and making their own decisions. Ultimately, this human dimension is the most important of all – both the means and the ends of development. A population which is unschooled, unskilled and frequently also unhealthy is one of the most characteristic features of poor countries, both a cause and a symptom of underdevelopment.

A shortage of high-level skills creates very obvious problems. Countries which lack doctors, engineers, skilled administrators and so on will find it difficult to run modern enterprises or efficient administrations. Similar difficulties occur also at lower skill levels, arguably with greater economic consequences since these are the people who actually undertake most economic production. A farmer who has had even a little education will be more productive, more flexible and more open to new ideas than one who has not. One detailed study, by Collier and others, in Tanzania came to this conclusion: 'A household head who had completed primary education would produce around 27 per cent more output from given inputs than someone with no education' (Collier et al., 1990: 86).

In the past, there was a tendency among economists to regard expenditure on education or other basic human needs as a social expenditure, a cost rather than an investment, unlike classic investment in tangible physical capital. This is wrong. Moreover, when economists did get round to calculating the return on investment in primary education, just as they might do for investment in physical capital, the results showed surprisingly high returns. The World Bank's 1980 *World Development Report*, a controversial document within the Bank at the time, provided one of the early summaries of the evidence. It suggested, for example, that the social return on investment in primary education was well over 20 per cent (World Bank, 1980). More recently, Colclough has reviewed the available evidence and finds: 'These studies have consistently indicated that the social returns to primary schooling (which range between 18 and 35 per cent in each of the southern continents) are considerably greater than both those at higher educational levels and those associated with most industrial projects' (Colclough with Lewin, 1993: 26).

Further, countries with high literacy or life expectancy subsequently grow faster than those which do not. Eleven years after the earlier report, the 1991 *World Development Report* claimed: 'Research for this Report suggests that increasing the average amount of education of the labour force by one year raises GDP by 9 percent. This holds for the first three years of education; that is three years of education compared with none raises GDP by 27 percent' (World Bank, 1991: 43).

Similar conclusions apply to other forms of investment in human capital, such as health care. Workers who are carrying endemic or parasitic diseases cannot be as productive as those who are healthy. Women overburdened with pregnancies or the care of small children will be unable to grow sufficient food for their families. Children suffering in their early years from severe malnutrition may have their intelligence permanently impaired.

In short, although the link between human development and economic development is hard to define precisely, and, although some of the evidence is open to different interpretations, taken together it is compelling. It is also deeply disturbing for Africa. Few African countries, notwithstanding government developmentalist propaganda to the contrary, actually allocated many resources to human development of a basic kind – literacy, primary education, simple and preventive medical care, and nutrition, though they did open expensive and extravagant hospitals and universities, of reportedly dubious standard, in their capital cities. Since dozens of children can get a primary education for the same cost as teaching one university student, this tendency perpetuated the low average skill level in the population, particularly among country people, who, since they had been excluded from the political process, were in no position to protest.

Population Growth

Education and population growth are also linked in an important way. The population of Africa is growing at around 3 per cent a year, a rate higher than in any other part of the world. This is seen, by outsiders particularly, as a major problem eroding the little economic progress which is actually being made (refer to Figure 5.1). The argument is as follows. For there to be an improvement in average living standards the economy as a whole has to grow at a faster rate than the population. Indeed, few African countries have achieved sustained economic growth rates above 3 per cent a year during the 1980s. So, by simple arithmetic one way of achieving a greater increase in average living standards is to reduce the rate of growth of the population.

However, this argument is oversimplified. Much of the African economy consists of labour for agricultural production, so the more labour that is put in the greater is the economic output. Reduce the rate of growth of labour, that is of population, and the rate of growth of the economy may also fall. Those who have tried to examine the question econometrically have not been able to demonstrate convincingly that high rates of population growth lead to lower rates of income growth (Killick, 1992: 14).

Thus, it is important not to argue mechanically that Africa's besetting problem is high population growth, nor that Africa as a whole is overpopulated. Even so, in some countries, for example Rwanda,

Burundi, Kenya, and in many regions of other countries, increasing population is imposing pressure on agricultural land. Perhaps equally important is that the pre-colonial escape strategy from social tensions, drought or other disaster – to migrate elsewhere – is no longer open.

All in all, population policy is a question which it behoves outsiders to handle with some delicacy. This may indeed be one of the areas where Africans can justifiably complain of cultural imperialism on the part of foreigners. Family and kinship are immensely important. The freedom to produce and raise children is an aspect of human well-being and a source of status for women, particularly for those whose life is not otherwise greatly fulfilled, which is not to be lightly set off against some marginal increase in material wealth.

The question of female status is indeed the key to the problem. Populations have grown mainly because of improvements in basic medical care for children and babies, leading to a considerable drop in the infant mortality rate. In the meantime, women continue to have the same number of babies as in the past but more of them survive. Now many studies have shown that the way to reduce the female fertility rate is by more widespread female education, and not simply by providing family planning. Better-educated, better-off women have greater control over their lives. They have other opportunities for self-fulfilment open to them, apart from child rearing. They marry later. They understand the importance of child spacing and caring for the children they already have, and they know how to obtain and use contraceptive advice when they so wish. Evidence from other regions of the world shows that, as female education improves, the decline in infant mortality rate is followed in due course by a decline in fertility rates. There is some evidence that this fertility decline is already happening in Africa, for example in Zimbabwe and Botswana, countries which are investing heavily in schooling for all and in country-wide health care. The same trend may also be starting in Kenya, which has one of the highest population growth rates in the world.

However, the population of Africa will continue to grow rapidly for some time, since about half the people of Africa are children, compared with 20 or 30 per cent in countries with more stable populations. These children will grow up and in turn produce their own families. Consequently, the population of sub-Saharan Africa will carry on rising rapidly for several generations yet, even if female fertility rates do decline. It is perhaps the long-term inevitability of the continued high population growth, the consequences of which are incalculable, more than the immediate impact on economic growth and present-day living standards, which constitutes Africa's population problem.

Economic Adjustment

The great optimism in the 1960s for the new African sovereign nations, for their development and for the progress of their peoples had evaporated by the 1980s. The previous discussion has shown how, in reality, development got off to a bad start. An over-centralized approach to economic policy and decision-making, with excessive state interference in the economy and in production, was unsuccessful in economic terms. Low investment returns, dependence on a few export commodities with unstable markets, neglect of basic agriculture and growing external debt all exacerbated the problem. For many Africans, conditions of life are worse than they were when their colonial rulers departed. The more-or-less democratic constitutions which had been bequeathed to most of the states concerned broke down and gave way to massive political mismanagement and corruption and the loss of basic rights and freedoms. The relatively isolated and neglected country people, who suffered most as a result, could offer little opposition to the erosion of their rights and the neglect of their interests.

In response to the deteriorating economic situation most African governments decided in the 1980s that they had to adjust. In truth, they did not reach this conclusion on their own. Rather, they came under pressure from the IMF and the World Bank and other increasingly disillusioned external agencies. The precipitating event in each country was normally an acute balance of payments problem which would force the country concerned to turn initially to the IMF for a short-term stabilization loan, and then to the World Bank, for longer-term finance. IMF support, being like an overdraft, always involves some degree of conditionality imposed on the borrower to correct the underlying imbalances. The new element in the 1980s was the offer by the World Bank to make a new type of loan to the countries concerned. These new loans would not be for identified investment projects but would be available to the government for general purposes, as long as the government implemented specific changes in domestic economic policy. They were called structural adjustment loans.

The main thrust of these policy changes was to attempt to break down the centralizing, public-sector bias that had emerged over the previous two decades. It would be replaced with a more open economic system, both internally and externally, more responsive to individual needs and initiatives and to the discipline and guidance of market forces. The package of policy measures would be agreed between the country concerned and the World Bank and the IMF. Further financial support would then normally be mustered from other aid donors.

Experience with Adjustment

The remedies for different countries included many common medicines. Indeed, a criticism sometimes made, but which is not altogether fair, is that the same prescriptions have been unthinkingly applied by the World Bank and the IMF to different countries, regardless of their circumstances. Some medicines were easy to take and were supposedly quick acting. They were aimed at rapidly making the economy more competitive by 'getting the prices right'. These included, by means of devaluation, the price of foreign exchange in order to encourage exports and domestic production and discourage imports, the raising of crop prices paid to farmers, in order to stimulate agricultural production, and the removal of the import quotas and high tariff levels which had been artificially protecting inefficient domestic industries. All are reforms which directly attack some of the problems discussed earlier in this chapter. Measures aimed at making markets work more effectively would include the abolition of agricultural marketing boards, the removal of distorting taxes or subsidies, for example on food consumed by townspeople, the freeing of financial markets and the simplifying of labour and employment regulations.

Other policy measures, particularly those that involve some degree of institutional change, have been much harder and slower to implement. For example, many countries had allowed their civil services to expand – as a result of political patronage – to a point at which the size of the government's budget deficit was simply unsustainable. Thus, one necessary adjustment would be to reduce the size of the government budget deficit, partly by increasing revenue, for which the scope is limited, but also by reducing expenditure.

Normally, the initial reduction in expenditure would be directed at capital or investment expenditures. After that, apparently minor items would be cut back. As a result, schools would find themselves fully staffed but without textbooks, or hospitals would be without drugs. Since the much more difficult task of actually reducing public-sector manning levels presents political problems that might even lead to the fall of the government regime, it would usually be postponed. Few governments have yet made much progress at all in this direction. What happens instead is that public-sector salaries are allowed to get eroded away with inflation. This is an unsatisfactory compromise since, although it certainly reduces real government expenditure, it also increases the incentive for corruption and diminishes those for work and for the adoption of professional values by the civil service.

Similarly, the vast burden of the parastatals, which have become a dead weight on many economies, needed to be lightened. Some could be made efficient and would survive on their own or with only a little governmental support, some needed to be sunk, while others could be sold off to the private sector. However, across the continent privatization is moving very slowly. There has been some success in Ghana, Guinea, Senegal, Nigeria and Mozambique. In Uganda, a few plantations and factories have been returned to their original Asian owners, who were expelled in the 1970s by Idi Amin. In most countries, however, the absence of credible investors, the unprofitability of the enterprises, political lack of enthusiasm and the sheer complexity of the task have all combined to undermine progress. Talk of privatization in Africa is mostly empty rhetoric.

In the light of the discussion above, the failure to implement these institutional aspects of adjustment is unsurprising. In political terms, African governments simply cannot afford to lay off tens of thousands of urban employees, at least not without first winning rural support through an election. Public-sector employment, whether in government or parastatals, has become not merely a rich source of patronage but the basis of the whole urban economy. Most African politicians, lacking as they do real support and popular legitimacy from the rural areas, would be highly vulnerable to a disaffected urban population. For example, the Kaunda government in Zambia attempted in 1986 to reduce urban food subsidies but quickly retracted in the face of riots and protests from workers in the copperbelt. This set back economic reform in Zambia for several years and ultimately contributed to Kaunda's downfall.

Lessons from Adjustment

The first lesson from experience so far is that adjustment is more likely to work with clear and consistent political support, coming not just from a group of politicians but from the polity as a whole. It is better not to embark on policy changes that cannot be sustained than to reverse them in mid-course, since this merely undermines confidence in the process. Policy changes that are merely imposed from the outside may be superficially successful but in the end will be frustrated.

By contrast, Nigeria and Zimbabwe accepted economic adjustment only after much internal political debate. In Nigeria, one of the more open of African societies, the public debate led to a curious compromise. No IMF financial assistance was accepted, yet in 1986 the country introduced its own stabilization programme, which initially was a model of IMF rectitude. However, the policy was effectively abandoned two years later. Zimbabwe, whose financial plight is less desperate than many, also devised much of its own programme, which started in 1991. Notwithstanding the failure in Nigeria, such a domestically designed adjustment programme eventually has a greater chance of success than policy reforms which have merely been adopted as the latest political manoeuvre to get out of short-term difficulties.

Second, the sequencing of various economic policy changes has proved to be more important than originally thought. For example, it may not be possible simply to liberalize foreign trade, as long as the underlying supply and demand for foreign exchange are unbalanced. Lowering external tariffs to eliminate excessive external protection may well have an adverse effect on government revenue. Selective increases in the prices paid to farmers may increase production of one crop but at the expense of another, without raising overall agricultural production significantly, particularly if agricultural credit is limited or if inputs are unavailable. Many of these matters were only imperfectly understood even by the economists at the World Bank and the IMF.

Third, the pace at which the economy can change is relatively slow, and the supply response takes some years to materialize, certainly much longer than originally expected. Ghana was one of the first countries to embark on adjustment in 1983. It is widely considered to be the nearest African case to a success. Certainly, economic output has been growing in recent years at around 5 per cent a year, although starting from the very low base to which it had previously fallen. Yet a 1987 study on Ghana (Green, 1987) argued that adjustment would have to continue until the mid-1990s, a prediction which seems to be being fulfilled. In the meantime, there are continuing financial constraints. For example, debt service, although falling, still absorbed nearly half of its export earnings in 1990. Nevertheless, there are some glimmers on the Ghanaian horizon, one of the brightest being the growing interest on the part of the numerous and well-educated Ghanaian diaspora to return to their country or to invest in it.

No African country could be said to be a model of successful economic adjustment, and the initial high hopes for success have not been fulfilled. Although evidence is growing from some other countries, apart from Ghana, Uganda and Zambia for example, that their economies are beginning to recover, they are not doing more than recovering. Adjustment has not proved to be the golden key to unlock the door to sustained development and prosperity. Yet, by and large, countries which have not yet started to adjust are doing much worse.

Criticisms of Adjustment

Outside the refined circles of development agencies and ministries of finance, criticism of economic adjustment in Africa has been vociferous. It comes from within the continent itself and from outsiders such as academics and the aid charities (referred to as non-governmental organizations, or NGOs) who campaign for the poor. Some of this criticism is perplexing. For example, many argue against currency devaluation on the grounds that it hurts the poor. However, since the vast majority of poor people in Africa are to be found in the rural areas,

---

The CFA franc, the currency of most francophone West African countries, had been tied to the French franc at a fixed parity for many years. It had become very overvalued, but the option of achieving economic adjustment through devaluation was long rejected by the countries concerned and by France. An alternative means of adjustment, to reduce urban and public-sector salaries and wages in order to make their economies more competitive, was tried, for example in Côte d'Ivoire, but with limited results. Devaluation eventually took place in January 1994, but its success will depend on resisting urban political pressures for wage increases. In the meantime, the economies of all of these countries, several of which up to the mid-1980s appeared to be among the most successful in Africa, have deteriorated considerably.

and since devaluation tends to work against urban bias by raising the domestic prices for crops produced in the rural areas as well as for imported goods which are mostly consumed in the towns, it is not clear why it is believed that a lower exchange rate adversely affects the poor.

Part of the explanation is that on this matter, as on others, the public views of Africans are articulated by those who live in the towns. Nevertheless, it is also true that leads and lags in the economy may not work in the immediate interests of the poor. A devaluation may well raise import prices for a farmer more quickly than he sees a rise in his earnings from his export crop. Moreover, since the poor are widely dispersed and have no real political power, the powerful may still find ways of exploiting them even after a currency devaluation, the effectiveness of which is as much a matter of the balance of political forces as it is of economics.

The conclusion from a number of studies on this matter (Morrisson, 1992) is that, while any economic change is bound to have winners and losers, structural adjustment does not have to be detrimental to the poor as a whole. It all depends on the particular policy choices taken and especially exactly how government spending is reduced – whether it is the more extravagant urban expenditures or basic social services in the rural areas that are cut. We come back to this point below.

A second line of criticism seems to suggest that adjustment has caused the economic problems which it sets out to solve; it confuses the illness with the medicine. It must be said that adjustment to deteriorating economic circumstances takes place whether or not a government introduces an adjustment programme – designed either at home or in Washington. If resources are not available to a country its people go without.

In the face of a deteriorating economic situation, whatever its cause, the real choice is between orderly or haphazard adjustment. Not to adjust is in fact a choice for the latter. One author refers to the 'dangerous illusions of non-adjustment' (Morrisson, 1992). The impact of non-adjustment or haphazard adjustment is arbitrary and anarchic and affects different groups in different ways. In the absence of orderly adjustment, government expenditure becomes increasingly ineffective – teachers without books, hospitals without medicines and so on. Governments attempt to balance their budgets by printing money, causing hyper-inflation. Commonly, the greatest burden falls on the rural poor, who have least political influence and who see their earnings, such as they are, eroded by inflation and experience the break-down of local social services. If goods and services come to be in short supply, it is the country people who go without first.

Orderly adjustment, or what has come to be called structural adjustment, aims to manage this inevitable process of change in a sensible way and at the same time to reduce some of the distortions and urban biases which have been the bane of African development. Those who see only the urban areas see only part of this correction. They observe falling wage levels in the formal sector of the economy and sometimes declining public-sector employment, reduced food subsidies, rising interest rates and factories and industries facing financial difficulties. They do not necessarily witness the small but significant improvement in living standards among the mass of the rural people as a result of higher prices for agricultural crops, the elimination of rapacious crop marketing boards, the increasing availability of consumer goods in the rural areas, and, finally, the resumption of modest economic growth.

Of course, there are different ways to achieve orderly adjustment, and the detailed choices made are extremely important. For example, there is almost always a need to cut back government expenditure if hyper-inflation, which is a form of haphazard taxation, is to be avoided. Governments can choose whether to reduce the numbers of civil servants, many of whom are usually underemployed, or their wage levels, or food subsidies to urban consumers, or military expenditures, or social services in the rural areas. Which choices are made will critically affect economic and social progress, in both the short and the long term. Since urbanized, vocal public-sector workers and the military are politically powerful, the choice in practice too often falls on the last item – the cutting back of basic social services. This decision is then justified under the euphemism of the 'social costs of adjustment'.

In choosing to cut back basic social services, there are legitimate grounds for criticism since, in reality, the resources required to provide for basic human needs, or, in other words, to invest in human capital, are relatively small and are supportable even by poor countries (Cornia et al., 1987). (We shall come back to this in the discussion of aid and social expenditure in the next chapter.) It is other areas of government expenditure which need to be cut back, not least the military commitments, which are very high in many African countries. The problem is essentially political rather than economic.

What Drives Development?

Indeed, the fundamental element of orderly adjustment is little more than good economic housekeeping, which unfortunately many African politicians have not seen to be in their narrow short-term interests. In this light, structural adjustment loans represent incentives to governments to pursue policies they should be following anyway, together with some compensation to tide the economy over the difficult transitional years.

Unfortunately, and here the critics of adjustment certainly have a case, some of the rhetoric, though not the practice, of economic adjustment had become too ideological. For a time in the 1980s, the World Bank seemed to be excessively influenced by right-wing Reaganite thinking. Although it never claimed that structural adjustment was a panacea, outsiders might have been excused for having got that impression. Certainly, there was an excessive degree of optimism about what liberalized economies, run by market forces, would deliver.

There was also widespread misinterpretation of the causes of the phenomenal success of the newly industrial countries of South-East Asia, such as Singapore, Taiwan, Hong Kong and South Korea. Those advocating the unfettered freedom of markets used these countries as examples of market-driven success, but more detailed studies later showed that, with the exception of Hong Kong, these were not highly liberal, *laissez-faire* economies but were instead subject to strong interventionist governments with firm but flexible objectives. Moreover, these governments enjoyed a high degree of legitimacy, even if not always democratic. They were driven by a concern for the public good and not merely by the private concerns of particular politicians. The same lessons could have been drawn from Africa's own success stories – Botswana and Mauritius.

Nevertheless, without some ideology, the changes that have occurred might never have begun. A restoration of market forces was an essential prerequisite for future development, a point now widely accepted throughout the continent, though practice still falls some way behind.

A greater threat now is that the pendulum will swing too far the other way. The continent will, as ever, be vulnerable to rampant exploitation by outsiders of the kind which the original independent governments saw it as their task to prevent. In domestic affairs, there will be instances of market failure which in a civilized society have to be dealt with. The protection of the economically weak and vulnerable, now largely undertaken through kinship networks and obligations, may increasingly be a task for governments. In addition, of course, the efficient functioning of markets requires the support of an over-arching, incorrupt legal and regulatory framework.

Thus, the original insight of development economics, that market failure is widespread in developing economies, is as true today as it was 25 years ago. Yet the nagging question which has been obscured by the somewhat ideological, and certainly short-term, debate on adjustment remains. What really drives development?

We do know some more of the answers to the question than we did then. We know now that old-fashioned socialist economies do not work, but we can also be sure that some non-market economic intervention by governments will continue to be necessary – particularly in the provision of physical infrastructure, in education and training, in the transfer of technology and in basic agricultural research. The Green Revolution has shown the potential rewards of publicly funded genetic research and experimentation. Such research now has to be applied effectively to African staple food crops. Economic diversification will still be important and with that will come some degree of industrialization. Governments will need to learn how to foster and promote industries but without protecting them or trying to second guess the market. Future industrial strategy will have not so much to 'pick winners' as to 'drop losers'. How to do this is still imperfectly understood. All in all, economic adjustment and development amounts to a great deal more than just 'getting the prices right', and plenty of scope remains simply for good government, which most of independent Africa has not yet enjoyed.

Yet the importance of the human dimension in accounting for Africa's past economic difficulties and in determining its future prospects cannot be overstated. In the end, all of the problems of underdevelopment revolve around this central issue. People who are uneducated, unskilled and unhealthy have limited resources to reach their own potential, which is what development is all about. Societies and economies grow because the people, of which they are made up, grow too. As economies expand, more resources become available for improving the health and education of the next generation.

Investment in people also has major political consequences. An ill-educated population is certainly more easily manipulated by small groups seeking power for themselves. Consequently, the elites who have governed Africa for the last generation without being subject to popular restraint have been able to spend vast sums on military hardware, while giving lower priority to basic human development. Further, much of the educational expenditure has been concentrated on providing university education for the few, often turning out scores of unemployable sociology and political science graduates, at the expense of primary schooling for all.

Thus, for both economic and political reasons, the vicious circle of under-investment in human capital which has affected Africa for the last generation needs to be turned around into a virtuous circle. In the end, some form of democratic government may well be required to do so. A government which depends on mass popular support, not just that of a few townspeople, has to allocate adequate resources for popular needs if it is to survive and is thereby much less likely to be subverted by particular interest groups. Within Africa, the history of Botswana, briefly outlined in Appendix A, illustrates this approach.

In all of this, external aid and development agencies also have an important role to play, but one rather different from that which they have adopted hitherto.

6 External Aid

> The widening gap between the developed and developing
> countries has become a central issue of our time.
> (Opening sentence of the 1969 *Pearson Report*)

External aid to Africa is equivalent to about ten per cent of the
continent's total GDP, though smaller countries tend to get a
disproportionately large share. Almost all official aid passes
through governments and, in many cases, is at least as much as
they are able to raise in domestic taxation. Hence external aid
has tended to give *de facto* support to African regimes, even
when their legitimacy is questionable. Moreover, it is too focused on capital investment, whereas it could be more approp-
riately used for human development, that is, building up people's
skills and basic potential. Such human capital formation is still
neglected and much remains to be done. Donor agencies should
set themselves a target of ensuring that every African child is
receiving an education by the year 2000. To achieve this they
should work through society as a whole and not just through
African governments.

Thus far, very little has been said about external aid. This is quite
appropriate. The domestic social and political circumstances which
have been the subject of previous chapters have been vastly more
important than the activities of external donors. So, although aid to
Africa has been substantial and growing, its impact is unclear and
ambiguous. It has certainly not brought about the economic transformation of African societies that was once expected. Instead, Africa
appears to have been pursuing its own agenda, which, although manifestly influenced by external ideas and forces, has not been dictated by
them.

Since Africa itself is widely perceived as facing a social and political
crisis, aid to the continent is criticized on the grounds that it appears

that the West has been pouring money into Africa with very little return. There is also increasing competition for aid resources from other parts of the world. Per capita aid donations to the Indian sub-continent, where people are just as poor, are very much below those for Africa. The countries of Eastern Europe and the former Soviet Union are also increasingly demanding attention.

This chapter starts by setting out the main features of aid to Africa, then considers some of the criticisms that are made about aid. It argues that a major impact of Western aid has been the maintenance and sustenance of African states which may or may not have supported the development aspirations of their peoples. It concludes by propos-ing a radically different aid strategy in the future which would address the failings of the present approach.

What is Aid About?

Origins and Motivations

The colonial powers began to provide development aid to their colonies before the Second World War and, in the UK, the Colonial Develop-ment and Welfare Act of 1940 was a key milestone. The concept of aid freely given by one independent country to another was greatly boosted by the implementation of the Marshall Plan at the end of the Second World War. The United States made very substantial low-interest long-term loans, worth about US$ 70 billion at today's prices, to the war-torn countries of Europe, including Germany, so that they could restructure their devastated economies. It was an expansive gesture of generosity. There was no obligation on the part of the United States to assist in the rebuilding of Europe, but there was an awareness of the mistake made at the end of the First World War in insisting on German war reparations, which then became one of the causes of the Second World War. Moreover, Western Europe could not be allowed to go communist. Thus, the Marshall Plan was motivated by a mixture of generosity and imaginative practical politics, and this has been true of much aid-giving since.

The Marshall Plan is generally viewed to have been a great success. European recovery, especially in Germany, was rapid. Aid under the Marshall Plan was not the whole explanation for this recovery, but it certainly played its part. Thus, as the European powers began to prepare their colonies for independence, partly under pressure from the United States, the idea gained ground that the approach could be repeated. With the help of external aid from the West, these new countries could also move quickly to independent economic viability.

Aid is now taken so much for granted that we perhaps forget what an important step it then was. For the first time, one aspect of international statecraft was motivated in part by generosity towards another independent nation rather than merely by the political interests of the donor. Of course, there are other justifications for aid: it expiates guilt for colonialism; it encourages trade; and it buys political interest and sometimes votes in the UN Security Council. All of these are essentially secondary arguments. There is no particular reason, at this distance in history, for feeling guilty about colonialism, and there are many other, more direct, ways of pursuing trade and political objectives without requiring development aid. In short, none of these secondary arguments provides an essential justification for the aid that occurs now.

In 1969 the Pearson Commission, which is discussed further below, musing on these matters, asked: 'Why should the rich countries seek to help other nations ...?' and replied: 'The simplest answer to the question is the moral one: that it is only right for those who have to share with those who have not' (Pearson, 1969: 8). The report goes on to acknowledge that, of course, as with the Marshall Plan, the motive was not a purely moral obligation. There was the 'appeal of enlightened and constructive self-interest', but let that not obscure the altruistic aspect.

Where does this altruistic motivation come from? For some, the common Christian heritage of Western civilization is sufficient justification. Helping the poor or those in need is clearly a Christian virtue which is acknowledged even by those who themselves would argue in more humanistic terms, for example in terms of human solidarity or personal dignity. Others look for more philosophical arguments, of which the American philosopher John Rawls's *A Theory of Justice* is one of the most promising (Riddell, 1987).

Whatever the source of this motivation, aid is clearly not just a matter of money and economics. It is also a cultural export, profoundly imbued with Western values – especially the importance of the individual *vis-à-vis* society and his right to impartial treatment. Also implicit is the notion of universality, that, in principle at least, poor people have a claim on Western aid simply because of the fact that they are human beings. There is not supposed to be discrimination

The strongest theoretical argument for overseas aid which does not fall back on abstract morality is probably to be found in the philosopher John Rawls's *A Theory of Justice* (1973). He argues that social justice should be based on the way in which we would all agree to order society (or by extension international relations) if we did not know in advance what position we would occupy in that society. This is not an argument for absolute equality. An analogy would be for an architect to design a city, knowing in advance that one of the houses would be his, but not knowing which.

on grounds of race, or national or tribal affiliation, or religious belief. That at least is the ideal.

It is unsurprising, therefore, if aid is sometimes viewed as a form of cultural imperialism, purveying the values of a particular bourgeois Western culture with its emphasis on individual rights and on private property. That such values are written into the UN Declaration on Human Rights is of little consequence, since this Declaration was itself drawn up by the dominant Western nations.

These matters may seem pedantic until situations arise in which the objectives of the aid agency are not shared by the recipients – or more often their governments. This, for example, was the case in 1991 in southern Sudan when the World Food Programme, a UN agency, tried to get food to the Sudanese refugees there. Its efforts were impeded by the Sudanese government, which preferred bombing the refugees to feeding them. Such difficulties will always arise where the interests of the political elite in a country do not appear to coincide with those of their people. The problem then is: who represents the people? Sometimes there will be no alternative but for outsiders to arbitrate or for the aid agencies to follow their own judgement.

Such issues are not at all straightforward. Aid agencies may well consider that they can achieve more for the people of a particular country by continuing to cooperate with its government, however unrepresentative or tyrannical it may be. Such cooperation may be the only way of continuing to provide humanitarian assistance. Yet at the same time it may give sustenance and respectability to the regime in question. Moreover, donor agencies have too often taken political stability to be evidence of underlying popular consent; the colonial period should have warned them against that. Growing awareness of this dilemma has encouraged debate on the subject of political conditionality, or using aid as a means of promoting political change in the recipient country, a topic to which we return in the final chapter.

Definitions

Aid is normally taken to be the sum of all gifts and low-interest, or soft, loans made by governments or official institutions – such as the United Nations, the World Bank, the African Development Bank, or the European Community – to poor countries. It is often referred to as Official Development Assistance (ODA), and figures on aid flows from all Western countries are compiled by the Development Assistance Committee (DAC) of the Organization for Economic Cooperation and Development (OECD), which is the club of the Western developed countries.

The volume of aid provided by OECD countries, nearly US\$ 56 billion in 1990, has increased by about 20 per cent in real terms over the course of the last decade, though it is still a long way from the ancient target of 0.7 per cent of each individual country's GDP. The USA and Japan are the largest donors, each providing about 20 per cent of OECD aid. The 12 member countries of the European Community combined provide about a half of all aid from OECD countries. Their share of aid to Africa is higher than this, about 55 per cent of the total (Marin, 1992), because of their particular historical interest in this part of the world. Total aid from the OPEC oil producers reached nearly US\$ 10 billion in 1980, or about a third of that provided by the OECD countries at the time. With the subsequent decline in the oil price, it has since fallen away very substantially. Arab aid has always been primarily destined for Muslim countries; there is little pretence at universality here.

It is important, for the later discussion, to be clear about what is excluded from the definition of aid. First, loans made on commercial terms are excluded. Thus, lending by the World Bank itself (IBRD loans) is not defined as aid – even though it is for development purposes. IBRD loans are raised by the World Bank on the world's capital markets and are therefore not concessional. In fact, the World Bank has a sister institution, the International Development Association, which makes highly concessional loans available (IDA credits); these are part of total aid. IDA credits are financed by the governments of Western countries, that is by their taxpayers. From an operational point of view, no distinction is made between IBRD loans and IDA credits – the same staff and procedures are involved. A country receives one or the other, depending on its level of development. In the past, several African countries received IBRD loans. Nowadays, with the poor economic situation in the continent, very few are eligible for IBRD loans, and World Bank assistance to Africa now comes mostly from the IDA.

The loans made by the IMF are also not considered to be part of aid. The IMF is not a development institution. Its principal role is to maintain the convertibility of one currency into another, in order to encourage international finance and, indirectly, world trade. It does this by providing short-term financial facilities, overdrafts actually, to countries which find themselves in temporary difficulties. As with any good bank manager, the IMF provides its overdrafts on condition that the borrower agrees to take remedial action rather quickly. As with other banks, it sometimes gets more deeply drawn into situations which cannot be turned around quickly, as with much of Africa during the 1980s. Keynes, who was instrumental in setting up both the World Bank and the IMF, commented that the IMF was really a bank and the World Bank was really a fund.

Similarly, loans made by commercial banks or by export promotion agencies and direct private investment by individuals or companies do not form part of total aid, either. As was seen in the discussion of Africa's external debt, commercial bank loans were only ever important for a few countries, and scarcely any new ones are now being given.

Second, official aid statistics also exclude charitable donations to private development agencies, normally referred to as non-governmental organizations (NGOs) – Oxfam, Christian Aid, Save the Children Fund, etc. By and large, the volume of development finance from NGOs is about one-tenth of that from official sources (Clark, 1991: 48).

Figure 6.1 summarizes this discussion in a schematic way. The most important features are: first, the overwhelming importance of official aid to Africa compared with either commercial lending or charitable donations through NGOs; and second, the fact that almost all official aid flows to the governments of the recipient countries or their immediate agents, such as parastatal corporations.

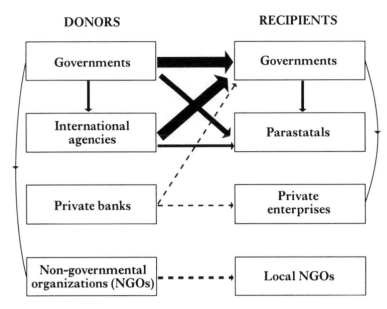

Figure 6.1 Financial flows to Africa

Reviews of Aid

Over the years there have been a number of major international reviews
of the aid process. In 1969 the Pearson Commission, headed by a
former prime minister of Canada, published its report *Partners in
Development*. The main concern of the report was that the total flow of
aid, which in the late 1950s had grown to about 1 per cent of GDP of
the Western countries, was falling. The Commission proposed the
international aid target of 0.7 per cent of an individual country's GDP,
which was later adopted by the United Nations. In fact, few countries
have reached this target, and certainly not the United States or the
United Kingdom. Much of the discussion of the report was rather
technical, concerned with aid methodology and procedures. There was
little questioning then of whether governments should be the main
engine for development, of whether government-to-government aid
was actually a good idea and still less of the basic legitimacy of the
African or other Third World governments, since many had only
recently come to power in pre-independence elections.

A decade later, in 1980, the Brandt Commission, headed by a former Chancellor of West Germany, produced its report *North–South: A Programme for Survival*. Brandt was concerned less about aid as such and more with international economic relations between rich and poor countries. The latter were particularly vocal at that time about the need for a new international economic order, in which the voice of the South, the poorer countries of the world, would be stronger. The report made much of the mutuality of interests between the North and South. Brandt himself, in the book's introduction, even mused on the possibility of some form of international taxation to pay for development.

> One might argue that it is hard to imagine international taxation without international government. But we believe that certain elements of what might be called international government are already called for to meet both mutual and national interests, and that by the end of this century the world will probably not be able to function without some practicable form of international taxation; and a decision-making process which goes a good deal beyond existing procedures (Brandt, 1980: 22).

In some ways, the Brandt Report was ahead of its time, and thus was largely ignored politically. Little has come of the new international economic order; market forces were as much the theme of the 1980s in international relations as in domestic policy. Mutuality of interests has only recently forced its way onto the international political agenda, with the awareness of global environmental issues – notably ozone depletion and global warming – with the more widespread availability of weapons of mass destruction – both nuclear and chemical – to small countries and petty dictators and with the threat of uncontrolled migration from South to North. Brandt's idea of paying for development through some form of international taxation is still some years away.

In the meantime, more prosaic worries about the effectiveness of aid continued. An intergovernmental task force commissioned a further study on the matter, which appeared in 1985 under the title *Does Aid Work?* (Cassen, 1985). This was a more down-to-earth and comprehensive view of aid methods and procedures than either of the two previous reports and drew on a number of more detailed evaluations of specific aid projects and programmes in many parts of the world. The answer given to the question in the report's title was: 'Yes, but ... ' The detailed, project-by-project studies showed that by and large aid did work, though it could certainly be made a great deal more effective.

This was a rather controversial conclusion. Most economists who had studied aid effectiveness at a macroeconomic level, for example by comparing the development performance of countries that had received much aid with those that had received little, came to a rather different conclusion from that of Cassen's project-by-project analysis. There was little or no macroeconomic evidence that aid was working. Countries that received a lot of aid did not seem to be growing faster than others, or to be notably more successful in alleviating poverty or overcoming the constraints on development. This was particularly true for Africa, where, as we have seen, development performance has been disappointing, but where aid flows have been proportionately higher than anywhere else.

This chapter aims to show some of the structural reasons why aid is not particularly effective in Africa and what should be done about it.

Mechanisms

Distribution by Country

Sub-Saharan Africa's share of total OECD aid has increased from a little over 20 per cent in the mid-1960s to around 30 per cent in 1990 (Pearson, 1969: 271). On the face of it, and assuming for the moment that aid does work, this is an encouraging trend for Africa. Development appears to be more intractable in Africa than in other poor regions of the world so it is appropriate that resources should be concentrated where the need seems greatest. However, the trend could well be reversed in the 1990s as the demands of the former Soviet Union and Eastern Europe move up the political agenda and as donor agencies and rich country taxpayers become more disillusioned with the lack of visible progress in Africa.

In absolute terms, aid to Africa reached US$ 17 billion in 1990, or the equivalent, on average, of about 11 per cent of the GDP of the countries concerned. On the whole, countries with small populations do better out of aid receipts than do large countries. This is illustrated in Figure 6.2, which plots aid receipts per head for different countries against the population of each country. (As in other diagrams, countries with a population of less than one million have been excluded.)

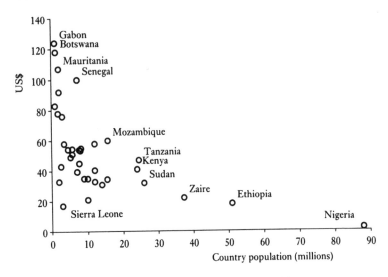

Figure 6.2 Aid per capita in sub-Saharan Africa, 1990

For the countries shown, aid per head in 1990 varied from over US$100 per head in some of the smaller countries (such as Mauritania, Gabon, Botswana) to only about US$3 per head in Nigeria, which had a population of nearly ninety million. However, this is still more than for large countries outside Africa. Per capita aid for India in 1990 was only US$2.

In matters of charity, of course, there is no rule that everyone should receive the same amount, but if aid is about helping poor people wherever they are, according to the principle of universality, then this uneven distribution of aid between countries is strong evidence that some people are not getting a fair share. For instance, the four most populous countries of sub-Saharan Africa – Nigeria, Ethiopia, Zaire and Sudan – together account for half of the population of the region but receive less than 20 per cent of its total aid. In three of these countries there have been special impediments to normal aid operations – civil war in the case of Ethiopia and Sudan and exceptionally corrupt government in the case of Zaire. Yet the very fact that people are in desperate circumstances ought to be a reason for greater humanitarian assistance rather than less. In short, these simple aid per capita statistics strongly suggest that aid needs to be redirected more towards where people are actually found – that is, the more populous countries. For the time being, we leave open the difficult, but inevitable, question of how people in situations of war or government breakdown are actually to be reached.

Project Aid

As discussed in Chapter 5, the prevailing view in the 1950s and 1960s was that capital investment was the major factor in economic growth and development. Certainly, this was what was most needed in post-war Europe. It was a cement-and-machinery approach to development. Consequently, aid was initially seen as being primarily a way of providing capital for investment. The normal procedure was that capital 'projects' would be identified and analysed and then financed by one or more of the donor agencies.

For similar historical reasons, aid was offered to governments, rather than to private enterprises. Governments, it seemed, had to take charge of the development of their countries. Economies would certainly not grow if simply left to market forces, or they would have already developed during or even before the colonial period.

However, one of the strange paradoxes of conventional project aid in Africa has been the growing difficulty in actually finding, designing and managing suitable projects in which to invest. The difficulty arose in part because of the self-imposed donor requirement to pass aid through the hands of the recipient government. The administrative capacities of most African governments were simply inadequate for the task involved. When roadworks squeeze motorway traffic down to a single lane, bottlenecks and queues develop; so it was with aid. Some agencies were better able to jump the queue and advance their own projects, but at the expense of further delaying those of others. An alternative would have been not to attempt to travel at all, but simply to wind down aid expenditures until the bottlenecks were removed. This option was not seriously considered until recently, as donor agencies have an interest in their own future. Moreover, as far as the World Bank was concerned, there was an increasing danger that, if new loans were to diminish, the repayment of past loans would be threatened.

Further, there was accumulating evidence that many capital projects were failing in their objectives. Some failed because they had been misconceived, either innocently or culpably by those who used aid for their private gain. Increasingly, project failure was also due to an economic policy environment in the recipient countries which frustrated normal enterprise with regulatory controls and poor administration. As we saw in the previous chapter, poor returns on investment were one of the causes of the African debt problem.

Programme Aid

In the 1980s, a new approach was born of this frustration. Project aid increasingly gave way to what is known as programme aid, which is essentially support for a country's balance of payments. Under programme aid, a grant or a very low-interest loan is made to the recipient government. The proceeds of the loan can then be used to buy imports needed by the economy. Sometimes the terms of the agreement specify what imports are eligible, and sometimes the choice is more or less left to the recipient. If the imported goods are required by the private sector – fertilizers for farmers or factory raw materials, perhaps – then the private individual or company concerned pays the government the appropriate price in local currency. These local payments are referred to as counterpart funds. They are, in effect, additional government revenue. Thus, even if the imports are for the private sector, the government itself receives the equivalent revenue in local currency. This is a most important point for further discussion below.

Programme aid is usually linked with specific agreements by the recipient government on economic policy reform, or structural adjustment. Apart from the IMF's short-term stabilization facilities, the lead on structural adjustment lending has always been taken by the World Bank, which then persuades other major donors to follow. As discussed in the previous chapter, the policy changes advocated have tended to be rather long-term in nature, only leading to results, if at all, after several years. The hope is that increased economic growth, as a result of the policy changes advocated, will eventually permit the borrowing country to repay the structural adjustment loans.

Technical Assistance

There are two further important types of aid – technical assistance and food aid. Technical assistance usually means sending skilled people from the donor country to work in the recipient country, with their salaries and expenses paid by the donor. Given the huge skill shortages at the time of independence, external technical assistance has always been important to independent Africa. Initially, much technical assistance consisted of teachers, both in secondary schools and for universities and similar colleges of further education. At the same time, foreigners continued to fill many of the African civil service posts even after independence. They have been gradually replaced by Africans, and expatriates are now more likely to work in advisory positions, as consultants, often for very short periods. This is expensive and may not be very cost-effective. Technical assistance to Africa still accounts for as much as 40 per cent of total aid flows, or about US$ 6 billion a year (UNDP, 1991). External skills are still needed in Africa, but many people doubt whether the present arrangements actually offer good value for money.

Food Aid

Food aid has also been highly controversial. Given that both the United States and the European Community produce more food than they consume and that most African countries produce less than they need, it seems only sensible for the former to give food to the latter. The problem is that dumping food on African markets may undercut African farmers themselves and ultimately undermine the incentive to increase domestic food production. The solution, which is increasingly adopted, is to require the donated food to be sold in the recipient country rather than simply given away. The proceeds from the sale are then kept by the African government concerned. This makes food aid rather like financial programme aid.

Nevertheless, there are still occasions when food should simply be given away. Emergency famine situations are an example, but even here the problem of longer-term incentives to food production needs to be considered. As noted in Chapter 1, famines are not usually caused by an absolute shortage of food. Instead, they result from problems of access to food and from loss of income (either at a national level or at an individual level), often as a result of war. Food to relieve famine is sometimes near at hand and does not always have to be imported from across the world. For example, food supplies have, in the past, been bought from Malawi and Zimbabwe in order to relieve famine in Mozambique. In this case, providing Mozambique with money to buy food from its neighbours was more appropriate than food aid itself.

It may also be appropriate to use food aid to provide primary

> *Pierre Pradervand quotes Demba Mansare, one of the founders of the Senegalese Committee to Fight for the End of Hunger:*
>
> It all depends on how [food] aid is used. If it aims at reinforcing the farmers' own efforts, it can act as a real leaven. But if it destroys the farmers' efforts to become self-sufficient in food production, it's harmful. Occasionally we receive food aid that is unadapted to habits of local consumption or that is even spoiled. Sometimes it even swamps the market, and all the prices take a dive. On the other hand, millet or rice enable us to build up pre-existing stocks. That's positive. But here again the grain must be of the kind that people are used to in the area (Pradervand, 1989: 53).

school children with a midday meal. Although primary education for all is vital for the future of the continent, sending a child to primary school involves real and immediate costs to poor families. The child is not available for other work – such as looking after goats, fetching water, or scaring birds from crops. Free school meals offer one way of offsetting some of those costs.

Criticisms

Aid is subject to a wide range of criticisms coming from different and indeed sometimes contradictory standpoints. Some will argue that Africa has received too much aid, which has been made too freely available. As a result, aid money has been wasted on financing projects and investments which are white elephants, yielding little or no return, or which are driven more by the desire to sell Western goods than by the economic interest of the recipient country concerned. It is not difficult to find examples in any developing country of such cathedrals in the desert, or mountains of unused or derelict equipment. Moreover, in so far as much aid is in the form of soft loans, if it is not well used it merely contributes to the African debt crisis. What is needed is to take more time and care in the preparation and implementation of projects and investments. The discussion in the previous chapter suggests that there is much truth in this argument.

Yet from the opposite perspective comes the undeniable macro-economic argument that African countries are poor, which means that

they are short of resources of all kinds, in need of physical infrastructure which aid can build and require a flow of imports which aid
can finance in order to develop and grow. Moreover, on occasions of
famine and human crisis, as Mozambique, Sudan and Somalia have
all suffered in recent years, the humanitarian assistance is almost
invariably too small. In the face of the poverty and suffering in Africa,
aid resources should be increased.

Another contradiction concerns the conditions which are attached
to aid. Thus, a complaint which comes particularly from within the
continent itself is that aid has too many conditions attached and is
thus a form of imperialism by which the West maintains its interests
and imposes its values on Africans. Others, especially those outside
the continent, argue that since many African governments have
become corrupt and unrepresentative it is perfectly proper for aid
administrators to impose conditions on aid to avoid it being misused
or improperly diverted. For these critics, donor agencies are insuf-
ficiently insistent concerning the manner in which aid is used.

The misuse of aid has been repeatedly substantiated in many books
and articles, and it is not intended to dwell on it here. Any human
enterprise is subject to failure, including human failure, and the
chances of failure in aid and development are at least as high as in an
any other human activity. Our purpose is rather to look for the more
systemic reasons why the whole approach appears to be having limited
success.

Aid and Governments

The type of criticism which is more germane to the present discussion
is that, notwithstanding any moral obligations we may have to help
others, aid is inherently unhelpful or even harmful. This is a more
serious charge since, unlike those above, it cannot be overcome merely
by learning from past mistakes, honing the procedures and doing
more careful project analysis. It is a view which is to be found on
both the right and the left of the political spectrum, though both are
concerned with the essential fact that aid is given to developing
country governments, rather than directly to poor people.

For those on the left, aid helps to maintain unrepresentative governments in power and by doing so either postpones the day of
revolution when they will be overthrown by an oppressed people or
perpetuates the colonial relationship in a new form. The Western

powers have certainly intervened frequently behind the scenes to ensure the continued survival of this or that African government. France has taken overt military action in support of particular African governments on a number of occasions. In the United States one of the most powerful, and least altruistic, political arguments for aid has been to keep the world safe from communism. This has led to some of the most scandalous abuses of aid, and the support of right-wing, dictatorial or military governments. There have been several examples of Western support continuing to be given to African governments long after their regime has passed the boundaries of human decency, including Bokassa in the Central African Republic and Mobutu in Zaire, to cite just two notorious examples.

At the extreme, these matters stray rather far from overseas aid in the commonsense way in which people understand it and move into the realm of power politics, which exists throughout the world, even where external aid is irrelevant. In such circumstances aid budgets and appropriations are simply being abused by Western powers to serve other political objectives.

On the right of the political spectrum, the economist Peter Bauer has been among the most influential and outspoken (Bauer, 1991: 38–55). In his view, excessive government interference in a developing economy, largely financed by external aid, inhibits the emergence of efficient markets and actually slows down the process of economic growth and development. The point is somewhat more economic and somewhat less political than the criticisms made from the left and is closely related to the case for economic adjustment made in the previous chapter.

The common feature of these views is that the state has come to be too economically or politically powerful *vis-à-vis* its own citizens. This conclusion is certainly consistent with the political analysis of Chapter 4. The important question is whether external aid has encouraged or promoted this excessive domination of the neo-patrimonial, undemocratic state. In economic terms, has aid permitted the continuity of an excessively large public sector, which has then become a dead weight on the rest of the economy and on society? The circumstantial evidence for this is rather powerful, at least as far as Africa is concerned.

To illustrate this, Figure 6.3 uses a concept which is referred to as net development finance (NDF), which is not the same as external aid, as usually defined. NDF includes all long-term loans to, or guaranteed

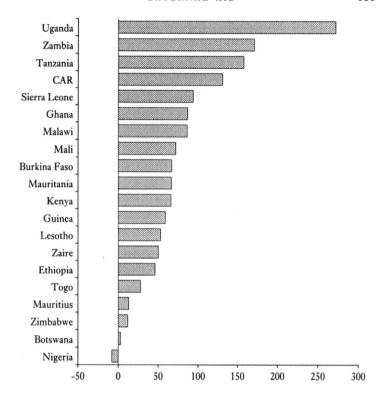

Figure 6.3 Net development finance as percentage of domestic revenue, 1990

by, an African government, even those on non-concessional terms, as well as financial gifts. It excludes technical assistance, since this is not received in the form of finance; indeed a high proportion of technical assistance expenditure actually occurs outside the recipient country.

It should perhaps be recalled that aid flows and those of NDF as defined here are received by governments not by private individuals. As we have seen, this applies even to programme aid intended to benefit the private sector, with the only difference that in this case the government's receipts are received indirectly in local currency in the form of counterpart funds.

The figure compares NDF with government domestic revenue from taxes, import duties and so on, showing the one as a proportion of the other. It demonstrates the extraordinary dependence of African governments on external finance. In 14 of the 20 countries for which suitable data were available, NDF was equivalent to 50 per cent or more of domestically raised revenue; in four countries it was over 100 per cent.

The point of this comparison between domestic and external finance is that a government's ability to raise taxation from its citizens is a real measure of its popular legitimacy. Taxation will be resisted where a government is not supported. The slogan 'No taxation without representation' has great political power. The rise of democracy in Britain revolved around the question of taxation, as did the American Declaration of Independence. In colonial Africa itself, as we have seen, taxation was one of the major sources of resentment of the colonial power. Thus, a comparison between domestic taxation and external finance demonstrates the extent to which governments have been able to sidestep this particular test of popular legitimacy. For a government to be highly dependent on external finance does not prove that it has lost popular support, but it certainly raises the question of whether or not it has – all the more so as most African governments had, until recently, also sidestepped the basic test of legitimacy: that of contested elections.

Without this external finance, it is doubtful, first, whether some of these governments could have survived politically and, second, whether the needed economic reforms could have been postponed for so long. Tanzania, for example, has long been urged by external donors to reduce the size of its inefficient parastatal sector, which represents a huge dead weight on the economy. Yet, at the same time these same donors continue to provide external development finance to the government on a scale which is 150 per cent of what it raises in domestic taxation. It is indeed paradoxical that external agencies have been providing such massive support to the public sector, while at the same time arguing for it to be slimmed down.

Finally, it will be noted from the figure that this problem tends to be less severe for the larger countries which generally receive smaller per capita allocations of aid. Thus, the flow of NDF to Nigeria in 1990 was actually negative since, in that year, Nigeria repaid more than it received.

An Alternative Approach

To summarize the argument so far: first, aid tends to be disproportionately allocated to smaller countries at the expense of larger ones; second, the channelling of aid through governments has created implementation bottlenecks, at least for project aid, which no doubt partly explains why projects so often fail; and third, most importantly, many African governments have become excessively dependent on external aid, which raises questions of whether external donor agencies are artificially maintaining in power governments which no longer have popular legitimacy.

Aid to the Private Sector?

One obvious alternative, which is being increasingly tried, is to use aid finance to support private business directly. This sector has the merit of being subject to the market discipline of success and failure, which the public sector is able to evade. Moreover, one of the major aims of economic adjustment is to revive the private productive sector.

There is some potential in this approach, though it creates a new set of problems. If money were to be thrown indiscriminately at the private sector, it would be encouraged to believe, as has the public sector in the past, that capital resources are abundant and almost costless. Moreover, there would be ethical problems. Who would decide which among potential entrepreneurs or businesses should receive such gifts of aid, which might well force competitors out of business? Finally, the private sector in Africa, long weakened in most countries by years of government regulation and political interference, is still small and not always very healthy.

In fact, there are some partial solutions to the problem. Rather than making grants and loans, donors can put up equity finance for the private sector – in other words finance which takes risks but also aims to secure rewards. Strictly speaking, if this were to be done in a commercial spirit, it would not be aid at all – except in so far as the

---

The Commonwealth Development Agency (CDC) is in many ways a model agency for supporting the private sector. It is financed by the British government on commercial terms and is required to act as a business and to make a profit. But its many operations bring development to the countries in which it invests. Further, the CDC is unusual in that it actively manages many of the projects it finances. Thus it has acquired real practical experience of what works in development terms.

willingness to take a long-term equity risk in Africa is not something that others are prepared to do. To succeed, aid agencies themselves, or at least those parts of them dealing with the private sector, would have to become very much more hard-headed and commercially minded than they are now. However, such mechanisms could not absorb the totality of funds which now flow through the public sector without again creating the same kind of systematic institutional distortions which now appear in the public sector.

There is a more fundamental objection to using aid finance in direct support of the private business sector. Aid flows are, in a real sense, a free good to the recipient economy. Even when aid is provided as a soft loan rather than as a grant, the real value of the loan which has to be repaid, perhaps over more than a 20-year period, is in economic terms very much less than the original amount lent. Consequently, aid is required to produce only a small financial return, or, in the case of grants, none at all. It is thus particularly suited to investments which have a long-term social or economic pay-off but little or no firm financial return. These are not characteristics of private business. In short, to give aid to business ventures is to waste some of its most valuable features.

Aid for People?

What types of investment or expenditure does aid suit? Some physical infrastructure investment, such as building roads, which has been a major focus for aid, would seem appropriate, though, unfortunately, many of these roads are now pot-holed and ruined. Other suitable investments might include environmental conservation or, as argued earlier, long-term agricultural research.

However, taxpayers in rich countries probably believe, or would like to believe, that the aid they provide helps poor people. Unfortunately, it is hard to produce evidence that official aid does so, though the record of the private aid agencies, the NGOs, may be better. As was stressed in Chapter 1, the poor are remote, isolated, powerless and difficult to reach. How could they be reached with aid funds? If we exclude the handing out of dollar bills – a more sensible strategy than it might at first appear, but unlikely to be politically appealing – probably the most effective strategy is to aim for basic human capital formation: universal primary education and community health care. As long as universality is aimed for, such programmes cannot be appropriated by the rich and powerful. Once people have some education it cannot be taken away from them. Moreover, human capital formation satisfies the criterion of having a high long-term social return but a highly uncertain private financial return. In other words, it is eminently suitable for the sort of finance that aid represents.

A major theme of this book is the overwhelming importance of the human dimension in development, though this is not necessarily the main argument for allocating aid to basic humanitarian goals. Rather, the specific characteristics of aid finance make it outstandingly suitable for investment in human capital formation. Other resources, domestic savings for example, can be used for investment in other sectors and for other purposes, including secondary and higher education and hospital-based health care. Further, it will be argued below that this strategy could also enable the link to be broken between external aid and its underpinning of government finances.

Aid and Social Expenditure

Previous chapters have shown that in the matter of human capital development much still remains to be achieved. The World Bank (IBRD, 1991) reports an infant mortality rate in sub-Saharan Africa of 107 per thousand, which although 50 per cent less than a generation earlier, is still 13 times higher than in OECD countries. With respect to primary education, the net primary school enrolment is only 47 per cent, which is probably an overestimate (see Figure 2.3). Only two or three sub-Saharan African countries have reached full primary school enrolment, and throughout the continent the quality of primary education is very poor. Figure 6.4 illustrates net primary school enrolment for a number of countries.

Could aid make a difference to the human objectives? The short answer is 'yes'; they are attainable and need not be expensive. The problem even now, at a time of adjustment and austerity, is more a matter of political will than of limited resources. This is a theme which the United Nations Development Programme has been pursuing in its annual *Human Development Reports*. The 1991 Report (UNDP, 1991) analysed and published for a number of countries, 25 worldwide, the proportion of national income which goes into basic social services of a priority kind, essentially primary education and basic health care; secondary and higher-level education and hospital medicine are excluded. This it calls the human priority expenditure

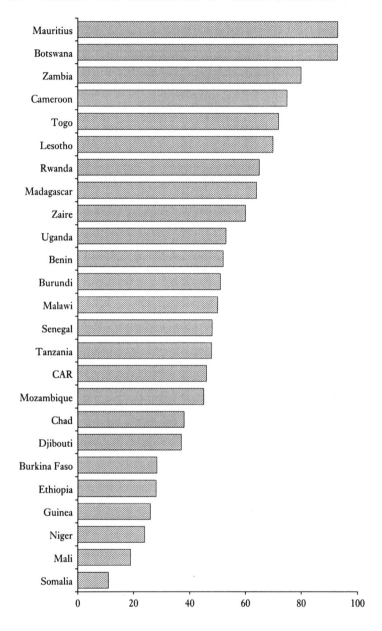

Figure 6.4 Net primary school enrolment in sub-Saharan Africa, 1989
(% of eligible age group enrolled in school)

ratio (HPER). Figure 6.5 shows this ratio as a percentage of GDP for the six African countries which were analysed, together with aid flows.

There are two conclusions to draw from the figure. The first concerns the HPER itself. In most developing countries, including those in Africa, expenditure on basic social services is remarkably low. For more than half the countries examined by the UNDP in its worldwide sample, the HPER was less than 3 per cent of GDP. For Africa, this is the case in the first four countries in the figure – Sierra Leone, Nigeria, Tanzania and Mauritius. Basic social expenditure is indeed frequently less than military expenditure; on average, in Africa military expenditure is equivalent to as much as 70 per cent of total public expenditure on health and education (UNDP, 1991). The precise figures may be contestable from one country to another, but the order of magnitude is not. The simple fact is that African governments have not given very high priority to basic human expenditure and, with the increasing economic difficulties on the continent over the last decade, it has often been the first to be cut back.

The case of the other two of the six countries – Zimbabwe and Botswana – is different. In these countries, basic social expenditures as a proportion of GDP are much higher, reflecting a greater priority attached to human capital development. Indeed, these two African countries, both incidentally multi-party democracies whose governments are maintained in power by a rural electorate, had a higher HPER than any of the other 23 countries in the worldwide sample.

The second conclusion concerns aid flows, where the picture is a little more complicated. Figure 6.5 shows that aid flows are greater than human priority expenditure (HPE) allocations for Sierra Leone and Tanzania. These represent the typical case of most African countries since aid on average now represents about 11 per cent of African GDP. In fact, the other four countries shown in the figure, for which aid is less than the HPE, are all somewhat atypical. Botswana and Zimbabwe, as noted above, have exceptionally high allocations of resources to human expenditure, while, for reasons of size and prosperity respectively, Nigeria and Mauritius have exceptionally low aid receipts.

It is perfectly clear that if we were to take the continent as a whole, external aid would be amply sufficient to provide every child in Africa with a primary education, which only half get now, and to provide simple health care for all babies and young children. Indeed, there would still be something left over for other things.

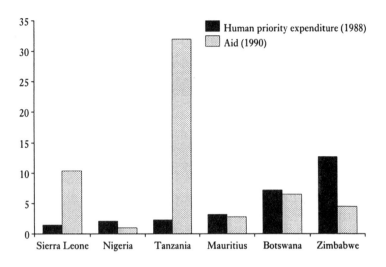

Figure 6.5 Human priority expenditure and aid as percentage of GDP

Such a reallocation of aid towards people and their needs would, of course, imply a major shift away from the present concentration on smaller countries towards the larger, such as Nigeria, since, as we have seen previously, the present distribution of aid does not correspond to where the majority of people live. It would also mean that mechanisms would have to be found to deliver aid, if at all possible, in countries where normal civil government had ceased to be effective – in Zaire, for example, which alone accounts for 8 per cent of Africa's population.

Using NGOs?

Some argue that the best way forward is through the non-governmental organizations, especially as they have a better reputation for reaching the poor – even though the very poor are almost unreachable by outsiders. If this is so, why have official aid at all? Even if we accept a moral obligation to help the poor, why is it assumed that this obligation is best exercised, in the case of overseas aid, through individual taxation and government-to-government assistance, rather than through private voluntary donations?

To answer this we need to go back to Figure 6.1. It was noted that the amount of money raised and administered by the charitable NGOs is only about a tenth of that of official aid. It would seem that, just as people in rich countries accept the principle of taxation for social security payments for the poor and disadvantaged within their own society, they are also prepared to discharge whatever obligation they feel towards the poor elsewhere in the world through taxation by their own governments. If this is the case, then to abandon official aid would be a backward step. It would lead to a reduction in resources available for Third World countries.

The problem of government-to-government aid does not therefore arise on the side of raising aid revenues, but rather on the side of its expenditure through African governments, for whom aid flows have become distortingly large, as we have seen. Should the large NGOs therefore be asked to administer the aid raised through taxation? This already happens to an increasing extent and is a welcome trend. Indeed, in recent years the NGOs have become much larger and more effective and, at the same time, more professional as development agencies.

However, the total volume of funds spent by NGOs, even including that part of official aid which they administer, still remains very small by comparison with those of the official aid agencies. If the NGOs were to be called on to handle resources ten times larger than at present, they could not do so without changing fundamentally the nature of their intervention. Many indeed would not want to do so, preferring the satisfaction of doing small things well rather than great things ineptly. The efforts of the big NGOs are worthy, may be influential in a catalytic sense and in demonstrating new approaches, and have been particularly effective in short-term humanitarian relief. Nevertheless, the finance they administer is simply too small to have an impact on recipient countries as a whole, notwithstanding some exceptions – for example, in the educational sphere, Oxfam plays a major role in Uganda, ACTIONAID does in the Gambia, and mission schools have always been important in Zaire.

In short, as presently structured, the international NGOs could not manage even a significant fraction of the US$ 17 billion of official aid going each year to sub-Saharan Africa. They certainly have a role to play, and may become increasingly professional, but they will not achieve the social and economic transformation that external official aid ought to be aiming for.

Using Civil Society

The choice of intermediaries to receive and administer aid finance, however, need not be limited to governments on the one hand or the large charities on the other. The net could be cast more widely. One of the most encouraging trends in Africa's current political and social transformation is the growing strength of civil society. By this is meant the social fabric of voluntary associations of people coming together for particular purposes. It would include churches and religious organizations, newspapers and publishers, farmers' groups, trade unions, professional associations and chambers of commerce, sports and interest clubs, women's groups, charities and cooperatives and, not least, tribal associations, political pressure groups and political parties.

If, as argued earlier, the aid agencies were to focus much of their expenditure on human capital formation, they could easily cooperate with this emerging African civil society. In essence, they would offer to finance anyone or any group in the recipient country who was prepared to work towards the objectives of human development. This could include local governments, tribal authorities, local NGOs, churches, and even private individuals wishing to work in their own communities. After all, running a primary school is not that difficult. The result would be pluralistic, perhaps disorganized sometimes, but that need not matter. There may be waste and corruption, but so there is now under the present approach of aid though big government projects. At least important progress could be made towards some of the fundamental development objectives which will determine how Africa fares in the next century, and the emerging civil society in Africa would itself be strengthened.

Most importantly, this finance would not be limited to capital expenditures. Building schools is not as much of a problem as finding the resources to staff and run them each year. Participating organizations would instead be offered a long-term commitment, say for ten years or more, subject, of course, to a certain amount of managerial and financial auditing. The UK and the USA both have a long tradition of public objectives being achieved through local private organizations. This tradition could now be applied to external aid.

Such an approach need not be threatening to African governments, since they themselves would not be excluded. They too would be eligible to come forward and seek financing for their own primary education programmes and basic health care. They would have the option of expanding their own human development programmes and seeking sustained recurrent external finance along with anyone else. If aid agencies agreed to underwrite on a regular basis, say for at least ten years, this part of government expenditure, then domestic revenues would be released for governments to devote to other purposes. The difference from the present situation would be that national governments would be required to address the issue of basic human capital formation, which at present they are scarcely doing. The continued flow of aid to governments would be conditional upon their maintaining such programmes in potential competition with private or community initiatives. If governments were unwilling or unable to cooperate in this, they could hardly complain if others did so.

The key features of this strategy are that it should aim to be universal and, for at least five reasons, should stick to basics. First, aid resources are substantial but not sufficient to do everything. Second, simple programmes could reach the poor. Third, basic human expenditures, although they will ultimately change society, are not politically threatening within the relatively short perspectives which most politicians have. Fourth, the aid agencies would not be making any particular prescriptions for the eventual transformation of African society, but would rather be giving people the tools with which to determine their own destiny in due time – albeit including a greater ability to resist political repression in the future. Fifth, by making the aim of the strategy relatively simple, Africa's emerging civil society would have a greater chance of being able to respond to the challenge. For example, although there may be a shortage of qualified primary school teachers in Africa, there are many people who could teach others to read and write.

Three Donor Impediments

However, the established procedures and mentality of the official donor agencies impose three bureaucratic impediments to this type of programme of basic human capital formation. The first is that internal donor procedures, as they have developed and with a few exceptions, do not allow aid to be used directly for financing recurrent government expenditures, such as teachers' and nurses' salaries, books and medicines, which are obviously the major costs of schools and clinics. This rule originates in the early theory of the purpose of development aid. It was thought that what developing countries needed was a quick fix of capital injection over a period of a few years, after which the developing economies would take off into self-sustaining growth. The last thing that the donors wanted was to be trapped into financing indefinitely the year-in year-out costs of anything. Unfortunately, even after a generation of increasing aid flows to Africa, with no economic take-off in sight, such thinking still applies.

There is a double irony here. In the past, donors actually did finance a major part of recurrent social service expenditure, though not in primary schools, through their supply of expatriate teachers and medical personnel. However, that commitment has now largely fallen away. Even more ironically, external aid is still financing a major part of African government expenditure of a recurrent nature, as Figure 6.3 illustrated in a graphic way, mainly through counterpart funds from programme aid, but the donor agencies exercise very little practical control over such expenditure. Indeed, because of their refusal to countenance direct long-term recurrent cost commitments, they have thrown away the opportunity to target most of their assistance at the poor.

A second donor impediment to aid effectiveness, with even less justification, is the practice of many, though not all, agencies of limiting their aid to financing foreign exchange expenditures. This rule goes back to pre-1980s thinking about development, when foreign exchange was something to be kept apart, husbanded and eventually allocated by the platonic guardians of the Central Bank. In the more modern, market-driven economies which Africa is now adopting, such thinking is not justified, since foreign exchange and domestic currency are being made freely convertible. Aid finance flowing into an economy is always an inflow of foreign exchange, but it matters not at all whether the particular item for which that aid is earmarked is produced domestically or is imported.

The third impediment is the belief that official aid should usually flow through governments. As noted above, this attitude is changing somewhat, but the presumption remains that, where African governments have ceased to be effective, aid should be cut back. In reality, these may be precisely the circumstances in which the needs of the poor are greatest. Of course, it will always be more difficult to reach out and assist in such situations, but the argument made is that, even where national civil government has broken down, there are always African people themselves who have an understanding of their own society and their long history of resilient small-scale social organization. These are the people, the civil society, with whom the aid agencies should try to work.

In conclusion, this proposed strategy would appeal to rich country taxpayers, who provide the aid in the first place and who can be forgiven for wondering whether aid in Africa has all become a waste of money and effort. Reasonable and achievable targets could be set – for example, primary schooling for every African child by the year 2000. Official aid would then be more firmly directed towards the humanitarian goals to which it is best suited. First, however, the official donor agencies have to overcome their own long-standing internal prejudices.

7 Conclusions and Outlook

What is to be done for the country? How can the Government
be carried on?
(Duke of Wellington, 18 May 1839)

The Second African Revolution is under way. In some places,
this will lead to new forms of democratic government, while in
others there will continue to be conflict and strife. Donor
agencies will need to distance themselves from those regimes
which have lost legitimacy and provide aid more through civil
society. Their assistance should concentrate on human development, giving people the means to shape their own lives and
future. Where there is conflict and anarchy the outside world
cannot simply walk away and may even have to use force to
restore order and back up its humanitarian assistance. With
development increasingly in the hands of millions of ordinary
people, rather than an over-powerful state, there should be
greater economic and social progress. Nevertheless, the state's
essential role of protecting and supporting its citizens will remain immensely important.

It is easy to be pessimistic about Africa. The small, simple but resilient
societies which made up pre-colonial Africa have been overlaid first
with colonialism and later, in the First African Revolution, with the
dominant bureaucratic institutions of modern society. This overlay,
presenting Africa to the world as a series of independent nation states,
is still little more than a veneer, which has not fully impregnated the
material beneath and which easily cracks open and peels off. Indeed,
in the hands of the leaders of independent Africa, much of this veneer
has been prised off. In economic terms, also, little appears to have
changed. With the single atypical exception of Mauritius, African
economies are still overwhelmingly dependent on the export of raw
unprocessed materials, usually from agrarian smallholder producers.

Even worse, they are now also overburdened with debt and have to support a population which is beginning to press in on the land and the sustainable capacity of the environment. The continent seems threatened by disease, famine and warfare as never before – though, in truth, such matters were never previously so widely reported.

The Second African Revolution

However, there are also abundant grounds for optimism. Beneath the surface something fundamental is changing. Under the veneer, the wood, the texture of African society, has considerably matured. A Second African Revolution has started. It is quite different from the first, in which a small minority of leaders, most of whom had been educated abroad, struggled for independence from colonial rule, rallying their people with them. The first priority of these leaders of independent Africa was that of nation-building, and they directed domestic policy towards this end, at least until they fell to the temptations of personal enrichment and empowerment unrestrained by any political accountability.

By contrast, the Second African Revolution is much more spontaneous. The swelling of popular dissent is like a distant wave out at sea, of little consequence until it breaks upon the shore. This time people do not have to be rallied by highly visible leaders. The new movements come from within the population. Their support is nationwide and drawn from different groups within national society, although there is an inevitable tendency for townspeople to take the lead. They are not necessarily or initially ethnically based.

Importantly, Africans are now more widely and better educated than ever before, more aware of the rest of the world. They know that they no longer have to suffer the dictatorship of petty tyrants and kleptocrats. In this, they are drawing inspiration from the international political and cultural environment and particularly from one of the most powerful ideas of the modern world, that of popular sovereignty, the belief that government legitimacy can ultimately only come from the people themselves. Thus, they are making the great leap to modernity.

This Second African Revolution is not primarily concerned with nation-building. That phase of African history is now over. No one is any longer sufficiently in charge to have an overall policy on nation-building, if indeed anyone ever was. Our prototype president, who mused in an earlier chapter on the importance of holding the new nation together, now has altogether different concerns, if he has not already been overthrown. He is fighting for his own political survival or trying to secure a few more million dollars in his Swiss bank account before his regime goes down. The future lies in the playing out of the different social forces – those that draw people towards modernism and popular rule in a democratic sense, on the one hand, and, on the other, ethnic forces for a smaller, more personal basis of organizing society, which has served Africa well in the past.

Tribalism and the Nation State

What will be the outcome of this interplay of the different forces between the small and the large scale and between tradition and change? Will the present African nations survive in their present form?

Different countries may well go different ways. The widespread view that tribalism in Africa would be bound to destroy open, democratic societies, if these came into existence, should not be too hastily accepted. There is simply not enough sustained evidence one way or the other. As we have seen, pre-colonial African society was not tribal in the sense in which that term is now popularly understood. It rather consisted of thousands of small, rather isolated mini-states, held together by common kinship under a priest-king, as a small ethnic group or clan, which perhaps included a number of slaves. Permanent loyalty to a larger group was rare, though stronger states may have succeeded in exacting tribute from weaker ones, as long as they remained stronger. Thus, where larger states were assembled they were held together as much by force and by tribute as by loyalty. They were empires rather than nations, and they did not usually survive for long.

The sense of tribe, of a larger social group going beyond clan or kin, came with a growing awareness of similarity of language and customs across neighbouring mini-states. It was certainly promoted by the colonial authorities, with their implicit models of European feudalism, which led them to look for hierarchical social and political structures through which indirect rule could be exercised. Tribalism in Africa, as distinct from kin loyalty, is thus quite recent, perhaps somewhat artificial and almost certainly much less deeply rooted than outsiders somewhat patronizingly imagine. The recent warfare and turmoil in the former Yugoslavia suggest that tribalism may still be at least as powerful in Europe as it is in Africa. Moreover, the European

Chinua Achebe, one of Africa's leading writers, describes what being Nigerian means to him:

Nigerian nationality was for me and my generation an acquired taste – like ballroom dancing. Not dancing *per se*, for that came naturally; but this titillating version of slow-slow-quick-quick-slow performed in close body contact with a female against an elusive beat. I found, however, that once I had overcome my initial awkwardness I could do it pretty well. Nationality is an expression of identity, one of the many clothes it can wear.

And later:

Nigeria needs help. Nigerians have their work cut out for them – to coax this unruly child along the path of useful creative development. We are the *parents* of Nigeria, not vice versa. A generation will come, if we do our work patiently and well – and given luck – a generation that will call Nigeria father or mother (Achebe, 1992).

tendency to nurture vengeance from one generation to the next contrasts with the African capacity for reconciliation.

Of course, in any part of the world ethnicity, or tribal loyalty, can be either played up or played down. It will certainly dominate where no other basis exists on which to organize society or where nation states for one reason or another fall apart. Thus, if parts of Africa do descend into anarchy, tribalism may be the only apparent cohesive factor, but the important point is that it will not inevitably override all other forms of political and social organization on the continent.

Taking the argument further, since in pre-colonial Africa there were never strong allegiances to large social groups, it may well be that the post-colonial nation states are now as viable a basis for building such allegiance in the future as is anything else. Nation states do not replace ethnicity, nor even compete with it, but they do add a new, larger social dimension. They represent a completely different scale of social organization for which there are few previous African parallels. Since they represent a new dimension the survival of these nation states is not assured, but neither is their disintegration into tribal components. Moreover, the nation state has one great advantage

as an organizing unit for society. It is externally recognized; it is part
of the international system. If an African moves outside his or her
own country, it is as a Nigerian, a Somalian, a Malawian or whatever
that he or she finds international identity.

This view modifies the frequent assertion that the colonial map-
makers created completely artificial nations that cut across existing
tribal boundaries. The creation of nations was certainly something
new, but it did not replace any pre-existing, large-scale, social organization. The tribes, supposedly divided by the map-maker's pen, were
actually much less cohesive than that and usually much smaller-scale
social and political organizations than is the nation state.

It is unsurprising therefore that, by and large, the independent
African nations have not actually disintegrated and have indeed been
rather cohesive over the last 30 years. This success is normally attributed to a mutual agreement between post-colonial African presidents
not to get involved in border disputes with each other, but such a
modus vivendi between politicians would never have survived had the
forces for disintegration been strong enough. It is more likely that
Africans have tolerated the nation state to which they had been
allocated by the colonial map-makers, first, because after all it did not
touch their lives a great deal, but, more importantly, because they had
no overwhelming reason to break away from it. Nationalism did not
compete with any other similar type of allegiance.

Of course, there have been exceptions – Eritrea has broken away
from Ethiopia, and Sudan probably should break up. There have also
been many civil wars – particularly, in Zaire, Nigeria, Sudan, Ethiopia,
Chad, Mozambique, Angola and Somalia. In the case of Somalia the
war is between clans, led by warlords, in a nation which is actually
ethnically homogenous; Somalia is not an example of tribal disintegration. Nevertheless, the dominant pattern in Africa has been of
nations actually holding together rather than breaking apart.

The Changing Role of the State

Thus, nations may survive in Africa but their importance will change.
Hitherto, the state in Africa has purported to be all-embracing, repres-
enting the national will in all respects. This was a carryover from the
pre-independence nationalist movements' claim to be the embodiment
of the peoples' will for self-determination. Such claims, although
convenient for those in power, have become increasingly hollow. The

real popular legitimacy of African governments has been extremely limited among people who, as we have seen, have never had any historical loyalty to a national group. The ruling groups' legitimizing rhetoric of developmentalism, used initially for nation-building, became increasingly a cover for the distribution of the spoils of office among their members.

As central government has grown steadily weaker in Africa, overwhelmed by its own popular illegitimacy and inefficiency, local politics and local power – not necessarily formally organized as local government – have been quietly growing in importance. This may be part of an international trend, not just an African phenomenon, but it may be as important a political development as is the move back to democratic constitutions. The challenge is to harness and direct this trend, rather than to permit regional and local tendencies, which are perfectly legitimate in themselves, to break up nations as a whole.

Moreover, a greater role for local authorities in delivering services, such as for education and health care, may be a better way of drawing on the organizational strengths of African society, which has always functioned best on a small scale. National delivery of such services may have appeared tidier and more efficient to the bureaucratic mind, including those of external official aid agencies, which have hitherto worked almost exclusively through the state. The reality, however, is that the national authorities in Africa have been singularly ineffective in bringing government down to a local level, with most of the available resources of people and money actually being captured by the centre and remaining in the capital city. The time has now come to devolve this responsibility to local groups or authorities, in a way which would build on the traditional local structures of African society rather than undermine them, as has been the case for most of the last 30 years.

At the other end of the scale, many of the functions of the nation state are also being eroded by supra-national groupings of nations. Within the European Community, for example, decisions previously taken at national level are now taken in Brussels. The same applies even where there are no formal groupings of nations. To give just one example, no country can maintain a convertible currency and expect to have full control over its domestic interest rates. Money will flow in or out of that currency according to how its interest rates compare with those of other currencies. On the other hand, if it does not maintain a convertible currency it will not attract foreign investment.

These same forces for international integration are at work within Africa. Indeed, many matters of national economic policy have been mortgaged to the international institutions of the IMF and the World Bank – which raises some awkward questions of accountability since the officials of these institutions are no more accountable than are unelected governments. Even if this were not the case, no sub-Saharan African economy, except perhaps Nigeria's, is large enough to modernize in isolation. The scale is simply too small. They have to be part of a larger regional economy which pools the resources and markets of a number of independent nations. The alternative is to continue with semi-subsistence economies, highly dependent on one or a few export crops.

The implication of both of these trends, towards more localism on the one side and regional groupings of nations on the other, is that Africa only needs minimal government at the national level. It would do little more than the nineteenth-century European state. Its essential functions would be to:

1. maintain the external defence and international relations of the nation, by a diplomatic presence and, if necessary, a small army;
2. maintain civil order, and with it an impartial system of justice, in order to restrain lawbreakers and to enforce contracts. Civil stability is especially important for economic development;
3. provide such social and physical infrastructure which, of its nature, can only be organized at a national level, such as ports, major roads and a system for tertiary-level education;
4. administer the currency and maintain its value over time and vis-à-vis other currencies;
5. raise the taxes necessary to carry out the above.

The first of these roles is immensely important. In many ways, a nation state is defined not so much by what happens internally but by the relations it has with other nation states – diplomatic relations, treaty obligations, membership of international organizations and so on. In this area of international representation, international standards of education, of professional competence and of remuneration have to apply, even though it can be a heavy financial burden for a small nation. Nations can dispense with armies for their military protection, as Costa Rica still does, but they cannot dispense with diplomacy.

Political Nature of Economic Adjustment

Now, as it happens, this political slimming of the state coincides with one of the main aims of economic adjustment, which is to reduce the role of national governments in order to allow markets to function more efficiently and, at the same time, to eliminate unmanageable budget deficits.

In practice, during the course of economic adjustment the state tends to abrogate some of its functions, not so much formally but rather allowing its overall effectiveness to be reduced. Ideally, most African civil services should be a third or a quarter of their present size, and should consist of a disciplined and well-paid workforce, with strictly limited policy objectives, of the sort outlined above. However, almost without exception, structural adjustment is leading to only a modest reduction in the size of government administrations, and to a demoralized and dreadfully underpaid civil service, as their salaries are allowed to erode with inflation.

In many African countries public-sector salaries are now ludicrously low, and certainly insufficient to maintain an urban lifestyle. Officials nevertheless stay in their posts because of other non-salary benefits which they may receive – for example, the right to live rent-free in a government house or, for the more senior among them, the possibility of foreign travel and expense accounts. They also combine their government jobs with other activities, or they profit from the possibilities of patronage and corruption which their public positions offer. The economic signals these servants of the state are now getting are that it is the traditional values, of looking after oneself and one's immediate kin, that are rewarded and not the more modern impartial values of public service.

This trend is potentially disastrous, threatening to undermine the nation state as much as is tribalism. African countries need a reduced role for central government, but what remains should be effective government, and the residual functions must be carried out impartially. The state must be seen to be supportive of ordinary people and as existing to serve them in their day-to-day lives. Otherwise, African people, from presidents to peasant farmers, will continue to view it as something either from which to extract whatever profit they can or which is hostile to their interests.

An observer surveying the present shambles of government machinery in Africa might consider such ideas of slimming down, professionalizing and properly remunerating African administrations to be excessively utopian and unlikely to be achieved, but there is undoubtedly a great deal of administrative capacity and talent in African civil services which is now locked up and frustrated by the political system. Many fine African government officials, highly professional men and women, have made the transition from the social values and local loyalties of traditional society to the more anonymous professional values required to run a modern state. Nonetheless, they have been penned in by political circumstances, under pressure from grasping politicians and now under-paid as well.

The difficulty is to see how to get from the present situation to the one being outlined. Since one of the main objectives of neo-patrimonial government is to control and distribute patronage, chopping off the arms of the present octopus state is proving to be the most problematic aspect of economic adjustment. Rolling back the frontiers of the state reduces the possibilities for political largesse and undermines the power of the ruling group. The implication is that structural adjustment in Africa, having been embarked on for economic reasons and largely on the advice and insistence of powerful outsiders, such as the World Bank, may now require the Second African Political Revolution to see it through to the end. It may require governments whose constituency is a rural electorate to complete the job.

The aid agencies, by virtue of the fact that they finance a major part of government expenditure in Africa, also have a role to play here. At present much of their programme assistance is simply absorbed into government budgets. They certainly have a great deal more potential leverage than they have yet exercised to direct how their resources should be used and to insist on administrative reform. They could, for example, ease the transition to a smaller, more professional, and less corrupt public administration, by financing some of the massive redundancy costs which would be required if the African public service and the military establishment were to be cut back as much as they need to be.

Democracy and Civil Society

The problem of how to get from here to there is not limited to that of an efficient and effective government. Democratic change itself will not come easily, and nobody, certainly not outsiders, can draw up blueprints for African society or government. Moreover, democracy amounts to a great deal more than just writing new constitutions, which can be simply torn up or ignored by those bent on personal power. Effective democratic government has to include not just an electoral routine but a protective structure, both of the individual and of society as a whole. It requires the recognition of human rights and those of minority groups, an independent, impartial judiciary, not easily subverted and, more widely, freedom of speech and of association and a free press. Such institutions do not appear of their own accord. Human rights protection, in particular, is not achieved merely by legislation or by the signing of international conventions. It has to be fought for in particular cases and circumstances.

Thus, democracy's bedrock is a society in which the rights of citizens are well established and defended. This will only happen over time and with some struggle. How can a modern democratic political structure and social organization emerge, in which people will come to have sufficient confidence to enable them to set aside or play down their pre-existing ethnic loyalties?

The key is civil society, which was defined earlier as the totality of all forms of voluntary social organizations, from football teams to political parties and from village savings clubs to chambers of commerce, and certainly not excluding tribal or ethnic groups. Such associations are not necessarily supportive of the state or of a particular regime – indeed, they may be strongly critical of government – but they provide a depth to society and to social organization which is necessary for the efficient and proper functioning of a liberal democracy.

Colonial Africa had few such groups, and many of those that did exist were later involved in, or co-opted into, the nationalist independent movement. Since the independent African regimes then considered themselves to be the embodiment of the aspirations of their peoples they saw no particular need to maintain civil society. The state was all in all – a convenient philosophy for those who had their hands on the instruments of power. Consequently, freedom of voluntary association was largely proscribed or circumscribed. State-sponsored trade unions became the norm, the press and television were turned into mouthpieces for government propaganda, universities were frequently closed, and students were sanctioned whenever academic freedom led to views which were in the least bit subversive of the state. In some cases, for example with the *authenticité* decrees in Zaire, attempts were even made to bring the churches under the control of the state.

What we have just described is in the past. In present-day Africa, beneath the brutal and unproductive instability of much of the continent, a deep social transformation is occurring. Abundant anecdotal evidence is now coming from the towns, the villages and the countryside of people taking their destiny in their own hands. Pradervand writes:

> Activities such as managing a village granary or marketing vegetables, running a village mill or store, setting up a tourist camp or selling bamboo furniture, administering a village self-help fund, or organizing a chicken farm or nutrition centre call for the mastery of complex organizational skills ... The learning process inherent in 'getting organized' represents in itself a profound transformation of ways of thinking. The passage from a situation in which behavioral patterns have been traditionally mapped out to a situation in which innovation and bold creativity are the order of the day represents a gigantic conceptual leap that our African partners are making in less than two decades ... Today a silent revolution is under way. A dynamic and irreversible process that nothing will stop is in motion. The situation ... is more positive than any of the statistics would lead one to believe (Pradervand, 1989: 123).

The strength of such initiatives lies in their smallness, enabling them to draw on the great resilience of African society at this level. However, being small and remote, they are scarcely documented, nor do their results register yet in economic and social statistics.

The future for African civil society is by no means bleak, for three reasons. First, the greatly increased numbers of people with some education compared with a generation ago, even if still inadequate for the need, will steadily transform the structure of society. Education is the necessary germ for the political maturing of Africa, quite as much as for its economic development. Second, the towns, in which a third of Africans now live, are the cooking pots for civil society. Here, people are bound to rub shoulders with others of different ethnic backgrounds and, little by little, to build up social groups and structures which are based on factors other than ethnicity and kin. Third, no African government will find it as easy to be as dominating and authoritarian as over the past generation. This will be true even in countries which do not immediately become representative democracies; the democratic genie is out and about, and it will not be contained or repressed. Even in the past, few African governments – Nguema Macias's maniacal regime in Equatorial Guinea being one of the exceptions – have ever reached the heights of totalitarianism that were widespread in Eastern

Europe, with efficient networks of frightened informers reporting on neighbours and family. The African sense of kin loyalty would make that difficult, if not impossible. From now on civil association will be hard to suppress.

Limitations of Democratic Change

The impact of these changes on African society will be slow but sure, as a growing self-confidence and assuredness steadily permeates the continent. In the meantime, however, expectations for democracy may be running too high for several reasons. First, democracy will not guarantee egalitarianism, nor economic development, as it does not necessarily prevent the exploitation of minorities by a majority group. Further, most democratic governments, as other forms of government, are effectively captured by the rich and economically powerful, as the United States amply demonstrates. It is well to remember Winston Churchill's remark that: 'democracy is the worst form of Government except all those other forms that have been tried from time to time.'

Second, the African democracies which may eventually emerge will not necessarily replicate the adversarial Westminster model, which was criticized with some justification by early African leaders as being unsuited to the African consensual tradition. The French democratic tradition, with a directly elected authoritarian presidency, which exercises wide constitutional powers, and a relatively weak national assembly, may be more appropriate. In the end, Africa will have to find its own constitutional solutions. The pyramid of consensus from the village level up, which some observers believe is emerging in Uganda, may be a pointer to the future.

Third, democracy cannot create a nation state in the first place. If a particular society does not have a sense that it constitutes or is part of a nation, then a democratic constitution will not fill the gap. Nations are built on some sense of community and shared values. If one region or ethnic group is inclined to break away, then it may be persuaded or convinced not to push separatism to the limits, but the question cannot be resolved democratically. Poll society as a whole and you may get one answer; poll the separatist region and you get another. Which is the right democratic choice? The sense of nationality is altogether more subtle and cannot simply be voted into existence.

So, as the Second African Revolution continues, the limits and drawbacks of democratic change will emerge. In some countries, a sufficiently strong sense of nationhood may still be lacking. Even where it exists, there is no guarantee of an easy transition to popularly elected government and political stability. Some popular disillusionment will certainly set in, and there will be many, including some in external aid agencies, who will regret the passing of the former regimes and their apparent stability.

At that stage, perhaps by the late 1990s, it will be especially important not to draw the conclusion, as many outsiders are too prone to do, that democracy cannot take root in Africa, as it is bound to founder on ethnic or tribal division. Such an attitude is patronizing, implying that the system of government which Westerners believe best for themselves, whatever its practical difficulties, is too sophisticated for Africans. The basic right of people to change their rulers from time to time under a recognized constitutional procedure is fundamental, an essential part of the values of the modern world. We should not deny that right of citizenship to Africans, or deny their ability to exercise it.

The Outlook for South Africa

What does this analysis tell us of the prospects for South Africa, which is also moving towards a democratic system, though from a very different starting point than the rest of sub-Saharan Africa? First, the process of modernization has already gone a great deal further in South Africa than in other parts of the continent. The Boers first landed in South Africa almost three and a half centuries ago, and, although they themselves were a deeply conservative, pre-modern society, they were followed by other waves of more sophisticated settlers. Indeed, the modernization of South Africa could be said to have started with the diamond rush in the 1870s and the later gold rush, which for the first time brought Western industrial culture to South Africa.

Of course, the native Africans were allowed only a marginal stake in this industrialization as providers of relatively unskilled labour, but it must certainly have had an impact on their own culture and view of the world. The system of migrant labour to the mines and towns, socially objectionable though it was, exposed millions of South Africans, and Africans from neighbouring countries as well, to the modern industrial ethic. Meanwhile, throughout the present century, many black South Africans were acquiring an education, notwithstanding apartheid and the much more limited educational and employment opportunities that were open to them, relative to whites.

Moreover, within the white community some degree of opposition politics, of an independent press and an almost independent judiciary was maintained, even through the most repressive periods of apartheid. Overall, civil society is alive and flourishing in all groups of South African society.

These are all reasons why it might be expected that democracy will take root more easily within South Africa than in other parts of Africa. Of course, there has been a stirring up of ethnic loyalties, particularly by Chief Buthelezi and the Inkatha Freedom Party on the one side and the far-right white Conservative Party on the other. This has led to violence and bloodshed, which have actually grown worse as the prospect of a settlement has come nearer. It is likely that the present unrest represents, apart from just criminality, a jostling for political power over the transitional period, rather than any real threat that South Africa will descend into civil war between ethnic groups.

A second reason for hope is that the two parties which represent the middle ground in South Africa, and between them the over-whelming majority of the people – the African National Congress (ANC) on the one hand and the white National Party (NP) on the other – have, since they started negotiating, shown a determination to reach agreement at all cost. As Allister Sparks describes in his book *The Mind of South Africa*, the history of South Africa is essentially about different nations trying to maintain their separate traditions while occupying the same territory. At last, in the present negotiations the African *National* Congress and the *National* Party are seeking ways in which these different national traditions can be brought together in some democratic harmony.

For both parties the alternative of not reaching an agreement is too horrible to contemplate; those would be the circumstances in which the country might descend into civil war. So while both the ANC and the NP have had from time to time to rally their support at the edges – disaffected township dwellers on the one hand and conservative Afrikaners on the other – by provocative rhetoric, and, although there have been many incidents which could have been used as an excuse to halt the process, such as the June 1992 Boipatong massacre, they have grimly carried on negotiating. So by late 1993, agreement had been reached to hold a nationwide election in April 1994. This historic process of reconciliation will almost certainly be helped by the great African tradition of forgiveness, which is being witnessed again in South Africa as it has been at other times and places on the continent.

However, if the political outlook is encouraging, the economic one is much less so. Average per capita income in South Africa, at about US$ 2,500 (in 1990), is higher than in any other African country except Gabon, and national GDP is more than that of the rest of sub-Saharan Africa put together. Thus, sophisticated South Africans like to think that their economy is more similar to that of Latin American countries than to those of the rest of Africa. As far as having a highly skewed income distribution is concerned, this is certainly the case. The income disparities between the 5 million wealthy whites and the 29 million blacks, many of whom have been dumped in the so-called homelands, is as great as anywhere else in the world. It is estimated that the average income level for the whites is ten times higher than for blacks, for whom living standards are comparable with some African countries, such as neighbouring Zimbabwe, but much lower than others, such as Botswana (Lachmand and Bercuson, 1992: 7). Infant mortality and life expectancy, two key indicators of the quality of life, are worse for black South Africans than in either of these two neighbouring countries.

As soon as there is a political settlement, this imbalance has to begin to be redressed. As with the rest of Africa, there needs to be a massive redirection of resources away from the urban middle classes towards the basic educational and health requirements of the poor. Unfortunately, as with the rest of Africa, the economy is built on the export of raw materials and is not as strong as it used to be, as prices and international demand for its products have fallen. Also, as in the rest of Africa, since the early 1980s the economy has been growing at less than 2 per cent a year, lower than the rate of growth of population. The gold mining sector, in particular, once the mainstay of the economy, faces serious competition from new, cheaper sources of gold in other parts of the world. The industrial sector is more advanced than anywhere else on the continent, but, as with other African industry, it has been built behind protective tariff barriers and is largely uncompetitive with the rest of the world. South Africa will become a major supplier of industrial goods to the rest of Africa, as it already is for other countries in the southern African region. However, the total African market is not large enough for this to be sufficient.

Finally, the South African economy has been hampered in recent years by international sanctions, which have limited foreign investment and loans. With a political settlement the loans will return, as will foreign aid. Nevertheless, the experience of the rest of the continent should warn against expecting too much from aid. Also, private foreign investment will remain cautious until political stability is assured and until there is a track record of continuity in economic policy.

Stability may indeed be the greatest challenge for a new South African government. A whole generation of young black South Africans has grown up alienated from society and with little prospect of productive employment. Somehow, this underclass will have to be drawn back into the mainstream of society and given some hope and expectations, if it is not to turn to banditry – perhaps egged on by the politically disaffected. Yet fulfilling these expectations will be difficult: there will be very little time and, as yet, very few resources.

Zimbabwe, where the civil war was proportionately much bloodier than it has been in South Africa, offers a hopeful model. However, Zimbabwe remains a much more rural economy than South Africa. It is still possible for many Zimbabweans to live out their lives in a time-honoured African way, relatively apart from the modern world. In a thoroughly urbanized and industrial society, such as South Africa now is, that option is not really open.

The Anarchic Alternative

So far, we have concentrated on the hopeful signs for Africa. Yet, in some places another scenario is unfolding, one of complete social and political breakdown, normally accompanied by civil war and famine. One thinks, for example, of Somalia's suffering after the fall of the Barre regime in 1991. Many other countries are similarly disintegrating – Liberia, Sierra Leone, Angola, southern Sudan, Zaire, to name just the obvious cases. Altogether, perhaps a third of Africans live where effective government no longer exists at all, or where the regime has become so exploitive of its country and people as to have passed the norms for civilized behaviour. Alternatively, they are prey to the uncontrolled rampages of wandering bands of soldiers or bandits. Usually they have little or no access to the outside world or to health, education and other services.

Until quite recently the international community was little involved in such situations of governmental breakdown. Aid agencies tended to withdraw altogether, to be pushed out, or at best to intervene merely as the need arose, with emergency and humanitarian assistance. Although there may have been a crying need for humanitarian assistance, action was restrained by the doctrine of non-interference in the affairs of a sovereign state. However, with the ending of the Cold War and the precedent of the Gulf War, international law, or certainly practice, in these matters has changed rather radically. Indeed, before he retired, the former UN Secretary-General, Javier Pérez de Cuéllar, called for a reinterpretation of the UN Charter and the principles of sovereignty and non-interference to allow for humanitarian intervention in countries under certain circumstances (Weiss and Chopra, 1992). The use of military force under a UN umbrella to create safe havens in Kurdistan in 1991, at the end of the Gulf War, was a watershed. In some respects, this relief operation was clumsily carried out – for example many people were killed by food being dropped on them from the air – but the combination of relief and military protection became a model to be applied in other situations.

Since then, the number of occasions when international intervention has been required to make peace and help restore civil order has multiplied. So far, success has been very limited. The international community failed to act early enough in the former Yugoslavia, mostly because of differences of opinion among member states of the European Community. The UN did supervise an election in Angola but failed to stop the civil war. In Somalia, the initial success of the operation in distributing humanitarian assistance soon turned sour as it became clear that neither the United States nor the United Nations had any long-term strategy for restoring civil government.

Nonetheless, there have been some successes. In Cambodia, under circumstances at least as difficult as those found on the African continent, the UN set up a transitional government with a full administrative bureaucracy and successfully organized an election. There is also some hope that the mistakes made in Angola, principally that of not going in with a sufficiently strong UN force to disarm the opposing armies, will not be repeated in Mozambique. In all of these operations, the world is sailing into hitherto uncharted waters, and it is inevitable that some early expeditions will founder. As time goes on, however, coordinated international intervention of this kind, with a view either to restoring a measure of social order or to providing humanitarian assistance, will come to be seen as quite normal, and with each successive peace-keeping operation the UN's role should expand and its effectiveness increase.

One problem with this new international phenomenon is that the United States, and to a much lesser extent the European Community countries, have played the prominent role, even though they have been operating through the United Nations Security Council. It seems likely that NATO will also become involved in some cases. Smaller, weaker nations may well suspect a resurgence of neo-colonialism and fear that the UN has been captured by the stronger nations. But they should also be encouraged that the major powers are acting internationally rather than unilaterally, as would have been the case not very long ago. By doing so, they are implicitly accepting some restraints on their actions. In due course, the checks and balances on this type of intervention must become more effective. For example, the role of the International Court of Justice in the Hague, which should serve as an agency of restraint on the UN Security Council, could be strengthened.

In the meantime, the charge of neo-colonialism, although less often heard, is frequently made most loudly by those governments whose own legitimacy is questionable. Villagers harassed by marauding bands of soldiers or looters, as initially in Somalia, do not resist the arrival of a protecting force or of humanitarian relief on the grounds of neo-colonial interference. Rather, they welcome the restoration of some degree of stability in society even if it is imposed by an external power.

Yet the risk of outside intervention and interference in Africa, far less benign than that of the United States or France, persists. There are numerous private individuals, crooks and fanatics for the most part but often bankrolled with drugs money, waiting to move into power vacuums, where they can then hide behind the notion of national sovereignty or some local puppet government. This is not fantasy, but has already happened in a number of small countries around the world.

Thus, a more serious concern may not be that of neo-colonialism by the major powers but rather the opposite – whether or not they will continue to be interested in the internal affairs of disintegrating African countries. After the end of the Cold War, there are no more proxy battles to be fought on African soil. With the possible exception of cobalt supplies from Zaire, Western countries now have little economic interest in sub-Saharan Africa – though the case of South Africa may be somewhat different. The sad truth is that Africa is still marginal to the world economy, perhaps even more so now than ever,

The vulnerability of African states in times of internal conflict or uncertainty is illustrated by the recent history of the Comoros Islands, a former French colony in the Indian Ocean. In 1975, Ahmed Abdallah, President of the Council of Government, declared the islands independent. Abdallah was later overthrown but restored to power, or at least to puppetdom, in 1978 when a small band of mercenaries, led by Bob Denard, invaded and occupied the islands. For more than a decade, the mercenary-controlled government terrorized and tortured the islanders. In 1989, Denard assassinated Abdallah. At that stage, France intervened to remove Denard from the country.

though humanitarian considerations may continue to be a driving force, as in Somalia.

Nevertheless, although its capacity for intervention is increasing rapidly, the UN remains seriously underfunded and still has no military resources of its own on which to draw. Without the interest of one or other of the major powers, it is unlikely that the UN will be able to intervene in African conflicts on its own.

It therefore behoves the African states themselves to strengthen their own regional institutions and mechanisms for conflict resolution within Africa itself. In August 1990, a number of West African countries, led by Nigeria, jointly sent a military force to attempt to end the fighting and restore order in Liberia, though two years later it had still not managed to do so. A 50-man African military observer group from Senegal, Nigeria and Zimbabwe was established to monitor the ceasefire in the Rwandan civil war (it failed, as we now know).

These are welcome precedents, but some accountable agency for conflict resolution in Africa is still essential. Within Africa, Nigeria is increasingly seen by its neighbours as a local superpower, useful perhaps for peace-keeping operations but also to be feared. The harsh truth is that a group of suffering people may actually prefer the arrival of the French Foreign Legion to that of a Nigerian or other African force, unless the latter's actions are clearly accountable and professional. In this context, some observers have commented on the professionalism of the small contingent from the Botswana Defence Force among the UN troops in Somalia.

A reformed Organization for African Unity (OAU) might provide the answer. The OAU has allowed itself to be turned into a dictators' club and, for the moment, shows little sign of wanting to change. Nonetheless, if it did so, it could become the best and most appropriate agency for conflict resolution in the continent, as well as a force for the implementation of its own 1981 Charter on Human and People's Rights. Reform of the OAU is an important item on the agenda for any democratic states which do emerge on the continent in the coming years.

So far, thinking these situations through has not gone very far. Sending in the Marines or an OAU force wherever normal government has completely broken down, as in Liberia or Somalia, is only the first easy step. Setting in place a new civilian administration, sufficiently strong for the military men to withdraw, will always be a great deal more difficult. In some cases the territory may have to be administered by outsiders for a long time before an adequately representative national government can be formed. The magnitude and difficulty of these tasks should not be underestimated, as the Nigerian-led force found in Liberia or the UN discovered in Somalia.

However, the consequences of not acting may eventually prove more costly, especially to neighbouring African countries as refugees and armed bandits begin to pour over their own permeable borders, but also to the rest of the world. In a world which is threatened with global environmental, health and security problems (drugs, tropical forest destruction, AIDS, economic migration and so on), where news of human and environmental disasters is almost instantaneous and where ex-Soviet plutonium is already becoming available in the nether world of arms dealing, total withdrawal of the international community is no longer a politically viable option. In the modern globally interdependent world, no country can be allowed just to descend towards anarchy.

In due course, the notion of international trusteeship will have to be revived and fleshed out, following the precedent created by the League of Nations after the end of the First World War for the former German colonies – Cameroon, Togo, South West Africa and Tanganyika. The difference today is that the mandated authority would not be one of the colonial powers, but could be a regional organization, such as a reformed OAU, which would then assemble a purely African administration to carry out its mandate. It is not inconceivable that, as the map of Africa at the end of the nineteenth century was largely coloured red, showing British colonial rule, at the end of the twentieth century large swathes will be coloured in United Nations blue, indicating a revived UN trusteeship. Liberia, Somalia, southern Sudan, Angola and Zaire seem likely candidates.

The question will arise as to how such operations should be financed, since the UN is already overstretched. There is no reason, however, why supporting conflict resolution, and if necessary the establishment of UN or OAU trustee territories, should not be a legitimate charge on existing development aid budgets. There is certainly no development where there is conflict.

The Role for Aid

Political Conditionality

Between the few countries moving effortlessly towards democracy and those reverting to anarchy lies the rest of the continent – struggling to build modern economies and effective social institutions, sometimes moving forwards and sometimes being set back. There will be much political unrest. Indeed, history may come to record the first 30 years of independent Africa as a period of exceptional political stability, notwithstanding the wave of popular discontent swelling up under the surface.

This superficial stability permitted aid agencies to believe, comfortably, that many African governments were legitimate, in the sense of having popular support, long after African people knew that they were not. Since almost all aid has been given to African governments, as distinct from African people, it has been highly supportive of a whole variety of African regimes to which aid agencies have become far too close. Aid officials have been too easily flattered by proximity to African presidents and ministers. It is difficult to avoid the conclusion that aid has sustained some African governments in power too long. In the future the question of government legitimacy promises to be a minefield for external agencies, which will need to be far more circumspect over which governments they deal with and how.

One consequence is that the agencies are already and increasingly using aid as an overt instrument for political change in Africa, making aid allocations dependent on whether certain political conditions are satisfied. One of the most prominent examples was the decision, in late 1991, to postpone granting further programme aid to Kenya until there was some evidence of democratic change. In 1993, Malawi succumbed to similar pressure. Outside the continent, Haiti was another contemporaneous example. The trend, however, is much wider than that. Behind these overt examples is a great deal of behind-the-scenes pressure on a number of countries in the same direction.

Inevitably, the question arises of the justification for using aid to encourage political change in the recipient country according to an agenda set entirely by the donors. African politicians may claim that such political conditionality is a form of neo-colonial interference, but if they themselves have not come to power in a democratic, representative process, they have no greater moral claim to make such judgements than has anyone else.

In the meantime, the aid agencies cannot avoid the issue. They have a fiduciary duty to use the taxpayers' funds responsibly. In Africa, they are already deeply politically engaged by the simple fact, as we have seen, that external aid provides a high proportion of government revenue. The aid relationship, unlike normal diplomatic relations, which are neutral, actually implies a high degree of political commitment and judgement. In some countries it is as much a political act to continue aid programmes as it would be to stop them.

Nevertheless, using aid to promote political change is not as easy as it may seem. Donor agencies tend, conveniently, to believe that aid is a much more finely tuned instrument for facilitating economic and political advance than it really is. The numerous detailed conditions attached to the World Bank's structural adjustment loans bear witness to this. In practice, many of these conditions have not been satisfied, particularly those which are administratively complex or which go against the political or economic interests of well-organized groups (Mosley et al., 1991). Yet, even where economic policy conditionality has clearly failed, the aid agencies have been extraordinarily slow to walk away from supporting the regime concerned, though that is now happening more frequently, as in the case of Sudan and Zaire.

In other words, aid has proved a rather blunt instrument for encouraging economic change and is at least as likely to be so for promoting political reform. While there may be scope for gradualism and policy debate in matters of economics, in many areas of political reform that simply cannot be. An aid agency cannot sit down with an African government and draw up a formally agreed programme under which, say, torture would stop in six months' time or political prisoners would be released by the end of the year.

As the instrument is blunt it might as well be used directly and straightforwardly. Overt political conditionality may well be more realistic than supposedly fine-tuned diplomatic pressure behind the scenes, which no one sees, and certainly not those who are oppressed by a particular regime. Clear signals are required, such as insisting that a contested election is held, to prevent aid funds from being diverted elsewhere. In all of this, one important touchstone should be the willingness of the recipient government to cut back on excessive military expenditure.

If this does not work, donor agencies do, as we have argued, have the choice of not working through governments at all. Even if one believes that Western aid to Africa is a moral obligation which cannot simply and capriciously be avoided, that obligation does not necessarily have to be discharged through the regime in the country concerned, which may be pursuing quite different objectives, such as building up military strength or extracting a private rent from the country and its resources. Indeed, in such circumstances the moral obligation to help people may be even greater.

In the end, aid, as an instrument for change, can do no more than support a social undercurrent which is moving in a particular direction. The real impetus will always have to come from local people themselves and from their own society. Donor agencies can choose either to give aid to African governments or not to do so, but they cannot substitute for them. They can facilitate change but they cannot direct it.

The Development Impact

This applies just as much in the economic sphere. Although external aid to Africa has been substantial, it has certainly not achieved the economic and social transformation that was expected of it. Much effort and finance has been dispersed into nugatory capital investment and expensive technical assistance, with very little real return. Further, the aid donors, having been reluctant to make longer-term recurrent expenditure commitments, have consequently thrown away the opportunity to target their assistance on basic services, such as those of education and health, which would have had a direct impact on poverty. In many ways, the official aid agencies have really lost their way. They continue to use the old formulae and procedures, as in the past, but with less and less conviction. Get any aid official over a beer in the 1990s, and he will soon be questioning the effectiveness of what he is doing in Africa.

Much of the problem, in terms of development as well as of politics, arises from the channelling of aid through governments, but, for different reasons, neither the private business sector nor the NGO sector offers adequate alternative channels for aid funds. To give aid to the business sector on a substantial scale would be to undermine the very market disciplines that are essential to a healthy private sector. Moreover, aid resources are more fittingly deployed where the returns are essentially social and economic rather than financial, which excludes much business activity. As far as NGOs are concerned, they are still just too small to manage the magnitude of funds which the official aid agencies provide, though some aid resources could be, and indeed are being, used to build up local African NGOs as well as other institutions of civil society on the continent.

Is the answer perhaps that external aid is no longer really required or that it is no longer useful? Given the tide of economic and political reform now washing over the continent, perhaps African economies will get stronger, will be able to slough off their external debt and will grow without the need of external assistance. However, although the economic outlook is better, there will be no rapid economic transformation or dramatic reduction of poverty. Even if the whole continent were to grow at a remarkable rate of 5 per cent a year between now and the end of the century, real per capita incomes would, because of population growth, only be a little over 10 per cent higher at the end of the millennium than they are now.

Thus, if the original motivation for aid – assisting those in poverty – still holds, then on humanitarian grounds the need for external assistance will continue for a long time – indeed indefinitely. Aid agencies' present procedures, however, are the product of a belief, now a generation old, that the need for external aid was strictly temporary and would fall away. They must now revise their ways of operating and redirect their effort towards people and the reduction of their poverty – which has scarcely been the case up until now.

Making a Long-Term Commitment

The previous chapter argued that the best chance of facilitating (but not directing) long-term social and economic change was for aid to finance, over a whole generation, a major part of social expenditure in Africa – that of basic human capital formation. Such a reorientation of aid should take place with or without the cooperation of the African governments or local authorities concerned. The general principle would be that long-term financial commitments for primary education and health care would be offered to civil society as a whole, alongside African governments. There would be few requirements laid down in advance. The woman with a little education herself who wanted to pass this on to the children of her village, under a tree if necessary, would be as eligible as the primary school programme of a whole district. The innovator who wanted to try modern distance-teaching methods could also be considered. All would be subject to inspections and audit, which were appropriate to the particular circumstances, for funding to be renewed from one year to the next. Although the supervisory effort would be considerable, much of it could be carried out by local staff employed by the agency concerned.

Such a commitment is readily affordable under present aid budgets, as long as it remains limited to basic education and health. The services have to be basic since, if resources were to be diverted, say, into secondary education or city hospitals, they would cease to have much chance of reaching the poor. Higher education and more advanced health care, together with infrastructure spending and so on, are necessary also but should be financed in a different way – from taxation or by the private sector. Indeed, to the extent that African government expenditure would be reduced as a result of aid financing of basic services, other government revenue would certainly be released for other purposes.

However, the geographical distribution of aid would be very much changed. A country such as Tanzania, which now receives aid equivalent to about a third of its GDP, enabling it to continue supporting a vast panoply of uneconomic public enterprises, would receive very much less, while Nigeria and other large countries, but not necessarily their governments, would take rather more.

Such a change of strategy would have a major impact on the Western taxpayers who provide the finance and who are increasingly questioning what is being achieved with their money. Much present aid expenditure is frankly indefensible, the product of an aid establishment which has run out of fresh ideas, but cynically goes through the old routines and is unprepared to rethink its operations or address its government clients with some hard truths. A new vision is required to revitalize the effort so that, after another generation has passed, the donors and their supporting taxpayers will then be able to look back and say: 'Something has been achieved.' This cannot be said of the last generation of aid to Africa.

Direct Transfers?

The vision of the Brandt report went further than this, mooting the idealistic proposal of automatic transfers from rich countries to poor, a sort of international social security system. However, such automaticity, which is taken for granted within a nation, does not yet normally occur. Indeed, as long as undemocratic patrimonial politics, which further the narrow interests of the ruling elite, remain the norm in Africa and other Third World countries, aid providers cannot and should not simply pass resources on to recipient governments with no strings attached.

There may be other possibilities, however. Ironically, much that has been learnt over the last 30 years about how aid does and does not work in Africa leads to the uncomfortable conclusion that the 'helicopter' method of distributing aid would be the most effective. Under this approach, dollar bills (not local currency, whose value can be manipulated) would be thrown out of a helicopter in a regular, even pattern as it traversed the African countryside. The approach seems ludicrous and somehow distasteful. Yet, it would certainly put modest resources directly into the hands of the poor, which present procedures do not. Economic research suggests that the poor would invest these windfall resources more effectively, perhaps in simple tools and equipment, than their governments now do. By and large, people know what their needs are. Nobody would be favoured above anyone else – the values of universality and impartiality would be met. Of course, some of this aid would fall into the hands of the better-off, but not as much as occurs now. Since people would have to go to the trouble of picking the banknotes up, and, since anybody would be free to do so, there would be little chance of their becoming concentrated in the hands of a few. By providing new purchasing power directly in the rural areas, rural services would certainly improve, as traders, teachers and health workers would be drawn to sell their skills there. The aid programme would be simple to run and would not be overburdened with administrative costs.

Such an approach would not be practical politics, but it is worth considering why it seems objectionable. Is it any more than a paternalist belief that the giver knows better than the receiver what his help should be used for? Yet, if aid is about enabling people to develop their own potential in their own way, can such paternalism be justified? In any event, whatever new approaches to aid may emerge in the future, the helicopter method offers a standard of efficiency and effectiveness against which they should be assessed. For example, it might be worth simply putting simple capital assets in the hands of the poor – hand tools for agriculture and building, buckets, wheel-barrows, efficient cooking stoves, hand maize mills, and sewing machines. This would be a second-best approach because it would run the risk of not providing people with what they most need, or of inappropriate technological choices. Nevertheless, it might be more satisfying to the aid establishment than throwing money out of an aeroplane and certainly more likely to improve the lives of the poor than highways or large-scale hydroelectric schemes.

The Economic Outlook

A theme of this book has been that development is about people and comes from them, with individuals and societies being aware of choices and taking them. It proceeds at the pace people choose and cannot be imposed by the authorities or by outsiders, yet the social and political environment can either promote or frustrate that process of development. The colonial period in Africa, with its authoritarian but reasonably impartial and predictable government, was probably more supportive of this people-centred development than it is normally given credit for, while the arbitrary and patrimonial governments of independent Africa have been less conducive to development than was hoped or imagined. There are good reasons for thinking that, in the future, a reduced role for national governments, combined with greater economic cooperation with neighbouring states, and internally greater devolution to community and local groups and organizations would again be a more fertile environment for development. At least in theory, these propositions are now widely accepted, including that of giving more scope for the working of markets.

Nevertheless, the state still has a crucial role in economic development. Although we have argued for a slimming down of the state in Africa, what remains to be done is vital. The first requirement is to provide a stable legal and regulatory environment with an uncorrupt administration and the possibility of enforcing contracts through the courts if necessary. Because the state in most African countries has been captured by narrow interest groups, few countries in Africa enjoy these advantages now.

Moreover, sensible economic policy pays dividends. An unfortunate consequence of the way structural adjustment is being implemented, with loans being used as bribes to introduce certain policies, is the impression it creates that if a list of conditions is worked through and ticked off, then the economy will simply respond. The economic system is more complex than that – it works as a whole. Good policy in one area feeds off and reinforces good policy elsewhere. It is not just a matter of working through a set of conditions, accepting a few here or fudging a few there; it is a question of getting the whole economic machine running and humming, free from irrational interference. This point is as yet scarcely understood.

Good Housekeeping

A major government responsibility is the good housekeeping of its own budget – those resources which are directly under its control. How a government manages its own affairs is the touchstone of its overall economic competence and orientation.

The ability to raise taxation is a measure of a government's popular legitimacy – hence the emphasis given in the previous chapter to the high proportion of African government revenue which is actually coming from external aid. Few African governments are yet in a position to raise taxation more than the equivalent of about 10–20 per cent of GDP, and perhaps a bit higher where there is a large mining sector. Of course, it is not difficult to pass legislation which would theoretically raise more taxes than this, but the opportunities for avoiding or evading taxes in Africa are considerable – from smuggling farm produce over the border, to bribing customs officials or filing fraudulent company accounts. Thus, there is a social and political limit on a nation's taxable capacity, and attempting to go above this simply encourages further evasion. The rather modest taxable capacity of most African economies is yet one more indication of the need to slim down the governmental function at the national level to its main essentials.

Limited revenue implies that careful expenditure choices are crucial. How a government spends its resources certainly affects the path of development. One choice is between expenditure which encourages people to grow and develop and that which keeps them down – between human capital formation or military and security expenditure. Another choice, as has been stressed above, is that between a shambling, underpaid, unmotivated civil service and a slimmed-down, well-remunerated professional body. African governments have so far scarcely addressed these issues, and external aid agencies, although indirectly providing a high proportion of the finance, have been reluctant to get deeply involved, other than through exhortation of the governments concerned. Many of those who criticize adjustment in Africa in the abstract could more usefully analyse the minutiae of government expenditure in particular countries. The devil is in the details.

Debt, Population and Trade

Given a stable, responsive and uncorrupt political environment, many of the other economic problems of Africa are eminently solvable, or at least manageable. Foremost among these is the debt problem, about which there has been a great deal of posturing and shadow boxing. Posturing has occurred because all the parties concerned now recognize that, whoever is to blame for the external debt, most of it is not being and never will be repaid. The remaining questions are how the burden of unpaid debt should be shared among the various creditors, most of whom are ultimately other national governments not private banks, and what quid pro quo can be extracted in the process. The rapid write-off of government debt is probably a prize, waiting for those countries which can quickly introduce representative government. For example, Zambia was able to negotiate better terms for its debt restructuring following its democratic change of government in 1991.

On a different timescale, the population problem is also manageable, notwithstanding a great deal of Malthusian pessimism concerning overpopulation. Africa certainly has the highest population growth rate of any region of the world, but it is also a vast continent, whose agricultural potential has not yet been fully exploited. So, viewed as a global or continental problem, there is still time. The solution involves giving people real control over their lives and the resources to make their own judgements and decisions. It is not acceptable that African women should be bearing children year after year, simply in the hope that a few of them will survive through to adulthood, or because this is the only way in which they can achieve some kind of social status. The most important element in changing this situation is sustained investment in health and in female education. Educated women have more choices. Here, we have one more argument for the revised aid strategy which is being advocated, that of concentrating resources directly on human capital formation. Moreover, the aid agencies should take no more notice of Islamic reluctance over female education than they do of the official reservations of the Catholic Church over contraception.

Overcoming Africa's dependence on a few primary commodity markets also requires a long-term strategy, since the only solution is through the growth of new sectors and types of production, leading to economic diversification. We come back to the questions of agricultural production and industrialization below.

In the meantime, we have argued in Chapter 5 that short-run price instability in these markets is at least as important as any long-term secular decline in commodity prices. This is a complication for economic management in Africa far greater than in advanced Western economies. Where income and foreign exchange earnings in the latter may vary by a few percentage points from one year to another, and in doing so call forth a great deal of frothy discussion about booms and recessions, African governments and peoples have to cope with far wider variations in the level of economic activity. Many of Africa's economic problems come from internal factors – the interplay of historical forces and politics, leading to poor economic management, but the problem of price instability decidedly does not.

Some solutions are discernible. Simply understanding the nature of the problem helps, since it may then be easier to save during the good years of commodity boom in anticipation of the bad. There may also be a case for reviving the unfashionable proposals for international price stabilization mechanisms as long as these are not viewed as a means of sustained price support.

A Brown Revolution?

In the agricultural sector, notwithstanding the devastation throughout the continent of failed rural development schemes – mostly initiated and financed by external agencies – there are nevertheless grounds for hope. The current trends towards economic liberalization, including getting the prices right, while not a panacea, will unlock a great deal of productive potential. Indeed, it is already happening. Agricultural output since the late 1980s has begun to rise, and there are a number of small but surprising new initiatives by farmers – such as Zambia's exports of cut flowers and Kenya's of runner beans. Agricultural production in Africa was never totally stifled by state interference; the farmers are too independent and robust for that. Nevertheless, if they were now to be actively encouraged, supported and educated, the results could be surprising.

For the longer term, greatly increased genetic research on the basic African food crops is needed. It should be directed not so much towards higher yields but to drought resistance and adaptation to poor soils. The hope lies in the enormous strides in genetic science which have been made in recent years and the successes which have been achieved with other crops. So far, similar research on African food crops has not been particularly clearly focused or well directed. Again, this is an activity which is crying out for more, and more effective, external agency finance and would be well affordable within the present aid budgets.

The fruits of such research cannot be guaranteed, but we can be sure that any such 'Brown Revolution' would be taken up by African farmers without requiring much external persuasion or coaxing, as long as agricultural markets are allowed to operate without inter-ference. A Brown Revolution would certainly exacerbate the many issues which need to be addressed throughout the continent – of land rights, water rights, rights to trees, and to wild animals – just as the Green Revolution in Asia threw up social issues and changed the balance of power between various groups. In the Western world, these matters would be solved by legislation. In Africa local *ad hoc* resolu-tion, drawing on long-established knowledge and custom, opaque though the process may be to outsiders, is more likely to be effective.

Industrialization

The industrialization of Africa, the original starting point for much economic growth theory, remains deeply intractable. Certainly, a num-ber of industries have been established across the continent in a modest way, notably in textiles and food processing, and manufacturing typic-ally accounts for about 10 per cent of national product. Further industrial deepening will occur as and when African countries open up their markets to each other. Certainly, Africa does have its entre-preneurs, but, like its farmers, they have not been encouraged or empowered.

Nevertheless, Africa accounts for less than half a per cent of world-wide manufacturing industry, and its participation in global industry will remain very limited for some years to come (*Financial Times*,

1993). At one time, international footloose industries used to migrate to countries where labour costs were lowest, but the international location of industries is increasingly determined by proximity to particular centres of technology or to major markets. Low labour costs alone are no longer a major incentive. Moreover, technical development in many industries, even in basic industries such as textiles, is unrelenting and tends to reward those who are already ahead. In these respects, Africa has little to offer.

Theories of development still have very little to say about how to achieve industrialization in such circumstances. The previously fashionable ideas of the state as itself an entrepreneur, owning factories and enterprises, have been thoroughly discredited around the world. Similarly, excessive financial subsidies or levels of trade protection have failed to promote viable industries. Nevertheless, there is still a role for the state. It involves, first, the creation of a stable political and commercial framework – an obvious point but one which has yet to be achieved in much of the continent. It may also require much greater efforts at training, systematic marketing of whatever potential a country may have, and attention to detailed negotiation, for example, over the transfer of technology through technical licences, joint venture agreements and the like. Much can be learnt from those countries such as Korea and Singapore which have pursued successful industrialization, as well as from examples like Mauritius which are closer to home. Success is not assured and will at best take a long time.

The Final Word

There are those who would not regret Africa's failure to industrialize, arguing that the Western model of a highly materialist, consumer society is not replicable or sustainable across the whole world without doing irreparable damage to the global environment. That may well be, but it is a problem that the West, not Africa, has to solve. It is also not a satisfactory reply to the several hundred million people in Africa, and Asia too, who still live in absolute poverty and have yet to enjoy the fruits of human progress.

Thus, we end where we began. Although precise formulae for the spread of human knowledge from modern societies to the rest of the world remain somewhat elusive, Africa cannot be left behind. Yet, if we look backwards there clearly has been progress. Indeed, change and development in Africa, as elsewhere, have been accelerating, with each significant period being notably shorter than the one before. State-building and significant trading contact with the outside world go back only a thousand years or so; the colonial period started about a hundred years ago and ended a mere 30 years ago. The independent nation states which then emerged may have expected to survive indefinitely, but they soon found that the unfettered autonomy of nation states everywhere was beginning to be limited and circumscribed as the world struggled hesitantly towards some type of global order – the phase of history in which we now live. The Second African Revolution may not deliver democracy throughout Africa, but the collective will of the people is now a great deal more important and powerful than it has been. Of course, this idea of historical acceleration is not acceptable as a serious theory; recent events may only seem more important than those much earlier, but it is a warning against merely extrapolating the past into the future.

So, is the optimistic or the pessimistic scenario most likely in Africa into the next millennium? Will the forces for construction and cooperation, which slowly build up civil society and more democratic states, dominate over those of destruction and disorder, which are tending to break up some of the emergent African nations? The outcome will be different in different places. Hitherto, plausible generalizations, such as those in this book, could be made about Africa as a whole. They were justified on the basis of historical similarity, from pre-colonial society, to the colonization of Africa during the ten years from 1885, and the subsequent emergence of the continent as a series of independent countries in the 1960s. As time goes on, however, social, political and economic change is bound to diverge between one country and another. By the next century, generalizations about Africa as a whole will be increasingly untenable.

Appendix A
The Success Story of Botswana

Kgosi ke kgosi ka morafe
A chief is a chief by the will of the people
(Tswana proverb)

History

Botswana is a large landlocked country, about the size of France, in southern Africa. Much of it consists of the Kalahari desert. The Tswana-speaking people first came to the eastern edge of the desert in the eighteenth and nineteenth centuries, moving north and west from the Transvaal region of South Africa. Many no doubt came with the great movement of tribes in southern Africa which started in the 1820s. There they met older established groups, including the Khoisan hunter-gatherer groups often referred to as Bushmen, who had lightly populated the region since time immemorial, whom they dominated, enslaved and intermingled with or pushed further into the desert.

Like most people of southern and eastern Africa outside the tsetse-infested regions, the Tswana kept cattle, which were their main form of wealth and their pride and joy. However, they were not a nomadic people. Rather, they settled in large villages, small towns even, perhaps clustered around a source of water, while the cattle were grazed in the surrounding region often many miles away. This settlement pattern is unusual in eastern and southern Africa, though it is also found in parts of Zimbabwe.

As in other African societies, the Tswana were ruled by chiefs and kings, but, like the Ashanti in Ghana, there also seems to have been some concept of popular sovereignty. A Tswana proverb says: *kgosi ke kgosi ka morafe*, or a chief is a chief by the will of the people (Sillery, 1974). On important matters, the chief was expected to consult with all the men of the tribe, who would gather together in the *kgotla*, a sheltered place designated for the purpose and which was always partly encircled by a fence of stout wooden stakes. The *kgotla* also served as

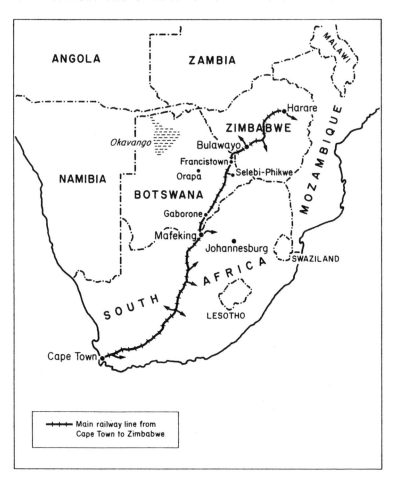

Map of Botswana

a law court. This was not democracy but it was consultation. Schapera, who studied the Tswana, has this to say of the *kgotla*:

> The relative frequency of the assemblies, and the fact that all tribesmen may attend and are sometimes compelled to, helps to explain why Tswana chiefs are seldom autocratic; they are directly and often in contact with the mass of their people, and it is difficult for them to remain indifferent to a publicly expressed threat of opposition (Schapera, 1956: 151).

Schapera may in fact be overstating the power of the *kgotla*. He studied the Tswana during the colonial period and there is some evidence that one of the effects of the colonial administration, in Botswana at least, had been to strengthen the *kgotla* relative to the chiefs (Mgadla and Campbell, 1989).

Moreover, the Tswana had a strong sense of constitution and of legality, or customary law as the colonial administration termed it. This too was studied by Schapera. However, history needs to be interpreted with some caution here. Had the laws of all African societies been studied by a scholar of his ability, the Tswana case might not seem so unusual among pre-colonial African societies. Be that as it may, a strong legalistic tradition certainly runs through all recorded Tswana history.

During the latter half of the nineteenth century both eastern and southern Africa were in political turmoil. The eight major Tswana societies, within the area of what is now Botswana, found themselves threatened by the Boers, groups of whom were pushing up from the south, trying to escape British rule in the Cape. During this time the Tswana chiefs, advised by missionaries among them, repeatedly asked the British government for protection. This at least is the conventional view, though some modern scholars question whether the Tswana chiefs were quite so enthusiastic for British interference. In any event, in 1885 this was granted, and the Bechuanaland Protectorate was established.

Shortly afterwards a new threat appeared in the form of Cecil Rhodes, who was pursuing his own ambition, independent of the British government, of extending British domination northwards through the middle of Africa and between the Portuguese to the east and the Germans to the west. His immediate objective was the gold and fertile land of what is now Zimbabwe. The newly created British Bechuanaland Protectorate lay in his path and along his line of communication between the Cape Colony and Zimbabwe. The obvious thing to do was to transfer the responsibility for the protectorate from the British government itself to Rhodes's British South Africa Company. The Tswana, however, saw Rhodes as an ambitious, ruthless man and were bitterly opposed to the proposed transfer. Eventually, in 1895 the three principal Tswana chiefs, Khama, Sebele and Bathoen, went to London to plead with the British government and to appeal in a series of public meetings directly to the British people. Here, with their public relations skilfully organized by the London Missionary Society, they argued their case, which was eventually won.

The incident is extraordinary for a number of reasons. First, the three chiefs, rivals though they were in other ways, cooperated in their perceived common interest. Second, they took advice from the European missionaries in their midst. Third, they actually made the long, difficult journey to London. Fourth, most of all, they perceived that negotiation, rather than, say, resorting to warfare, was in their best interests. This same pattern of mutual cooperation, of listening to outside advice and of believing in the efficacy of negotiation is repeated over and over again in the subsequent history, first, of the Bechuanaland Protectorate and, later, after 1966, of independent Botswana.

The colonial administration of the protectorate was minimal. It was not even governed from within the protectorate, but from the then Mafeking, over the border in South Africa. The British had no particular interest in the territory and were more or less content to allow the pre-colonial authority and government to continue. Perhaps because the Tswana had sought British protection in the first place, there was a sense of legitimacy about the colonial regime which was rarely paralleled elsewhere in Africa. For example, when the chiefs were in dispute with the colonial administration, they tended not to resort to civil disobedience or other forms of protest but rather took the colonial administration to court, where the original Protectorate Proclamation would be cited in evidence.

For most of the first half of the twentieth century, it was proposed that the ultimate future of the protectorate, as of Lesotho and Swaziland which were in a similar position, would be incorporation into South Africa. For all of this time, the Tswana campaigned against the proposal, all the more so as the South African government turned more racist and introduced apartheid. Eventually, when South Africa left the Commonwealth in 1961, it was finally apparent that Bechuanaland should be prepared for independence as a nation state in its own right.

Thus, Botswana did not need to struggle for independence. Its first president, Sir Seretse Khama, once commented that the Tswana asked the British to come and in due course asked them to go. He himself was the hereditary leader of the Ngwato, the largest of the Tswana subgroups. He had been banned by the colonial authorities from the territory following his marriage to a white woman in 1948. During his absence in Britain he was called to the Bar – the legalistic tradition again. When in 1956 he was finally allowed to return to Bechuanaland, he did not take up the chieftainship, which he could by then have done, but chose national politics instead, creating the Botswana Democratic Party (BDP). A few years later, the BDP won a convincing majority in the pre-independence elections.

With most of the people of independent Botswana belonging to different Tswana subgroups, it was a rather homogeneous country, in which the great majority of people shared the common Setswana language. It was led by a nationally elected president, who would otherwise have been the hereditary chief of the largest tribe. Thus, there was a great deal of continuity between pre-colonial society and the subsequent nation state, far more so than in most other African countries. Finally, it was a nation which already carried some democratic and certainly some legalistic tradition from its past.

There was no doubt that all of these elements gave the independent government a great deal of inner strength. Botswana could, like Swaziland has more or less done, have reverted to an essentially pre-colonial system of government and authority. Instead, the government unequivocally opted for modernity and, as in other African nations, immediately set about undermining traditional authority and the institution of chieftainship, which represented a potential future threat to its power and authority. At the same time, it defused potential conflict by also co-opting these traditional structures into the national framework, for example by giving chiefs a constitutional role in local government.

Altogether, unlike the case in most independent African states, there was little need to divert energy into nation-building. The politicians could turn to the task of development and were sufficiently self-confident to be able to listen to the advice of outsiders, of whom there have been a great many in Botswana, yet to make up their own minds and pursue their own course.

Economic Development

At the time of independence, 1966, the country had few economic prospects. It was a thinly populated, semi-desert, cattle country in the middle of a long drought during which about a third of the cattle died. Botswana was talked about in those days in the sort of apocalyptic way that is now reserved for, say, Mozambique or Somalia. Of physical and human capital, there was practically none. A small capital city, Gaborone, a village really, had been built by the British just before independence. Scarcely any Batswana had a university degree. Out of the whole of the country's half a million people, only two thousand were pupils in secondary school – one in every 250 people. The only industry was an abattoir, desperately trying to buy up and slaughter the emaciated cattle before they died on their feet, so that the meat could at least be sold. The country's only export was beef. Domestic taxation was insufficient for the needs of the administration, and the independent government continued to rely on an annual grant from the British government to cover its day-to-day expenditure, never mind financing for development projects.

Thus, the government's first priority was to increase its revenue. Since 1910 the three British protectorates in Southern Africa, now Botswana, Lesotho and Swaziland, had been in a customs union with South Africa. Under the terms of that agreement customs revenues

---

In economic terms the 1969 Southern African Customs Union Agreement (SACUA) is a model of its kind. The advantage of customs unions is that, by creating a larger market, they encourage efficiencies and economies of scale from which all the partner countries in the union benefit. The disadvantage is that economic production tends to be drawn to the economic centre of the union rather than to the periphery. SACUA takes this into account and financially compensates the peripheral countries for this economic loss by making transfer payments from South Africa to the smaller countries. Within nation states or federations, such as the United States, such compensation normally works automatically through taxation and subsidy and welfare payments. Within the European Community no permanent or fully satisfactory resolution of the problem has yet been reached.

were collected centrally by South Africa and shared out between the four countries. However, the details of the arrangement were increasingly unfair to the three smaller countries. On the other hand, such was South Africa's domination of the region that to reopen the agreement carried the risk for the smaller newly independent countries of losing what benefits they already had from the Union. They were all heavily dependent on South Africa for their external trade and transport and could not easily go it alone.

However, Botswana, supported by the other two countries, chose to renegotiate the agreement. As it turned out, the South African government proved to be sufficiently enlightened to see that supporting the prosperity of these three small neighbouring nations in this indirect way was also in its own broad interest. So in 1969 a new agreement was reached which was much more favourable to the three smaller countries. Within two years Botswana's revenue from this source more than doubled and thereafter continued to expand with the country's increasing prosperity. The Tswana characteristic of achieving an objective by negotiation, even with difficult partners, had again been vindicated.

The next step in the government's strategy was the opening of a copper and nickel mine at Selebi-Phikwe. This was a far bigger project than the country had ever contemplated before; the investment was equivalent to more than the country's previous annual GDP. All the finance had to be raised externally, from private investors for the mine itself, and from the World Bank and other development agencies for the associated infrastructure. The negotiations were extremely complex. In the end no less than 42 separate agreements between the various parties were drawn up, but they were so interrelated that none could be signed before any of the others; they were all signed simultaneously in Gaborone on 7 March 1972.

In the event the Selebi-Phikwe project was a financial failure for all the parties involved – not everything undertaken in Botswana has been successful. However, the important point again was the government's sureness of its own purpose, its trust in legality and negotiation and its willingness to draw in and use external advice without being dominated by it.

In the meantime the De Beers Corporation had been quietly prospecting for diamonds in the Kalahari and announced to the government when it was immersed in the complex Selebi-Phikwe project negotiations that a diamond pipe had been discovered which they wished to mine. A mining agreement was quickly reached. There were no complications in this case, since De Beers would pay for everything, which they did. The Orapa mine was opened in 1971 and within three years the company had made so much profit from it that it had already recovered its initial investment (Colclough and McCarthy, 1980: 150).

Thus when, shortly afterwards, De Beers sought a mining lease for another diamond mine, the government responded that it wished first to renegotiate the Orapa mine agreement, which it was entitled to do under an exceptional circumstances clause – the exceptional circumstances being the mine's extraordinary profitability. By this time it was clear that Botswana was a major diamond province and would be as important to De Beers, which has worldwide control of uncut diamond sales, as De Beers's investment would be to the economic future of Botswana. So both parties were negotiating for high stakes. The agreement eventually reached in 1975 set up a new diamond mining company, Debswana, which is 50:50 owned by De Beers and Botswana. The equal ownership by the two parties was a deliberate symbol of partnership rather than domination by one or the other. The full details of the agreement have not been published, but overall they give the country 'not less than 65–70 per cent' of the gross profits of diamond mining, with De Beers taking the other 30–35 per cent (Harvey and Lewis, 1990: 125).

During this period, while Botswana's mining sector was expanding in cooperation with the multinational corporations, most of the rest of Africa's mining industry, notably in Zambia, which Botswana took as a model not to follow, had been nationalized and was beginning to run down. Mineral prospecting, the necessary preliminary to a mining industry, has practically ceased in most of the rest of Africa but continues apace in Botswana. By the time other African governments were ready to contemplate foreign private-sector investment again, at the end of the 1980s, it was too late; investor confidence had evaporated.

Botswana has been the fastest-growing economy in the world. Between 1965 and 1989 Botswana's per capita income grew at a rate of 8.5 per cent a year, albeit from a very low starting point. Per capita income growth in the miracle economies of Singapore and South Korea was only 7 per cent a year, while in Hong Kong it was 6.3 per cent (IBRD, 1992).

Thus, Botswana became a diamond-based economy, with the diamond sector dominating both national income and government revenue. By the mid-1980s diamonds provided more than 50 per cent of government revenue and more than 75 per cent of total exports. Outside observers accordingly tend to attribute the country's economic success merely to diamonds, but mineral wealth does not inevitably guarantee economic success. The reality is that Botswana would not have achieved what it has without the national unity which came from its own history, together with enlightened, relatively uncorrupt leadership. Sierra Leone also has major deposits of diamonds, but, in economic terms, has stagnated, and, as we have seen, has the second lowest human development indicator in the world.

Investing for the Future

Of course, any economy which is so dependent on a single commodity is extremely vulnerable to downturns in the market or to other catastrophic circumstances. The only defences against this are, first, to husband resources prudently and, second, to use them for long-term economic diversification – the conversion of natural capital into other forms of productive capital. Botswana has certainly husbanded its resources. At the end of the 1980s its holdings of foreign exchange reserves were substantially more than annual GDP. It has largely avoided wasting resources in the sort of prestige projects that litter so many African countries. At the same time it has been investing, for the long term, in human capital. By the end of the 1980s over 90 per cent of Botswana's primary school age children were actually in school, compared with 47 per cent in Africa as a whole. The net secondary school enrolment rate was 37 per cent, amounting now to 55,000 students, compared with a rate of only 17 per cent Africa-wide. Only Ghana, Zimbabwe, Swaziland and Mauritius have higher recorded rates of secondary enrolment.

This book has said rather little about employment in the modern sector of the economy, since economic life in Africa is too complex for this to be a very useful target or concept at the present stage of development. Nonetheless, Botswana has reached a degree of modernization where national employment data do begin to mean something. It is estimated that on average every family or household now has at least one member in formal paid work. Further, at the end of the 1980s, the number of people employed was growing faster than the labour force; in other words more and more people who wanted work were able to get it (Harvey, 1992). That can be said of no other African country except Mauritius, which has already reached full employment.

It is not certain yet whether this strategy of human capital investment will work. One may ask the question: what will all the educated Batswana do landlocked in a semi-desert country north of South Africa? Is the growth in employment really sustainable? The answer is not obvious, just as there was no obvious answer 20 years ago for Mauritius, a small isolated island in the Indian Ocean, when it too had a growing educated population and a stagnant, increasingly uncompetitive sugar sector. Indeed, one of the mistakes of development strategies in the past has been to believe that such questions could be answered in advance and that the future could be laid out in some way by government strategy.

In the end geography and natural resources are not the determining factors in development; the important factors are the people and the social institutions which they create for themselves. Economies grow and societies develop as a result of individuals and groups finding ways of using their potential – as long as they enjoy a certain degree of economic and political freedom and political stability. All of these benefits are ones which the people of Botswana have now enjoyed for a whole generation. The more schooling they get the greater their potential.

Democracy

It may not be by chance that the countries which have attached the greatest emphasis to human development have also been the longer-standing multi-party democracies in Africa – Botswana, Mauritius and Zimbabwe. (The Gambia, a very small country, has also been a multi-party democracy since its independence in 1965 and Senegal claims to have been a 'guided' multi-party democracy since the mid-1970s, though there the opposition parties are constrained in a number of ways which limit their effectiveness.) However, in neither Botswana nor Zimbabwe has the party of government yet changed, so the constitution has not yet been fully tested. In Botswana's case the diamond revenues have enabled the government to meet many of its electorate's rising expectations without demanding great sacrifices from any group of the population. The democratic test will really come when economic growth slows down, which it will certainly do in the 1990s, with the end of the current expansion of the mining sector.

Yet Botswana politicians do take the democratic process seriously. The country has a free press, which in 1991 exposed a land deal scandal and led to the resignation of the country's vice-president and two other ministers. Opposition politicians are generally accorded respect and courtesy – not detained without trial as elsewhere on the continent. Moreover, the BDP government is fully aware that it has to be re-elected every few years by the population as a whole. In fact, the country people tend to vote for the BDP, while the townspeople support the opposition. As a result, rural interests have been more influential in Botswana than in most other African countries.

One observer comments as follows:

> The continued electoral success of the BDP is explained in a number of ways. Of prime importance is the fact that the BDP government has an outstandingly successful record to campaign on ... This has been translated into a massive extension of social services, health education and so on, especially in the rural areas ... The government has an excellent record on human rights and civil liberties and has established a considerable reputation for efficient, incorrupt administration. A good example of the high level of BDP government performance is the way in which it has managed to cope with a succession of serious droughts. In other parts of Africa the sort of drought experienced in Botswana has led to mass starvation only partly mitigated by humanitarian aid from the outside world ... the determination to succeed with drought relief is not just due to bureaucratic efficiency but is directly related to the existence of a freely democratic system (Wiseman, 1990: 46).

Finally, the Batswana themselves, having enjoyed an open democratic society for a generation now, and would not lightly accept a more repressive political system. Surveys in Botswana show that the younger people are, and the better educated they are, the stronger is their endorsement for modern pluralist government rather than for traditional patterns of authority (Somolekae, 1989). So, while the country has certainly benefited from its continuity with the past, time is on the side of modernity.

Lessons from Botswana

There are two lessons to draw from Botswana's experience. The first is that development is a dynamic interlocking process in which success in one sphere reinforces that in another. An open, pluralist society, with an uncorrupt government, encourages outside involvement of aid agencies, and of big international investors such as De Beers, not as exploiters but as partners, but most importantly allows ordinary people to take some control of their own lives. Resources extracted from the ground and reinvested in people sustain the process, in the expectation, or at least the hope, that one day the economy will become less dependent on mineral extraction. For real holistic development all the development indicators, whether economic or human, tend to move together in the same direction.

The second conclusion is that development is certainly achievable on the African continent. It helps if political and social energy does not have to be diverted into resolving social conflicts or invested in nation-building. Much of Botswana's success can be attributed to its particular historical circumstances – an ethnically homogeneous society, an apparent tradition of legalism and constitutionalism, and a continuity between the pre-colonial order and the modern nation state. Much of the development and political failure in the rest of Africa is the outcome of a rather different history of African societies which did not have these advantages.

Appendix B
A Menu for Aid-Givers

Although this book argues that the influence of external aid-givers is limited, at various points specific tasks have been identified which they could usefully do. These are summarized below.

Type of Programme	Why?
Primary education for every child by the year 2000, and	Because without education people cannot take their destiny in their own hands or begin to reach their potential.
Village-level basic health care *References*: Chapter 6 – An Alternative Approach Chapter 7 – Making a Long-Term Commitment	Educated and healthy people are more productive. *Comment*: Work through civil society as well as through governments. Finance recurrent as well as capital expenditures.
Finance redundancy programmes for the public sector and military *Reference*: Chapter 7 – Political Nature of Economic Adjustment	Because a massive reduction in the size of the public sector and the military is the most difficult unfinished business of structural adjustment, and because it is politically very difficult to do. External finance could facilitate the task. *Comment*: Aid agencies would have to be convinced that the government concerned was committed to the objective of creating a smaller, more professional, better-paid civil service.

Type of Programme	Why?
Genetic research on African food crops *References*: Chapter 5 – Agriculture and Food Production Chapter 7 – A Brown Revolution	Because modern biological science offers great promise, but no African government could afford or manage such a programme on its own. *Comment*: This is high technology transfer, though with an uncertain outcome, hence very suitable for aid finance.
Disseminate agricultural and other hand tools *Reference*: Chapter 7 – Direct Transfers?	Because this puts productive capital in the hands of the poor. *Comment*: A second best solution to giving people the cash to make their own decisions as to what they need.
Finance peace-making and peace-keeping where government has broken down *Reference*: Chapter 7 – The Anarchic Alternative	Because there is certainly no development in the midst of war. *Comment*: Much needs to be learnt from the mistakes made in Somalia.

Bibliography

Abedian, I. and Standish, B., 1992, *Economic Growth in South Africa: Selected Policy Issues*, Oxford University Press, Oxford.

Achebe, C., 1992, 'Words of Anxious Love', *Guardian*, London.

Amnesty International, 1991, *A Guide to the African Charter on Human and Peoples' Rights*, London.

Arthur, W. Brian, 1990, 'Positive Feedbacks in the Economy', *Scientific American*, February.

Baer, W., 1961, 'The Economics of Prebisch and the ECLA', *Economic Development and Cultural Change*, Vol. 10, No. 2.

Balasubramanyam, V.N. and Lall, S., 1991, *Current Issues in Development Economics*, Basingstoke.

Barnett, T. and Blaikie, P., 1991, *Aids in Africa, Its Present and Future Impact*, Belhaven Press, London.

Bartelmus, P., Lutz, E. and Schweinfest, S., 1992, *Integrated Environmental and Economic Accounting: A Case Study for Papua New Guinea*, World Bank, Environment Working Paper No. 54. Washington DC.

Bauer, P., 1991, *The Development Frontier: Essays in Applied Economics*, Harvester Wheatsheaf, London.

Becker, Charles M., 1990, 'The Demo-Economic Impact of the AIDS Pandemic in Sub-Saharan Africa', *World Development*, Vol. 18, No. 12, London.

Bennell, P., 1990, *British Industrial Investment in Sub-Saharan Africa: Corporate Responses to Economic Crisis in the 1980s*, Development Policy Review, London.

Berthelemy, J.C. and Morrisson, C., 1989, *Agricultural Development in Africa and the Supply of Manufactured Goods*, OECD Development Centre, Paris.

Bevan, D., Collier, P., and Gunning, J.W., 1991, 'The Macroeconomics of External Shocks', in Balasubramanyam and Lall, eds, *Current Issues in Development Economics*.

Bourguignon, F. and Morrisson, C., 1992, *Adjustment and Equity in Developing Countries*, OECD Development Centre, Paris.

Brandt, W. and Associates, 1980, *North–South: A Programme for Survival*, Pan, London.

Cassen, R. and Associates, 1985, *Does Aid Work?*, Oxford University Press, Oxford.

Chirimuuta, R. and Chirimuuta, R., 1989, *AIDS, Africa and Racism*, Free Association Books, London.

Clapham, C., 1990, *Third World Politics, An Introduction*, Routledge, London.

Clark, J., 1991, *Democratizing Development: the Role of Voluntary Organisations*, Earthscan, London.

Cockcroft, L., 1990, *Africa's Way, A Journey from the Past*, I.B.Tauris, London.

Colclough, C. and McCarthy, S., 1980, *The Political Economy of Botswana*, Oxford University Press, Oxford.

Colclough, C. and Manor, J., 1991, *States or Markets?*, Oxford University Press, Oxford.

Colclough, C. with Lewin, K., 1993, *Educating All the Children*, Oxford University Press, Oxford.

Collier, P., Radwan, S. and Wangwe, S., 1990, *Labour and Poverty in Rural Tanzania*, Clarendon Press, Oxford.

Collier, P., 1991, *From Critic to Secular God: the World Bank and Africa: A Commentary upon Sub-Saharan Africa: From Crisis to Sustainable Growth*, African Affairs, London.

Cornia, G.A., Jolly, R. and Stewart, F., eds, 1987, *Adjustment with a Human Face, Protecting the Vulnerable and Promoting Growth*, Oxford University Press, for UNICEF, Oxford.

Dahrendorf, R., 1990, *Human Rights Today*, Oxford Project for Peace Studies, Oxford.

Davidson, B., 1992, *The Black Man's Burden, Africa and the Curse of the Nation State*, James Currey, London.

De Chardin, P.T., 1959, *The Phenomenon of Man*, Wm. Collins, London.

Deng, F.M. and Zartman I.W., eds, 1991, *Conflict Resolution in Africa*, The Brookings Institution, Washington DC.

Economist, 1991, 'The IMF and the World Bank', London, 12 October.

Economist, 1992a, 'How Malawi Says Hello', London, 11 April.

Economist, 1992b, 'Democracy in Africa', London, 22 February.

Economist, 1993, 'The Final Lap: A Survey of South Africa', London, 20 March.

Elbadawi, I.A., 1992, *World Bank Adjustment Lending and Economic Performance in Sub-Saharan Africa in the 1980s*, Policy Research Working Papers of the World Bank, Washington DC.

Fallers, L.A., 1964, 'Social Stratification and Economic Process in Africa', in Bendix, R. and Lipset, S.M., eds, 1967, *Class Status and Power*, London.

Fieldhouse, D.K., 1986, *Black Africa 1945–1980: Economic Decolonization and Arrested Development*, Unwin Hyman, London.

Financial Times, 1993, 'Africa: A Continent at Stake', Financial Times Survey, London.

Gordon, D. and Lancaster, C., 1993, *The Implications of Political Change in Africa for SPA Donors*, USAID, Washington DC.

Grace, J. and Laffin, J., 1991, *Fontana Dictionary of Africa since 1960*, Fontana, London.

Green, R.H., 1987, *Stabilization and Adjustment Policies and Programmes, Country Study 1, Ghana*, World Institute for Development Economics Research, Helsinki.

Griffith-Jones, S. and Van der Hoeven, R., 1990, *Debt – The Unwanted Heritage of Today's Children*, Institute of Development Studies Discussion Paper, Brighton.

Griffith-Jones, S., 1991, 'International Financial Markets: a case of market failure', in *States or Markets?*, Oxford.

Grove, A.T., 1991, 'The African Environment', in Rimmer, ed., *Africa 30 Years On*, London.

Gwassa, G.C.K. and Iliffe, J., 1967, *Records of the Maji Maji Rising*, Historical Association of Tanzania, Dar es Salaam.

Hampton, J., 1990, *Living Positively with AIDS*, ActionAid, Amref and World in Need, London.

Harden, B., 1990, *Africa, Dispatches from a Fragile Continent*, W.W. Norton, New York.

Harvey, C. and Lewis, S.R. Jr., 1990, *Policy Choice and Development Performance in Botswana*, Macmillan with OECD, Basingstoke.

Harvey, C., 1992, *Botswana: Is the Economic Miracle Over?*, Institute of Development Studies Discussion Paper, Brighton.

Hastings, A., 1976, *African Christianity*, Chapman, London.

Healey, J. and Robinson, M., 1992, *Democracy, Governance and Economic Policy*, Overseas Development Institute, London.

Healey, J., Ketley, R. and Robinson, M., 1992, *Political Regimes and Economic Policy Patterns in Developing Countries, 1978–88*, Overseas Development Institute Working Paper 67, London.

Hill, P., 1986, *Development Economics on Trial*, Cambridge University Press, Cambridge.

Hirsch, F., 1977, *Social Limits to Growth*, Routledge & Kegan Paul, London.

Hirschmann, A., 1958, *The Strategy of Economic Development*, Yale University Press, New Haven, Connecticut.

Humana, C., 1986, *World Human Rights Guide*, Economist Publications, London.

IBRD, 1989, *Sub-Saharan Africa: From Crisis to Sustainable Growth*, Washington DC.

IBRD, 1989a, *Africa's Adjustment and Growth in the 1980s*, IBRD and UNDP, Washington DC.

IBRD, 1991a, *Trends in Developing Economies, 1991*, Washington DC.

IBRD, 1992, *World Development Report 1992: Development and the Environment*, Oxford University Press, Oxford.

IBRD, 1993, *Global Economic Prospects and the Developing Countries, 1993*, Washington DC.

IIHRDA, 1991, *Towards Africa's Second Liberation: Democracy, Popular Participation and Human Rights in Africa*, Report of the Inaugural Conference, International Institute for Human Rights and Democracy in Africa, London.

Kane-Berman, J., 1990, *South Africa's Silent Revolution*, South African Institute of Race Relations, Johannesburg.

Killick, T., 1978, *Development Economics in Action, A Study of Economic Policies in Ghana*, Heinemann, London.

Killick, T., 1991, *The Development Effectiveness of Aid to Africa*, Policy Working Papers of the World Bank, Washington DC.

Killick, T., 1992, *Explaining Africa's Post-Independence Development Experiences*, Overseas Development Institute, London.

Kingsley, M., 1897, *Travels in West Africa*, Macmillan, London.

Knight, J.B., 1990, *Public Enterprises and Industrialisation in Africa*, mimeo, Oxford.

Knight, J.B., 1991, 'The Evolution of Development Economics', in Balasubramanyam and Lall, eds, *Current Issues in Development Economics*.

Lachman, D. and Bercuson, K, eds, 1992, *Economic Policies for a New South Africa*, International Monetary Fund, Washington DC.

Landell-Mills, P., 1992, *Governance, Civil Society and Empowerment in Sub-Saharan Africa*, mimeo, Society for the Advancement of Socio-economics, Irvine.

Leys, C., 1975, *Underdevelopment in Kenya*, Heinemann, London.

Lipton, M., 1977, *Why Poor People Stay Poor, Urban Bias in World Development*, Temple Smith, London.

Lipton, M., 1992, *Food Production and Poverty*, mimeo (to be published in B. Harris and R. Hoffenberg, eds, *Food*, Blackwell, Oxford).

Lugard, F.D., 1922, *The Dual Mandate in British Tropical Africa*, Frank Cass, London.

Maasdorp, G. and Whiteside, A., 1993, *Rethinking Economic Cooperation in Southern Africa: Trade and Investment*, Konrad-Adenauer-Stiftung, Occasional Papers, Johannesburg.

McEvedy, C., 1980, *The Penguin Atlas of African History*, Penguin, London.

Mallaby, S., 1992, *After Apartheid*, Faber and Faber, London.

Marin, M., 1992, 'Duty and Self-Interest Dictate Europe's Policy on World Aid', *European*, London, 7 May.

Marsden, K., 1990, *African Entrepreneurs: Pioneers of Development*, International Finance Corporation Discussion Paper 9, Washington DC.

Mazrui, A., 1990, *The African Condition*, Heinemann, London.

Mbiti, J.S., 1990, *African Religions and Philosophy* (second edn), Heinemann, Oxford.

Meadows, D.H., Meadows, D.L. and Randers, J., 1972, *The Limits to Growth*, Universe Books, New York.

Meadows, D.H., Meadows, D.L. and Randers, J., 1992, *Beyond the Limits*, Earthscan Publications, London.

Mgadla, P.T. and Campbell, A.C., 1989, 'Dikgotla, dikgosi and the protectorate administration', in Molutsi and Holm, *Democracy in Botswana*.

Molutsi, P.M. and Holm J., 1989, *Democracy in Botswana*, Botswana Society, Gaborone.

Morrisson, C., 1992, *Adjustment and Equity*, OECD Development Centre Policy Brief No.1, Paris.

Mosley, P., Harrigan, J. and Toye, J., 1991, *Aid and Power, The World Bank and Policy Based Lending*, Routledge, London.

Nazih-Ali, M., 1990, *The Roots of Islamic Tolerance, Origin and Development*, Oxford Project for Peace Studies, Oxford.

Nyerere, J.K., 1968, *Freedom and Socialism; Uhuru na Ujamaa. A Selection from Writings and Speeches 1965–1967*, Oxford University Press, Dar es Salaam.

Oliver, R. and Fage, J.D., 1988, *A Short History of Africa*, Penguin, London.

Oliver, R., 1991, *The African Experience*, Weidenfeld & Nicolson, London.

Overseas Development Institute, 1991, *Aid and Political Reform*, Overseas Development Institute Briefing Paper, London.

Overseas Development Institute, 1992, *Explaining Africa's Development Experiences*, Overseas Development Institute Briefing Paper, London.

Page, S., Davenport, M. and Hewitt, A., 1991, *The GATT Uruguay Round: Effects on Developing Countries*, Overseas Development Institute, London.

Palanza, F., 1989, *Africa's Debt: An Analysis of the Crisis in the Eighties and of its Possible Remedies*, EIB Papers, Luxembourg.

Pearson, L.B. et al., 1969, *Partners in Development: Report of the Commission on International Development*, Praeger, New York.

Pradervand, P., 1989, *Listening to Africa, Developing Africa from the Grassroots*, Praeger, New York.

Prebisch, R., 1963, *Towards a Dynamic Development Policy for Latin America*, United Nations, New York.

Repetto, R. et al., 1991, *Accounts Overdue: Natural Resource Depletion in Costa Rica*, World Resources Institute, Washington DC.

Rawls, J., 1973, *A Theory of Justice*, Oxford University Press, Oxford.

Riddell, R.C., 1987, *Foreign Aid Reconsidered*, James Currey, London.

Rimmer, D., ed, 1991, *Africa 30 Years On*, The Royal African Society, London.

Rostow, W.W., 1990, *The Stages of Economic Growth: A Non-Communist Manifesto* (third edn), Cambridge University Press, Cambridge.

Sarkar, P. and Singer, H.W., 1991, 'Manufactured Exports of Developing Countries and Their Terms of Trade Since 1965 , *World Development*, Vol. 19, No. 4.

Schapera, I., 1956, *Government and Politics in Tribal Societies*, Watts, London.

Sen, A., 1980, 'Famines', *World Development*, Vol. 8.

Sen, A., 1981, *Poverty and Famines: An Essay on Entitlement and Deprivation*, Oxford University Press, Oxford.

Shivji, I., 1989, *The Concept of Human Rights in Africa*, Codesria, London.

Sillery, A., 1974, *Botswana: A Short Political History*, Methuen, London.

Singer, H.W., 1992, 'The Prebisch-Singer terms of trade controversy revisited', *Journal of International Development*.

Somolekae, G., 1989, 'Do Batswana think and act as democrats?', in Molutsi and Holm, *Democracy in Botswana*.

Sparks, A., 1991, *The Mind of South Africa: The Story of the Rise and Fall of Apartheid*, Mandarin, London.

Tordoff, W., 1993, *Government and Politics in Africa* (second edn), Macmillan, Basingstoke.

Transparency International, 1993, *Corruption: The Misuse of Public Power for Private Profit*, Berlin.

UNDP, 1991, *Human Development Report 1991*, Oxford University Press, New York.

UNDP, 1992, *Human Development Report 1992*, Oxford University Press, New York.

Vidrovitch, C., 1988, *Africa: Endurance and Change South of the Sahara*, University of California Press, Berkeley.

Weiss, T. and Chopra, J., 1992, 'Sovereignty is No Longer Sacrosanct: Codifying Humanitarian Intervention', *Ethics and International Affairs*, Vol. 6.

Wenner, K., 1970, *Shamba Letu*, Houghton Mifflin, Boston.

Wiseman, J.A., 1990, *Democracy in Black Africa; Survival and Revival*, Paragon House Publishers, New York.

World Bank, 1980, *World Development Report 1980*, Oxford University Press for the World Bank, Oxford.

World Bank, 1991, *World Development Report 1991: The Challenge of Development*, Oxford University Press for the World Bank, Oxford.

World Commission on Environment and Development, 1987, *Our Common Future*, Oxford University Press, New York.

Index